David Hare

'Britain's leading contemporary playwright.' *The Times*

David Hare was born in Sussex in 1947. His first play, *Slag*, was produced in 1970. A year later he first worked at the National Theatre, beginning one of the longest relationships of any playwright with a contemporary theatre. Since 1978, the National has produced eleven of his plays. Four of his best-known plays, *Plenty*, *The Secret Rapture*, *Racing Demon* and *Skylight*, have also been presented on Broadway. The first of his six feature films, *Wetherby*, which he also directed, won the Golden Bear at Berlin in 1985.

by the same author

Plays
PLAYS ONE (Slag, Teeth 'n' Smiles, Knuckle, Licking Hitler, Plenty)
BRASSNECK (with Howard Brenton)
THE GREAT EXHIBITION
PRAVDA (with Howard Brenton)
RACING DEMON
MURMURING JUDGES
THE ABSENCE OF WAR
SKYLIGHT

Screenplays for Television
LICKING HITLER
DREAMS OF LEAVING
HEADING HOME

Screenplays
WETHERBY
PARIS BY NIGHT
STRAPLESS
PLENTY
THE SECRET RAPTURE

Opera Libretto
THE KNIFE

Prose
WRITING LEFT-HANDED
ASKING AROUND:
background to the David Hare trilogy

DAVID HARE

Plays Two

Fanshen
A Map of the World
Saigon
The Bay at Nice
The Secret Rapture

Introduced by
the Author

faber and faber
LONDON · BOSTON

This collection first published in 1997 by
Faber and Faber Limited
3 Queen Square London WC1N 3AU

Photoset by Parker Typesetting Service, Leicester
Printed and bound in Great Britain by Mackays of Chatham plc, Chatham,
Kent

A CIP record for this book
is available from the British Library
ISBN 0–571–17835–9

2 4 6 8 10 9 7 5 3 1

Contents

Introduction

The editors at Faber and Faber talk to the author about the plays in this collection.

Q: *You wrote* Fanshen *in 1974 for the Joint Stock Company. It's the only play of yours which is based on a book.*
Yes. A couple of years before, Max Stafford-Clark and I had joined up with the producer David Aukin to form a travelling theatre company. The plan was to continue the work of Portable Theatre, which had recently gone bankrupt. Max then brought in William Gaskill from the Royal Court. Bill had always been frustrated at the Court that he couldn't create a genuine ensemble. Nor had he had time to do the exploratory work with actors that he so loved. So together he and Max began some casual evening workshops, using a book Heathcote Williams had written about the men and women you see speechmaking at Hyde Park Corner. After several months, they collected together this distinctive mix of written word, improvisation and direct observation, and mounted a wonderfully lively play called *The Speakers*. When I saw it, I knew they were on to something really exciting, and, quite simply, I wanted to be part of it.

Q: *So was* Fanshen *your idea?*
Not at all. The actress Pauline Melville had read William Hinton's book and taken it to Gaskill, saying she thought it would make an interesting play. Bill was understandably daunted by it. It's a six-hundred page history of the experiences of one village during the land-reform

programme that transformed China at the end of the 40s. It tells how a backward peasantry was given the chance to use techniques of public appraisal and self-criticism to take control of their own affairs. At the heart of it is the eternal question of how a democracy should police itself to ensure that it is genuinely democratic. Hinton was a farmer from a radical background. He was sent as a tractor technician from the US to help with the programme. Being a polymath, he had accumulated an extraordinary amount of detail. So it was with great caution that Bill gave me the book some time in 1974 and asked me if I thought I could make anything of it.

Q: *I believe the Joint Stock method was to do a preliminary workshop with a group of actors and then to send the writer away for a period on their own.*
Well, yes, that's what the method became. It was trial and error. As Joint Stock became more celebrated, so the method evolved. Like all good methods, it was flexible. Gaskill had run this country's leading new play theatre. Max had also presented many living playwrights. So there was never any question of interfering with the authorship of the play. Actors and directors contributed, but they did not dictate. The workshop was there to enrich and inform the play, but it was not intended to provide you either with structure or dialogue. Of course as the writer, you were expected to argue for your point of view – I remember the first reading of the finished play as a particular disaster and finding my back against the wall for several weeks after it – but, finally, you knew you were working with people who had an almost moral sense of the supremacy of the playwright's imagination. From the perspective of the 90s, with the rise of director's theatre and the stultifying condescension of so-called 'writers' workshops' which are all the rage in the US – and which consist mostly of directors who can't write interfering with playwrights

who can – it's impossible not to be nostalgic for those days.

Q: *When the play was finished and in performance, William Hinton came over and insisted on some changes to the text.*
Yes. I had no problem with that. After all, the book had taken him fifteen years to write. His notes had been seized, first by the US Customs, then again by the Senate. When we had asked to make a play from his book, he had not expected us to succeed. Others had tried before and failed. But as soon as he read the reviews he was on the plane. He was a Marxist, and I wasn't. So, inevitably, there was some trading about emphasis. But I believe the final play achieves a classical balance.

Q: *A number of critics have observed, however, that* Fanshen *is quite unlike your other plays – that it has a distinctive tone of voice. You wrote differently for the group than when you wrote for yourself.*
Yes, I think that's fair.

Q: *The play is frequently revived. How does it play now, in the less heady climate of the 90s?*
What's so interesting is that although you see it from a different perspective, it works just as well. Hinton's book brilliantly foreshadows the questions which went on to grip all political leaders in the last part of the century. Can you have equity without abundance? How do you reconcile the demands of plenty and the demands of justice?

Q: *This argument, of course, carries on in* A Map of the World. *Why was this play premiered in Adelaide?*
I almost never do commissioned work. Like a lot of writers, I feel uneasy when asked to write to order. If you say anything at all in advance about a play you're planning, then you create an idea of it in the producer's

imagination. They're invariably disappointed when they don't get what they're expecting. It's always seemed to me a playwright should work alone and in silence. That way, when you hand it in, it's a gift, not a let-down.

Q: *But you broke your rule with this play?*
I liked Jim Sharman so much. He is the son of an Australian circus-owner and had directed *Jesus Christ Superstar*. He had taken over the running of the Adelaide Festival for 1982. He wanted an American play from Sam Shepard and an English play from me, to run side by side. I had been very struck by reading something the Goncourt brothers said. Somewhere they express their admiration for medieval Japanese painters who, once they had perfected a style, not only started out on a new one, but actually changed their names when they did so. This way they hoped to avoid becoming what the brothers call 'prisoners of a reputation'. It was irresistible for me to be asked to travel ten thousand miles to try and re-make myself into a different kind of playwright.

Q: A Map of the World *almost overflows with subject matter.*
Perhaps I took on too much. A Martian visiting this planet would of course observe that a minority of us live in great luxury and comfort, and that the majority of us live in squalor and deprivation. Two-thirds of us have never made a telephone call. But I think they would also observe how few of us in the minority ever make any mention of these facts. The wretched of the earth are, for some reason, rarely thought to be a suitable subject for the arts. I was ambivalent about being able to represent the poor themselves. But I did feel qualified to write about our attitudes to them. The centre of the play is a debate in a Bombay hotel between a famous writer, Victor Mehta, who has an exquisite contempt for the crasser side of militant Third Worldism, and a young journalist, Stephen

Andrews, who has an equally eloquent anger at people's readiness to accept the world as it is. Almost any decent writer will recognize something familiar in Victor's cultivated fastidiousness. And then the balance, I hope, is provided by Stephen's well-grounded indignation.

However, plays of Shavian argument always leave me dissatisfied, because they perpetuate the false idea that human beings can be reduced to their opinions. I wanted to add another layer, to address the problem of subjectivity. Those of us who have spent our lives on the left are prone to banging on about something called 'the truth'. Yet, if we're honest, we know that the truth is a difficult thing to establish outside an unreliable context of memory and opinion. So there is a second plot. A film is being made years later. It is based on the book Mehta wrote about the original events, but it travesties them. What once seemed certain and clear has by now slipped out of everybody's grasp.

Q: *The play weaves in fact between the two locations – the hotel itself and the film-set of the hotel.*
That's right. It sounds complicated, but in my opinion, it plays very clearly. The problems of the play come much more from the figure of Peggy Whitton, the young actress who volunteers to give herself to whichever of the two men wins the argument. Peggy was played first in Australia by Penny Downie, then in England by Diana Quick, then in New York by Elizabeth McGovern. All three reported the same hostility from the public. Nothing they did would make the audience accept the basic likelihood of Peggy's action.

Q: *Throughout your writing, there are examples of twin plays – one for the stage and one for television.* Licking Hitler *and* Plenty *are an obvious couple. And now again,* A Map of the World *and* Saigon: Year of the Cat.

It's true they were produced at the same time. And yet I think of them as very different. There is no governing metaphor in *A Map of the World*. It's far too complex and diffuse for that. *Saigon*, on the other hand, is about a place which is as much in the mind as in historical reality. When I had visited Vietnam during the phoney peace in 1974 – between the Paris Peace Agreement and the final fall of the South – I had been intensely moved by the town of Saigon. What struck me was that everyone went about their life as if it would go on for ever. And yet in their hearts people knew that the end was near. They just refused to acknowledge it in their daily behaviour. What's more, when the end did come, the Americans, at least, could not cope with the reality of it. They simply could not accept or understand the fact that they had been defeated. So this suddenly seemed to me the occasion for a wonderful, almost Chekhovian theme: how a whole society may be bent on denying reality.

Q: *Your Vietnam is quite unlike any other film-maker's. There's so little violence, so little war.*
The war is there by implication. If you went to Saigon itself then what struck you most most was how absent the war was, not how present. The city still was extraordinarily attractive, almost languorous. The old French avenues, clubs and restaurants still worked their charm. And for many people life remained exceptionally pleasant. It seemed to me a great idea to look at the war from the point of view of a non-combatant – a middle-aged Englishwoman, Barbara Dean, working in a Vietnamese bank.

Q: *It's one of the few films about the war in which the Vietnamese themselves seem to be human beings, not just vicious dots to be blasted off the screen.*
Good, I'm glad you feel that, because that was the intention. I was tired of films from the American point of

view. All about what a tragedy the whole thing was for America. Oh yes? Well, it wasn't so great for the Vietnamese. By chance, I went back to Vietnam recently and I found its spirit essentially unchanged. They still are a stunningly likeable people, with a very distinctive mix of melancholy and purposefulness. The Cercle Sportif which features so strongly in the film is still there, but now open to a different, more down-at-heel clientele. By a great irony, as I approached the American Embassy where so much of *Saigon* is set, the Vietnamese were wheeling filing cabinets down the front path. They, in their turn, were now evacuating the building, with the intention of handing it back to the Americans! My visit was a miracle of timing.

Q: *There are these three works which are all about Asia, and then suddenly in* The Bay at Nice, *you write a play about Russia. Where on earth does this one come from?*
It's a rogue play, in every sense. But it's one of which I'm extremely fond. I wanted to write a double bill: one play was to be set in Russia, the other in the US. It was to offer a kind of cold war contrast. Then I had a second notion, which didn't work at all. In the Greek manner, an essentially serious play would be followed by something erotic. Pornographic, in fact. But stage pornography is incredibly difficult, and I abandoned the task. So instead I ended up with a kind of bastard comedy about spoilt Americans. It was called *Wrecked Eggs*. It's not a play I want to preserve in this volume. It was satire, and what's worse, it was tepid.

Q: *But the first half of the bill was* The Bay at Nice?
All through the 80s I became more and more interested in the visual arts. I remember visiting a Lucien Freud exhibition and experiencing a blind jealousy that a painter could achieve exactly the kind of dramatic portraiture I sought in the theatre, but with an infinitely more effective

economy of means. Plays are so much *labour*, compared
with painting.

Q: The Bay at Nice *is set in the Hermitage Museum in
Leningrad. An older woman, a former pupil, is called in to
authenticate a painting of Matisse's.*
Yes, and crucially you must add that it's set in the 1950s. I
wanted to contrast the heady days at the beginning of the
century when Valentina studied with Matisse in Paris with
some of the deadliest moments of Soviet conformity.
Nothing is more exciting than that moment at which an
avant-garde first makes its breakthrough. There's always a
curious innocence, even when – as with Man Ray, say, or
Picasso – the subject matter is ostensibly quite dark. At
one level, of course, *The Bay at Nice* is about the
relationship between the everyday and the sublime,
between mediocrity and genius – with, I hope, an equal
amount of respect for both. For someone like Valentina's
daughter, Sophia, just to get through the day in the
hideous reality of mid-century Russia is as great a
triumph, in its way, as any painting of Matisse's.

Q: *There is a very definite change of tone here in your
work. It's the first play of yours you could call sweet.*
It's a kind-hearted play, yes.

Q: *It also has a great virtuoso central role.*
By this time I'd worked with some of the greatest actresses
in the world. But there's never been one I admired more
than Irene Worth. She's slightly like Laurette Taylor – at
once legendary, and also caviare to the general. Everyone
else looks a bit vulgar beside her. You almost have to work
in the theatre to appreciate how extraordinary she is.
There's a bone-dry combination of austerity and
adventurousness in her acting. You never know what she's
going to do next. But she can break your heart with a
single phrase. I still meet people who boast they were

lucky enough to see Irene Worth and Zoë Wanamaker in *The Bay at Nice*.

Q: The Bay at Nice *was followed very quickly by* The Secret Rapture.
I've never written a play so fast in my life. I had thought about it a good deal, haunted, as usual, by an opening image – the daughter grieving at the bed of the father. But once I began to write, it was as if my whole spirit had been taken over. I knew I had stumbled on this magnificent theme: that good people bring out the worst in all of us. As I have said before, God does not have to *do* anything in *Paradise Lost*. It is his very existence which drives the Devil crazy. Once I had hit on this idea, I just couldn't get the words down fast enough.

Q: *Isn't there a danger when a writer produces work at this speed? Can't it seem banal in the cold light of day?*
Ah, well, this is Middleton Murry's famous objection to *King Lear*. Murry hated *King Lear* because it scared him. He said it gave the impression of a writer possessed. The author, he said, was not in control of his material. It was in control of him. Now, to me, that is of course the glory of *King Lear* – that the greatest of all playwrights produced a work which I'm fairly sure even he did not wholly understand.

Q: *What does the title mean?*
There is a great deal that I cannot justify or explain in the play. The title itself is a mystery. I believed that I had read a theological work which explained that the moment when a nun would finally consummate her marriage to Christ – that's to say, the moment of death – was technically known as the secret rapture. But when a researcher was set to finding the origin of this phrase, he established that no such term actually exists.

Q: *So you've contributed the concept to theology?*
You could say! But, at some deeper level, the play is
embedded in the irrational. After all, its mainspring is the
injustice of love. We can never say why we will do
something for one human being which we will not do for
another. For some reason, Isobel is willing to make
sacrifices for Katherine which she is unwilling to make for
Irwin. It is this basic unfairness which Irwin cannot
understand, and which finally drives him to violence.

Q: *Although the play darkens as it goes on, the first half
contains a great deal of social satire about the 80s. The
older sister, Marion, seems to arrive almost full-blown
from your similar portrayal of a Tory MP in the film* Paris
By Night.
I'd had this extraordinary experience. I was staying with
some friends in the country, and a junior minister came to
dinner, freshly exhausted from the Conservatives' third
election victory in 1987. As we were eating, everyone fell
to talking about how much money they'd made from their
investments in the previous eighteen months. And I sat
there like an idiot, the only person in the room who hadn't
realised that this fantastic financial boom had been going
on. I'd missed the gravy train. And my first feeling was not
one of contempt or of anger, but of utter foolishness, of
exclusion. Open, boastful money-making was now woven
into the fabric of middle-class English life. At that moment
I suppose I knew something had definitively changed.

Q: *In performance,* The Secret Rapture *comes across as
one of the most passionate of your plays.*
By what turned out to be a fortunate coincidence, I was
away filming during the rehearsals of the original
production. So the work was shaped in my absence. The
play had been somewhat rushed on, and the director was
Howard Davies, whom at that time I barely knew. Not
only was I not on hand to watch the work develop, but,

interestingly, I also couldn't do my usual re-writing.
Howard was then kind enough to arrange a run-through
at a time I could manage. To my amazement he had
directed the play as if it were by Tennessee Williams – at
an emotional pitch far higher than I was expecting. In
particular, the row at the beginning of the second act
between Isobel and Irwin was electric. The whole thing
was a revelation. I shall always be grateful to Howard for
it. He showed me something I only half-knew was there.

Q: *It's also the first of a whole series of plays you write
which are concerned with the idea of goodness.*
In defiance of theatrical lore, I see no reason why goodness
should not be interesting on the stage.

David Hare
London
August 1996

FANSHEN

Based on the book by
William Hinton

Fanshen was first performed in London by the Joint Stock Theatre Group at the ICA Terrace Theatre, on 22 April 1975.

Company: Philip Donaghy
Paul Freeman
Cecily Hobbs
Roderic Leigh
Tony Mathews
Philip McGough
Pauline Melville
David Rintoul
Tony Rohr

Directed by William Gaskill and Max Stafford-Clark
Designed by Di Seymour

Act One

Fanshen *is an accurate historical record of what once happened in one village four hundred miles south-west of Peking.*

Every revolution creates new words. The Chinese revolution created a whole new vocabulary. A most important word in this vocabulary was 'fanshen'. Literally it means 'to turn the body' or 'to turn over'. To China's hundreds of millions of landless and land-poor peasants it meant to stand up, to throw off the landlord yoke, to gain land, stock, implements and houses. But it meant much more than this. It meant to enter a new world. That is why the book is called Fanshen. *It is the story of how the peasants of Long Bow built a new world.*

This version of William Hinton's book should be played with about nine actors taking the thirty or so parts. There are no sets, and no lighting cues. It should be performed using authentic props and costumes. At one end of the acting area is a small raised platform on which certain scenes are played. The rest of the acting area thrusts forward into the audience.

SECTION ONE

When the audience are in, the actors appear one by one with a piece of information. Then they begin to work on stage at their land, or washing, or begging, or watching until they form a whole picture of the village.

Ch'ung-lai's wife The village of Long Bow is situated four hundred miles south-west of Peking. One thousand people live there. In 1946 nearly all the people lived off the land. Landlords claimed from fifty to seventy per cent of their tenants' crop in rent. The rate of interest on loans went as high as one hundred per cent every twenty days. I am Ch'ung-lai's wife. I have no land.

Cheng-k'uan A family might possess a few sections of house, each section six foot by nine, made of adobe and straw. Each person might own a quilt, a quilted jacket, cotton trousers, cotton shoes. A bowl.
  I am Cheng-k'uan. I have one acre.

T'ien-ming The soil of Long Bow was poor. Without manure nothing would grow. The main manure was human manure, the foundation of the whole economy.
  I am T'ien-ming. I have half an acre.

Hu Hsueh-chen Chinese peasant women had their marriages arranged by their parents, and were often sold as children into landlords' households. Only when a woman became a mother-in-law in her own home did she command any power in a household. All the older women had their feet bound when they were young and could only move short distances.
  I am Hu Hsueh-chen, beggar. No land.

Fa-liang In Long Bow landlords and rich peasants owned two acres or more per head. Middle peasants owned one acre, poor peasants half an acre per head. Hired labourers owned no land at all.
  I am Fa-liang, a hired labourer.

Shen Ching-ho By far the largest building in Long Bow was the Catholic church, a Gothic building built in 1916 by Belgian Catholics. It acted as a bank and orphanage. Many of the poor of Long Bow bought their wives from the orphanage because it was cheaper.

I am Shen Ching-ho, a landlord. Twenty-three acres.

Man-hsi For thousands of years China was ruled by emperors. When the Japanese invaded most of the country was controlled by the Nationalist Party, the Kuomintang, under Chiang Kai-shek. Throughout the Japanese occupation, the most successful and only lasting resistance was organized by the Communist Eighth Route Army. By 1945 when the Japanese left, parts of China were controlled by the Nationalists and parts by the Communists. Long Bow was at the edge.

Man-hsi. Half an acre.

Yu-lai (*holding up a copy*) This is the book *Fanshen* by William Hinton.*

I am Yu-lai, an ex-bandit.

Tui-chin Literally the word 'fanshen' means to turn the body or to turn over. This is a record of one village's life between 1945 and 1949. Many of the characters are still alive.

The peasants work. The landlord on the platform watches.
Then he leaves.
The house lights go down.

1

T'ien-ming boxes the compass with a megaphone from on top of the church tower.

T'ien-ming There will be a meeting. There will be a meeting today. In the square after the noon meal. There will be a meeting.

The men look up from their work.

---

*The actor should give publisher and current price.

7

Fa-liang A meeting.

Tui-chin Twenty years ago we had a meeting.

Cheng-k'uan About the church, about who owned the vegetable garden.

Tui-chin shrugs and smiles.

Tui-chin Another meeting.

They move from work and gather in the square. They squat down and wait till they are joined. Meanwhile the following scene is played simultaneously. Kuo Te-yu is being guarded by Man-hsi. He carries his rifle like a hoe with a red tassel on the end. The scene is played on the platform. T'ien-ming comes in.

T'ien-ming A battle. Eight miles away. Outside Changchih.

Man-hsi Are we winning?

T'ien-ming Not yet.

Man-hsi Then we can't go ahead.

T'ien-ming Tie him up.

Man-hsi T'ien-ming.

T'ien-ming Tie him up. We have messages telling us the Eighth Route Army have liberated fifty million people. Three hundred thousand square miles.

Man-hsi But for how long?

T'ien-ming It doesn't matter. Elsewhere the Japanese are handing over only to the Kuomintang.

Kuo Te-yu moans.

Be quiet. The Kuomintang are leaving in wartime puppet governments, puppet troops. They even have the Japanese

8

fighting for them against us in places.

Man-hsi Then we must wait till we know . . .

T'ien-ming The Kuomintang are throwing their troops into regaining the Liberated Areas. Civil war.

Man-hsi If it's still going on, the people will be frightened to . . .

T'ien-ming What else can we do? Get that leg up.

Man-hsi Can't we wait? Can't we wait for victory before we begin?

T'ien-ming No. Above our heads?

Man-hsi Very good.

T'ien-ming Make a show.

They hoist the trussed Kuo Te-yu above their heads.

There is a crack in history one inch wide. We fought for it and we must use it.

They hoist Kuo Te-yu down from the platform. They carry him out and throw him down in front of the crowd.

Countrymen. Your eight years' suffering, your eight years at the hands of the Japanese are over. Their troops have gone. Now – revenge on traitors.

Cheers from the crowd.

Kuo Te-yu was head of the village for the last two years of the Japanese occupation. He was a collaborator.

Peasants Kill him. Rape his mother.

T'ien-ming Yes. But with your help.

Man-hsi stands back from the bundle.

T'ien-ming You all suffered under this man. You all know what he did. I therefore am asking you to speak it out. We are asking for your help. No one has ever asked your help before. Look at him. There's nothing to fear. You can touch him. Everyone here has a grievance, everyone here has the right to accuse, we all have the same thoughts in our heads. Those of us who fought in the resistance are now asking for your help. You must be the ones to beat down traitors, you must accuse. Who will be the first to speak?

Silence. People move slightly away from the bundle.

Fa-liang, what are you thinking? Cheng-k'uan? Tui-chin, have you . . .

Silence.

Release him.

Man-hsi He . . .

T'ien-ming Untie the ropes.

Man-hsi starts to undo the bundle. The people watch. Then Yu-lai gets up slowly.

Yu-lai Why not just take him up into the hills . . .

T'ien-ming No . . .

Yu-lai And do whatever you want, shoot him, it's your . . .

T'ien-ming He must be tried, in public, by the peasants of Long Bow, by the people he's oppressed . . .

Yu-lai You're just afraid to kill him yourself . . .

They start speaking simultaneously, each riding over the other's sentences. Yu-lai lecturing at T'ien-ming.

T'ien-ming No . . .

Yu-lai Because the Kuomintang are eight miles away . . .

T'ien-ming I'm asking for your help . . .

Yu-lai And if they come back . . .

T'ien-ming No one has ever asked anything of you before . . .

Yu-lai Then Kuo Te-yu will be reappointed . . .

T'ien-ming I am asking you to speak out your memories . . .

Yu-lai And anyone who has spoken at the meeting today . . .

T'ien-ming That's all, to say what we all know . . .

Yu-lai Anyone who has taken part in the struggle . . .

T'ien-ming Just to speak it out.

Yu-lai Will be shot. Tell them that.

Pause.

T'ien-ming So what are you saying?

Yu-lai What are you saying?

T'ien-ming Would you prefer to live under the Kuomintang? Would you like Kuo Te-yu reappointed? Your harvest seized, your goods impounded, your friends in the resistance shot? You want to see more of your friends hanged by the hair until their scalp comes away from their skull? (*Pause.*) Then what are you saying?

Yu-lai I'm saying . . .

T'ien-ming Yes?

Yu-lai Those who accuse collaborators may themselves be killed.

T'ien-ming Yes. (*Pause.*) So will you speak first?

Pause. Yu-lai stuck. T'ien-ming smiles.

Wang Yu-lai?

Yu-lai Don't laugh at me.

T'ien-ming I'm not laughing.

Yu-lai If you . . .

T'ien-ming Of course, if you're frightened . . .

Yu-lai Wait. I'm thinking.

The villagers smile, enjoying Yu-lai's difficulty. Then slowly he sits down.

Give me time to think.

Kuo Te-yu is now untied. T'ien-ming stares hard at the crowd.

T'ien-ming The resistance worked eight years. Some of you . . . silently supported us, in secret. Now the war against the Japanese is over, a civil war may begin. If we cannot beat down the traitors . . . (*He moves towards Kuo.*) You're frightened of him. There's nothing. Look. (*He puts his finger inside Kuo's mouth, between his teeth. Holds it there. Looks at the crowd. Takes it out.*) There's nothing there.

Yu-lai You've paid him not to bite you.

T'ien-ming Come here.

Yu-lai No.

T'ien-ming Come here.

Yu-lai looks round, then walks up. T'ien-ming places him dead opposite Kuo Te-yu.

Was this man a collaborator?

Yu-lai nods.

Did you suffer at his hands?

Yu-lai nods.

Did he steal your harvest?

Yu-lai nods.

Did he butcher your friends?

Yu-lai nods.

Accuse him.

A pause. Then Yu-lai strikes Kuo Te-yu across the face. Then he smashes a fist under his jaw. Kuo Te-yu falls back. Then Yu-lai picks him up, hits him again.

Accuse him.

Yu-lai stands him unsteadily on his feet, then takes a pace back.

Yu-lai Shen So-tzu was tortured for eighteen days, starved and shot. He was responsible. He betrayed him to the Japanese. I saw the body. I know it happened.

T'ien-ming Name him.

Yu-lai Kuo Te-yu.

Yu-lai goes back and takes his place in the crowd. Silence. Then a voice from a man still sitting in the crowd.

Cheng-k'uan Kung Lai-pao was cut to pieces with a samurai sword.

T'ien-ming Stand up.

Cheng-k'uan (*stands*) It was his treachery. Kuo Te-yu.

Fa-liang I was made to hand over three bags of grain or told the Japanese would burn my whole crop. He took it away and kept it.

T'ien-ming Name him.

Fa-liang Kuo Te-yu.

Tui-chin He sent me to work in the fields, I was never paid. One day . . .

Then an outbreak of shouting in the crowd, all on top of each other.

Cheng-k'uan Kill the donkey's tool.

Tui-chin Rape his mother.

Man-hsi Kill him.

They all rush forward on Kuo Te-yu and start a huge brawl. T'ien-ming throws himself in to try and protect Kuo Te-yu.

T'ien-ming Leave him. Leave him. He's only a puppet.

Kuo Te-yu (*screaming now*) I carried orders, I was only carrying out orders.

T'ien-ming Leave him.

He manages to clear a space for Kuo Te-yu.

He took orders. Let him testify.

Kuo Te-yu I was told what to do.

Yu-lai Who told you?

Kuo Te-yu Wen Ch'i-Yun . . .

T'ien-ming Commander of the puppet garrison, Long Bow fort.

Kuo Te-yu Murderer. Killed many in my sight. Shen Chi-mei . . .

T'ien-ming Head of Fifth District Police . . .

Kuo Te-yu Killed many. Ordered many dead. Took prisoners. Cut their hands, their fingers. He ran the camps.

Silence.

Tui-chin Shoot them.

T'ien-ming Nobody will be shot, nobody, until they have been tried by you. You have taken their lives into your hands, you, the peasants of Long Bow. It lies with you. Do you understand?

2

The peasants gather to watch. Still figures. Two men are lined up with sacks over their heads.

T'ien-ming Down with traitors, down with Kuomintang agents, liquidate the bloody eight years' debt.

Man-hsi cocks his rifle.

Arrested, tried, found guilty by the people. Wen Ch'i-Yun, commander of the puppet garrison, Long Bow fort. Shen Chi-mei, head of the Fifth District Police.

Man-hsi shoots them. They fall. The people watch as T'ien-ming and Man-hsi strip the bodies of their clothes. They then hold the clothes out to the people.

Here. The fruits of struggle. What we have seized from traitors. Take them. You have earned them. You deserve them. You have played your part. You have condemned the traitors, you have executed collaborators.

The people look at the clothes, but they turn away and will not take them. Then Shen Ching-ho, the landlord,

15

passes across the back of the stage. They scatter. T'ien-ming and Man-hsi are left holding out the goods.

Take them. Take them.

There is no one left.

SECTION TWO

I

Slogan: ASKING BASIC QUESTIONS

Secretary Liu appears, to address three cadres from Long Bow: T'ien-ming, Man-hsi and Yu-lai. They sit in a square.

Slogan: THE VISIT OF SECRETARY LIU

Liu An island in the centre of China. A province held by the Eighth Route Army. Now – a short ceasefire in the war between the Kuomintang and ourselves. During this time the possibility of a coalition is to be explored. But for a time our ground is safe. Our army protects us. In Lucheng County there is a People's Government. Our duty, the duty of all village leaders, is to consolidate the successes of the Anti-Traitor movement. The history of China is a history of bloody and violent rebellion. But always the blood runs down the gutter and nothing is changed. How are we to make sure this time, in this tight circle, the overturning holds?

The difference is, this time, we think. We ask questions. We analyse. This is why I have come to talk to you. Today you must consider a single question. Who depends upon whom for a living?

Man-hsi What's the answer?

Liu No, you must think.

*T'ien-ming gets up and crosses to another part of the
stage where he is joined by the peasants from the
previous scene: Tui-chin, Ch'ung-lai's wife, Hu Hsueh-
chen, Fa-liang. There are now two meetings which are
played antiphonally for the rest of the section.*

Slogan: THE FORMING OF THE PEASANTS' ASSOCIATION

T'ien-ming If we peasants are to organize ourselves we
must know why. We must start with questions. We must
find an answer to the most important question. Who
depends upon whom for a living? Well, can anyone . . .

Man-hsi We depend on the land.

Liu On whom?

Man-hsi On the person who owns the land.

Liu The landlord.

Man-hsi Yes. We depend on the landlord for a living.

Liu Yu-lai?

Man-hsi If the landlord didn't rent us land, we'd starve.

Liu But who gave him the land?

Man-hsi He bought it.

Liu How did he make the money to buy it?

Yu-lai If . . .

Man-hsi No, let me, leave this to me. It's not . . . Listen
. . . I've forgotten what I was going to say.

Fa-liang Why do we need to know?

T'ien-ming You must not just do things. You must know
why you do things.

Fa-liang Why?

T'ien-ming Because you need a theory . . .

Tui-chin What's a theory?

Man-hsi The question is . . . I don't see it. Why ask it? What answer do you want? What do you want me to say?

Liu You must work it out for yourself. If you want to serve the people you need to think.

Man-hsi Collaborators, yes, I could understand, should be executed; this, I don't understand.

T'ien-ming Fa-liang. Tell us something of your life.

Fa-liang My life?

T'ien-ming Yes. Just tell us.

Fa-liang I was fourteen when I went to work for Shen Ching-ho. My mother had been ill, my father had to borrow four dollars from the landlord to buy medicine. So to guarantee the loan he lent me to the landlord to work for seven years. I was always hungry. Twice I was ill. But no matter how hard I worked I couldn't begin to pay off the debt. By the time I'd worked for him three years, we owed him fifteen dollars instead of four. And then, after seven years, by the time he'd taken off all the things he claimed I'd broken, all the time I was sick, what was left was not enough to pay even the interest on the debt. So I had no wages at all. I had worked seven years. And he gave me nothing. At the end I tore down two sections of our house, I tore out the timbers. And only then could I pay back the original debt.

Ch'ung-lai's wife I was sold at the age of nine to be Ch'ung-lai's wife. I then had to serve in his family for six years before I married him. I was a child wife, everyone beat me. One day my mother-in-law broke my arm. The water in the pot was boiling. I asked her what I should cook in it. She didn't answer. I asked her again. She picked up an iron poker and broke my arm with it. She said I annoyed her. I lay on the k'ang for a fortnight, couldn't work or move. Then Ch'ung-lai's family threw me out. Ch'ung-lai went to Taiyuan to get work pulling a rickshaw, I went to work as a cook for a landlord. After about six years we earned enough to buy one acre of land, but it only yielded two bags of grain. After we had paid taxes, there was nothing left.

Liu Why should one man have the right to say 'This land is mine' and then without doing any work himself demand half of what's grown on it?

Man-hsi He owns it. It's his, he can do what he likes.

Liu Is it right?

Man-hsi Listen. I work for a landlord. He feeds me. At the end of the year he pays me. If he had cheated me, then I could . . . discuss it with you. But as he doesn't . . . then . . . so.

Liu So tell me. Who depends on whom?

Man-hsi It's . . .

Yu-lai I . . .

Man-hsi Say the thing again.

Liu Who depends on whom?

T'ien-ming Hsueh-chen.

Hsueh-chen My father was a labourer but he sold me to a husband against my will. My husband could find no work, could barely live. So he gambled what money we had. We lost our only quilt, we were left with nothing. I've had three children. One I saw the Japanese kill, a soldier with his boot, then with his sword. The second died of worms crawling out of him. So I threw my husband out of the house, took my third child, begged alone. People give me nothing. I live in the fields, eat herbs, sleep in the straw. And my third child is alive.

Man-hsi There has to be somebody to give us work to do.

Yu-lai Why?

Man-hsi If there were no landlords we'd starve.

Tui-chin I once went to my landlord to ask for more wages. He said, if you're poor it's because the heavens will it, it's because your grave is poorly located. All you can do is wait for your luck to change. Select a more suitable spot for your own grave and hope that the eight ideographs of earth and heaven are in better conjunction when your son is born.

T'ien-ming What do you conclude?

Slogan: THEY TALKED FOR EIGHT HOURS

We have all suffered. But we've never asked why. If we had to suffer. Do you see?

Man-hsi I don't understand.

Slogan: THEY TALKED FOR THREE DAYS

T'ien-ming Think. All think of your lives. Think what you've endured, what have you suffered for?

Yu-lai What can they do which we can't? Nothing. What can we do which they can't? We can work. Our labour transforms their land. We make it valuable, we create their wealth.

Ch'ung-lai's wife We have all suffered for them.

T'ien-ming So who depends on whom?

Yu-lai We make them rich, they depend on our labour, they depend on us.

Ch'ung-lai's wife They depend on us.

T'ien-ming Yes.

Liu Yes.

Fa-liang They depend on us.

Yu-lai Take us away, they'd die. Take them away, we live.

T'ien-ming You do not depend on them. They depend on you. Understand this and everything you have ever known is changed.

Liu We have liberated a peach tree heavy with fruit. Who is to be allowed to pick the fruit? Those who have tended and watered the tree? Or those who have sat at the side of the orchard with folded arms?

Yu-lai We shouldn't even pay rent.

Slogan: THEY STOPPED PAYING RENT

Liu The policy in the Liberated Areas is to ask simply for a reduction in rents and interest charges. But here in Lucheng County, you – the leaders – will go ahead of the policy.

They shake hands with Liu and say good-bye. Then join the peasants.

T'ien-ming Now surely we can right the wrongs of the past. Already in many places the landlords have been beaten down. We have only to follow the example of others. Then we can all fanshen.

Above the platform they raise a red banner saying FANSHEN.

SECTION THREE

I

Slogan: SETTLING ACCOUNTS

At one end Ch'ung-wang sits with a pair of scales, ready to receive rent. At the other on the platform Ching-ho sits, his fingernails being tended by his Daughter.

Ching-ho Shen Ching-ho. A landlord.

Ch'ung-wang Kuo Ch'ung-wang. A landlord.

A group of peasants forms outside Ch'ung-wang's house. Then Tui-chin steps from the group and into the house.

Ch'ung-wang Rent.

Tui-chin The peasants have decided to stop paying rent.

Ch'ung-wang Come here.

Tui-chin We have decided it's wrong to pay rent. And we have decided you took too much in the past . . .

Ch'ung-wang Come here.

Tui-chin Through the war, you charged us too much. And we want it back.

Ch'ung-wang Tui-chin, the land you farm . . .

Tui-chin Also interest on loans, that was too high . . .

Ch'ung-wang You have just lost.

Tui-chin And we want that back. And land you seized when we couldn't pay our debts . . .

Ch'ung-wang The house you live in . . .

Tui-chin We want that back. Also there are to be penalties for when you hit us . . .

Ch'ung-wang You have just lost.

Tui-chin Or abused us or starved us . . .

Ch'ung-wang The clothes you are wearing . . .

Tui-chin If it's wrong to pay rent . . .

Ch'ung-wang You have just lost.

Tui-chin It must always have been wrong.

Ch'ung-wang Come here.

Ch'ung-wang rises to strike Tui-chin. At once the villagers invade the house.

Cheng-k'uan Elected Chairman, Peasants' Association.

Yu-lai Elected Vice-Chairman, Peasants' Association. Find his grain.

Ch'ung-wang Peasants' Association?

Fa-liang goes out to search for his grain.

Yu-lai You are to attend a meeting at which your past life will be reviewed. Everything you have taken from us unfairly since the war began – rent, interest, land – you will return. Everything you have done to us since the Japanese came you will pay for. In one day we will add up the bill for your life.

Fa-liang Look.

Yu-lai Until then we are seizing your grain as security for your debt. And we are posting militia on your land.

Fa-liang returns, throwing down a rotten bag of mildewed grain.

Fa-liang Look. Look.

Tui-chin It's rotten. Why? Why did you let it go rotten? How could you?

Fa-liang This was salt.

Tui-chin Salt. This was salt. (*He takes the jar and flings the contents in Ch'ung-wang's face. It has hydrolized.*) One year when I couldn't pay my rent you took my whole harvest. Now I find it's in here rotting. Why?

Yu-lai He was hoarding it. He was hoping to make money.

Fa-liang People died . . .

Yu-lai Wait . . .

Tui-chin Le-miao starved to death on your land . . .

Yu-lai Wait . . .

Tui-chin All the time this was here.

Fa-liang Once I came begging, I crawled for grain . . .

Yu-lai Wait . . .

Tui-chin Kill him. Cut off his hands.

Yu-lai Wait. Wait for the meeting.

Slogan: FIFTY-EIGHT ACCUSATIONS

> *The group re-forms. The other villagers go, leaving just Fa-liang, Tui-chin, Cheng-k'uan and Yu-lai facing Ch'ung-wang.*

Yu-lai The people have accused you. Now you must pay.

Fa-liang There are six good bags of grain. That's all I can find.

Cheng-k'uan It's not enough.

Tui-chin We've measured his land. Thirteen acres.

Cheng-k'uan Not enough.

Yu-lai He owes the village one hundred bags of grain. It's his blood debt. And his sweat debt. He must settle accounts.

Cheng-k'uan Look. Here is a list of everything you took from us. Where is it?

Ch'ung-wang I don't know.

Fa-liang You turned it into coins.

Ch'ung-wang I don't have any coins.

Fa-liang All your houses, all your stock, all your grain, your clothes are not enough to settle your account. Where are your coins?

Ch'ung-wang No coins.

Fa-liang Where are they?

Yu-lai clears a space. He hits Ch'ung-wang twice.

Ch'ung-wang Fifty dollars. In the stove.

Yu-lai Fa-liang. Stove.

Fa-liang goes off. Yu-lai nods at Cheng-k'uan.

Yu-lai Cheng-k'uan.

Cheng-k'uan moves round for his turn. Hits Ch'ung-wang.

Ch'ung-wang Forty dollars.

Cheng-k'uan Where?

Ch'ung-wang Back yard.

Yu-lai Fa-liang. Back yard.

Yu-lai nods now at Tui-chin who takes his turn at hitting Ch'ung-wang.

Ch'ung-wang Thirty. Under the stable.

Yu-lai Fa-liang. Stable. (*He turns and smiles at Tui-chin.*) All right?

Tui-chin Yes.

Yu-lai May we leave it to you?

Tui-chin Of course.

Yu-lai It may be slow.

Cheng-k'uan Good night.

Yu-lai Good night.

They smile and go off. Tui-chin looks at Ch'ung-wang, then kicks him again. Shen Ching-ho rises.

Ch'ung-wang Another fifteen. Under the tree.

Tui-chin Fa-liang. Tree.

On the platform Ching-ho suddenly speaks.

Ching-ho My oldest clothes. (*He changes and dirties his hands.*) One bag of white flour.

His daughter fetches it. He turns to her.

Kiss me.

She does so. Then they set off across the village. Fa-liang returns with the coins.

Tui-chin Did you get them?

Fa-liang Yes.

They look at each other.

Tui-chin When I was born my family wanted to celebrate.

26

But they had to borrow money for dumplings. And so before I could speak, I was already in debt to the landlord. A man stands up to his neck in water, so that even a ripple is enough to drown him.

The scene scatters, as Ching-ho stops at the door of Yu-lai and Cheng-k'uan who are sitting at home. He puts the bag down and gestures to his daughter to stay outside, unseen. Then he goes in.

Ching-ho New Year.

Yu-lai Yes.

Ching-ho I had to come.

He smiles. Yu-lai looks at Cheng-k'uan.

A new life. Just to say a Happy New Year, a happy new life.

Yu-lai Yes.

Ching-ho That's good. Thank you. (*He goes to the door, slips his hand out, brings in the bag.*) I know your life is hard. On this soil. The valuable work you are doing. Service to the community. But we are all . . . citizens of one village. Please no ceremony but . . . help yourselves to the flour and pass a Happy New Year. (*He puts the bag down and walks backwards away.*) If at any time you should meet any difficulty in your new life in any way you should know my door is as it has always been, open, and I am as I have always been, ready to help. (*He gestures his daughter in.*) This is my daughter. She has always wanted to . . .

Silence.

Yours. Good night. (*He goes out.*)

Yu-lai and Cheng-k'uan look at each other. The

daughter stands silent, dignified, ignored for the rest of the scene.

Yu-lai What does he take us for? Rats who can be bought for one bag of flour? One bag? I'm worth a thousand bags. I am a granary.

Cheng-k'uan looks at the impassive girl, then goes over to the flour, puts a finger in, licks it, then stares in the bag as down a deep well.

The richest landlord in Long Bow. In the famine year he gave us nothing, now suddenly we all belong to one village. And we are offered flour.

T'ien-ming appears on the platform.

T'ien-ming Never trust a landlord, never protect a landlord. There is only one road and that is to struggle against them.

A banner descends reading: NEVER TRUST A LANDLORD, NEVER PROTECT A LANDLORD, THERE IS ONLY ONE ROAD AND THAT IS TO STRUGGLE AGAINST THEM

2

Ching-ho is seized as he goes home, stripped, tortured. Silent tableaux of the scene as it is described.

Man-hsi When the final struggle began Ching-ho was faced with accusations from more than half the village. Old women who had never spoken in public before stood up to accuse him. Altogether one hundred and eighty people testified. Ching-ho had no answer to any of them. When the Association met to decide what he owed, it came to four hundred bags of grain.

Cheng-k'uan That evening all the people went to Ching-ho's courtyard to help take over his property. It was very cold. We built bonfires and the flames shot up towards the stars. It was very beautiful.

Yu-lai We dug up all his money, beating him, digging, finding more, beating him, digging, finding more. By the time the sun was rising in the sky we had five hundred dollars.

T'ien-ming We were all tired and hungry. We decided to eat all the things Ching-ho had prepared for the New Year. There was a whole crock full of dumplings stuffed with pork and peppers. We even had shrimp. Everyone ate their fill and didn't notice the cold.

Shen Ching-ho Of the seven landlords in Long Bow, three died after being beaten to death by the Peasants' Association. Two more died of starvation when they had been driven from their land. Shen Ching-ho was luckier: he ran away and became a teacher in a primary school.

3

Slogan: DISTRIBUTION OF FRUITS

Yu-lai speaks from on high. T'ien-ming stands beside him. Cheng-k'uan organizes the peasants while Man-hsi counts with an abacus.

Yu-lai We have seized the wealth from fifteen families. Two hundred and eighty-six acres of land, twenty-six draft animals, four hundred sections of house. And behind the temple doors: everything they own.

The peasants stand in single file while Cheng-k'uan explains.

Cheng-k'uan You'll be given a number.

Fa-liang Yes.

Cheng-k'uan The number will be the number of pounds of grain you've been allocated.

Fa-liang Yes.

Cheng-k'uan You may then either keep the grain or change it into any object you want from inside the temple. Each object has its price marked on it. A plough I think three hundredweight of grain. A shovel fifty pounds, a slipper two, a rattle one, so on.

Man-hsi A hundred and eighty.

Cheng-k'uan You may spend a hundred and eighty pounds of grain.

Yu-lai (*from above*) The poorest allowed in first.

Cheng-k'uan Ch'ou-har. Because you are poor and have many needs, we have put your number up.

Man-hsi A hundred and ninety.

Cheng-k'uan You may spend a hundred and ninety pounds of grain.

Ch'ou-har A hundred and ninety.

Cheng-k'uan Hsueh-chen. Your number is not as high as others. There are only two in your family. We know you suffered a great deal but you did not speak at meetings. You did not speak out your grievances at landlords.

She nods, too shy to reply.

How can we know unless you speak out? Anyway you've got what you need.

Man-hsi One hundred and twenty.

Cheng-k'uan You may spend one hundred and twenty pounds of grain. Go in. Next.

Tui-chin Tui-chin.

Cheng-k'uan Yes. Now, you have denounced many landlords. You have been active in the struggle from the start, spoken at meetings. This should ensure you a lot. But in every case we have also balanced people's grievances against their needs. And you are a single man, who has a lot of the implements he needs. So your number has come down.

Tui-chin What if I want a cow, but haven't been given enough grain?

Cheng-k'uan Then you'll get a share in a cow.

Tui-chin A share?

T'ien-ming Yes. Why not?

Tui-chin Share a cow?

T'ien-ming Four families, one leg each.

Tui-chin Very good.

Man-hsi A hundred and fifty pounds of grain.

Cheng-k'uan Next.

Ch'ung-lai's wife I am Ch'ung-lai's wife.

Cheng-k'uan Yes, yes I know. Many – grievances – yes – and also great need. Both. Grievances and need both high. Man-hsi?

Pause.

Ch'ung-lai's wife What do you get?

Cheng-k'uan What?

Ch'ung-lai's wife The leaders, what do the leaders get? You, the Chairman of the Association. Yu-lai over there, T'ien-ming, village head. What do you get?

31

T'ien-ming The leaders get less.

Ch'ung-lai's wife They get some?

T'ien-ming They get some but they get less.

Yu-lai has been listening to this last exchange.

Man-hsi Two hundred and ten.

Cheng-k'uan Go into the temple. Make your choice.

Ch'ung-lai's wife Thank you. Thank you. (*She goes in.*)

Yu-lai, Cheng-k'uan and T'ien-ming are left outside.

Yu-lai Why?

Cheng-k'uan Mm?

Yu-lai Why less?

Cheng-k'uan Less because . . .

T'ien-ming Less because you're the leaders and you must wait for the peasants to suggest you get some.

Yu-lai Wait for them?

T'ien-ming Yes.

Yu-lai Well it's not worth it. I'd be better off as a peasant.

T'ien-ming Yes.

Pause.

Yu-lai I think we should get something. Not for ourselves, more for expenses, for the Association. If we took over the inn, managed it, that would help pay for the school, pay for the oil we need for lamps for Association meetings. We're going to have to make some money somehow.

Cheng-k'uan Take over the inn?

Yu-lai Why not?

Pause.

Cheng-k'uan Put it to the people.

Yu-lai I thought we were waiting for them to put it to us.

They smile.

Cheng-k'uan Take over the inn.

The peasants begin to come out carrying loot. Some have bags of grain, some implements. Fa-liang is wearing a landlord's coat.

Hsueh-chen A quilt! A landlord's quilt!

Tui-chin comes out with a pot bigger than himself.

T'ien-ming Are you sure that's what you want?

Tui-chin Certain. I've always wanted it.

Fa-liang All my life I have been oppressed and exploited.

Tui-chin For all the grain I'm going to have.

He embraces T'ien-ming crying. Ch'ou-har has a huge bag of grain.

Ch'ou-har The bad life. The unbearable life of working for others.

Ch'ung-lai's wife We are moving from hell to heaven. To live in your own house, to eat out of your own bowl, is the happiest life.

Yu-lai looks at T'ien-ming and smiles.

SECTION FOUR

I

Night. T'ien-ming and Man-hsi walk up and down in silence, guarding the road to Changchih. T'ien-ming choosing his moment.

Slogan: THE PARTY

T'ien-ming Comrade. What do you think of the Eighth Route Army?

Man-hsi What do I think of it?

Silence.

What can I think? I used to have nothing, now I've fanshened. Everything I have the Eighth Route Army gave me.

T'ien-ming And the Communist Party?

Man-hsi Isn't that the same thing?

T'ien-ming Not exactly. The Party organized the army, in the army there are Party members. The Party directs the army, but most of the soldiers aren't in the Party. And it's the Party which led the battle against the landlords.

Man-hsi I see. (*He doesn't.*) Where is the Party then, where can you find it?

T'ien-ming I . . .

Man-hsi Do you know?

T'ien-ming Yes.

Man-hsi Well?

T'ien-ming It's many miles away, some hundred of miles.

In the countryside. Would you come with me?

Man-hsi Of course. Let's go tomorrow.

T'ien-ming It's a long way. And through Kuomintang country. It's difficult. Dangerous.

Man-hsi It doesn't matter, you say the Party led us to fanshen, so we must find it, let's go.

T'ien-ming Don't rush into it. You . . .

Man-hsi Go on.

T'ien-ming You may be risking your life.

Man-hsi Well?

T'ien-ming You may be risking your family's life.

Man-hsi I've made up my mind.

T'ien-ming Man-hsi . . .

Man-hsi Why do you talk about danger as if we weren't in danger already?

T'ien-ming In that case . . . your journey is over. The Party is here. I am a member of the Communist Party.

Silence.

Man-hsi Why did you trick me?

T'ien-ming Because the Communist Party is an illegal organization.

Man-hsi So?

T'ien-ming If the enemy returns we will all be killed. Membership is secret. Even if you are arrested and beaten to death, you must never admit you belong.

Man-hsi You deceived me.

T'ien-ming Listen . . .

Man-hsi Who else in Long Bow?

T'ien-ming You'd be the first.

Pause.

Man-hsi What do you hope to do? To take over the village?

T'ien-ming Never.

Man-hsi What then?

T'ien-ming The Party must be the backbone of the village. It must educate, study, persuade, build up the People's organizations – the Peasants' Association, the Village Government, the Women's Association, the People's Militia, it must co-ordinate all these, give them a clear line to follow, a policy that will unite everyone who can be united. Without the Party the village is a bowl of loose sand. So its members must get up earlier, work harder, attend more meetings, stay up later than anyone else, worry before anyone else is worried. We must become the best organized, the most serious group in the village. All in secret. We must lead, not by force but by example. By being good people. By being good Communists.

Pause.

Man-hsi I'd hoped for something . . .

T'ien-ming Yes.

Pause.

Do you see? Do you see how hard it is? And how far? And how dangerous?

In a series of tableaux on the platform Hu Hsueh-chen, her husband and T'ien-ming act out the story that Ch'ung-lai's wife tells.

Ch'ung-lai's wife Liberation and the settling accounts movement were to Hu Hsueh-chen what water is to a parched desert. She won clothes and threw away her rags, she won a quilt and threw away her flea-infested straw, she won land and gave up begging. Knowing that these gains were the result of struggle and not gifts from heaven, she attended every meeting and supported those who were active although she herself was afraid to speak in public. Then she met a revolutionary cadre who helped to make her fanshen complete. This man, a doctor, asked for her hand in marriage. She hesitated. She asked for a conference to tell him the whole story of her life. She told him she could not stand any more suffering or oppression at the hands of a man. He persuaded Hu Hsueh-chen that he was a man of principle, and that, most important, as a product of the revolutionary army and its Communist education, he believed in equality for women. They were married in February 1946. Her husband began even to cook his own supper so his wife could attend meetings – something unheard of in Low Bow. She became more active when he explained that fanshen could only be achieved through struggle. She finally mastered her shyness and became secretary of the Women's Association.

In late 1946 her husband had to move away. He wrote her letters urging her to work hard. 'When you run into trouble, don't be gloomy. For there can be no trouble to compare with the past.' One day Man-hsi came to talk to her about the Communist Party. Then later T'ien-ming came and asked her if anyone had spoken to her on the subject. She knew the Party was meant to be secret so she denied having been approached.

A few days later T'ien-ming came back with an application form and helped her fill it out. He asked if she would give her life for the Party.

Hsueh-chen I would.

Ch'ung-lai's wife And he enrolled her in the Party to which her husband, unknown to her, had long belonged.

SECTION FIVE

I

Slogan: THE END OF CEASEFIRE

A tableau of Man-hsi being sent to war. He stands at the centre.

Yu-lai
Glorious are those who volunteer
To throw down tyrants
March to the border when the millet sprouts
Fight for the people
Defend our homes and lands
Most glorious are the volunteers.

> *Man-hsi goes to war. The village disperse, leaving Yu-lai with Cheng-k'uan. Hsien-e is working in the house behind.*

Slogan: CIVIL WAR

Yu-lai What's wrong?

Cheng-k'uan Nothing.

Yu-lai Don't look so sad, he's happy to go. He's been given land, and we'll farm it for him while he's away.

Cheng-k'uan Yes.

Yu-lai Slut. Some soup. That's why we're going to win.

Because our volunteers don't have to worry about their homes.

Cheng-k'uan The Kuomintang . . .

Yu-lai (*turning away*) If we can keep things on the move.

Hsien-e serves the soup. T'ien-ming appears.

T'ien-ming There's a new directive . . .

Yu-lai Good.

T'ien-ming From the Party.

Cheng-k'uan What does it say?

T'ien-ming It says if the war is to be won, the peasants must be mobilized. They must take over the land to win food to eat, clothes to wear, houses to live in. It says many peasants have still not fanshened.

Yu-lai It's true.

T'ien-ming Serious feudal exploitation still exists.

Yu-lai There are hundreds in the village who still don't have enough to make a living.

Cheng-k'uan How's it to be done?

T'ien-ming The land must be further redistributed.

Cheng-k'uan What land?

Yu-lai We've scarcely begun. More soup.

Cheng-k'uan There aren't many gentry left in Long Bow. Two landlords, four rich peasants, it's not going to go very far.

Yu-lai Middle peasants.

Cheng-k'uan You can start on the middle peasants certainly . . .

39

Yu-lai Plenty of those.

Cheng-k'uan But if you take away their goods all you do is drive them over to the enemy side.

Yu-lai That's a risk.

Cheng-k'uan The middle peasants already don't work as hard as they should, because if they work hard they become rich peasants, and if they become rich peasants we take it all away. Like cutting chives.

Yu-lai Does that matter?

Cheng-k'uan So the people in the village who can actually make a living, who can look after themselves, who ought to be our strength, will drift over to the Kuomintang.

Yu-lai So what do you think we should do?

He strikes Hsien-e who has returned with more soup.

You're an idle cunt.

She goes.

The whole village is convinced the Kuomintang will return. The Catholics openly plot our assassination, peasants have begun to creep back in the night to return the goods that were seized from landlords, grenades go off in the hillside, you ask about fanshen, people have never heard the word. We're at war. What do you think we should do?

Silence.

Leadership. Strong leadership, Cheng-k'uan. We must keep things moving.

Cheng-k'uan Well . . . (*A pause.*) What does the directive say?

T'ien-ming Cut off feudal tails. This time we must examine family history. Anyone whose father or grandfather exploited labour at any time in the past will have their wealth confiscated.

Yu-lai Very good.

T'ien-ming We must go right back, right through the last three generations to look for any remaining trace of feudal exploitation.

Yu-lai Very good.

T'ien-ming Cheng-k'uan?

They look at Cheng-k'uan. Then Yu-lai goes up to him.

Yu-lai If you don't beat down the drowning dog, he jumps up and bites your hand. (*Then he smiles and calls into the house.*) Slut. My Luger.

Hsien-e brings him his gun.

And to work.

2

T'ien-ming The public meetings began again. All the remaining members of families already under attack had their last wealth seized. And families with any history of exploitation were added to the list. With the enemy troops so close and counter-revolution so likely, the campaign was emotional and violent. When there was no more land to be had, we ripped open ancestral tombs, leaving gaping holes in the countryside. It looked as if the country had been bombarded with shells.

Yu-lai But it was the living who bore the brunt of the attack. The gentry wives astonished us with their contempt for pain. We heated iron bars in the fire, but burning flesh held no terror for the women. They would die rather than tell you where their gold was hidden. They would only weaken, if at all, when their children were threatened.

Cheng-k'uan Slowly the advance of the Kuomintang was being halted. The military threat disappeared. And the campaign to find new wealth faded, a source of bitter disappointment to those of us who manned it. For when all the fruits had been divided, there were still many families who felt they had not fanshened.

3

Hu Hsueh-chen lying on the platform, her four-year-old daughter beside her. T'ien-ming at the door carrying his possessions.

T'ien-ming Hsueh-chen. Hsueh-chen.

She wakes.

I'm leaving tonight. Uh. Quiet, let me go quietly. I've been ordered to go and work at County Headquarters. You must elect a new secretary to the Party in Long Bow.

Silence.

Say nothing. I know what you're thinking. I can't help. One person doesn't make any difference. Hsueh-chen. I . . . two years ago I couldn't get a sentence out. The people . . . victory lies with the people.

Silence.

Good night.

He goes.

SECTION SIX

I

Slogan: NINETEEN FORTY-EIGHT

A single man working in the field. As at the opening of
SECTION ONE.

Cheng-k'uan on the tower.

Cheng-k'uan There will be a meeting. There will be a
meeting tonight.

Old Tui-chin stops and looks up.

Tui-chin Another meeting. Do the meetings never stop?

Cheng-k'uan Everyone to attend

Tui-chin 'Under the Nationalists too many taxes. Under
the Communists, too many meetings.'

*He picks up an enormous pile of stubble, twice his own
size and starts humping it home. He pauses. Yu-lai sees
him.*

Yu-lai Why aren't you at the meeting?

Tui-chin They can meet without me tonight.

Yu-lai Why?

Tui-chin I'm busy. I'm tired.

Yu-lai Come to the meeting.

Tui-chin There's no point, there's nothing left to dig up,
there's nothing. We'll just sit about and discuss
redistributing our farts.

Yu-lai Come to the meeting.

Tui-chin Listen, we all struggled for this land. Now we're not given time to work it because we're at meetings talking about where to find more land which even if we found it we wouldn't have time to farm because we're always at meetings.

Yu-lai Come to the meeting.

Tui-chin I haven't eaten.

Yu-lai The meeting is for your own good. (*He hits him across the face.*) It's in your interest. (*He hits him again.*) You think I don't have my work cut out without chasing up idle cunts like you?

Tui-chin stumbles away.

Where do you think your fanshen came from, you lazy turd?

2

The work team. Hou, Little Li, Ch'i-yun, Chang Ch'uer. Platform.

Slogan: THE ARRIVAL OF THE WORK TEAM

Ch'i-yun We paused for a moment to look down into the valley. A long flat plain, in the centre a complex of adobe walls under a canopy of trees, the yellow fields stretching away on all sides. In the semi-darkness we could just see the last actions of the day: a donkey straining at a plough, a man raking corn stubble, a barefoot boy spreading night soil, a child playing with some sticks in a ditch. Over our heads the warm, motionless air hummed and whistled as a flight of swallows swooped low. The four of us stood a moment, none of us knowing each other, none of us knowing what to say. Then we began our descent into Long Bow.

The work team enter the village.

Yu-lai (*off*) You. Get out of that ditch and get to the meeting. (*off*) Is everyone in?

Cheng-k'uan (*off*) All at the meeting.

Yu-lai appears, a broad smile on his face.

Yu-lai Perhaps we should lock the doors.

He looks up and sees the four of them, standing looking at him.

I don't know you.

Chi'-yun Comrade.

Hou I'm Hou Pao-pei, leader of the work team. We've been send by the government to supervise land reform in Long Bow.

Yu-lai I see. Wang Yu-lai, Vice-Chairman Peasants' Association.

Hou Ch'i-yun. Chang Ch'uer. Magistrate Li. Members of the work team.

Yu-lai Welcome to Long Bow. (*Pause.*) We are all at a meeting, you've chosen a bad time.

Little Li Is there somewhere for us to stay?

Yu-lai I'm sure.

Hou We will be starting work at once.

Yu-lai Yes?

Hou Talking to the people, finding out how they've prospered . . .

Chang Ch'uer Agricultural methods.

Hou Yes.

Chang Ch'uer Mutual aid schemes.

Hou Examining the progress of the movement. Elsewhere there have been shortcomings. Some landlords, rich peasants, riffraff, have sneaked into the people's organizations, where they abuse their power, ride roughshod over the people and destroy the faith of the masses in their new organizations.

Yu-lai You can sleep in the temple. I must go to the meeting. Mutual aid scheme. Discussion. You know.

He looks at them, goes out. The four of them left standing.

Hou Good, excellent, very good. Right.

Little Li Do you . . .

Hou Li, can you try and find the temple? We must know where we're going to sleep. (*He laughs.*)

Little Li Yes, of course.

Hou Chang Ch'uer, perhaps you could help, Ch'i-Yun and I will go and . . . find the meeting. Is that best?

Chang Ch'uer I think so.

Little Li Yes.

Hou Good, then tomorrow we start meeting the people of the village. There's a lot to be done. Good luck.

They scatter. Chang Ch'uer remains.

Chang Ch'uer The first day we watched each other, the four of us, unknown to each other, scrutinizing every reaction. The second day . . .

3

A man with a white scarf tied round his face runs on and

strangles Chang Ch'uer. They struggle for a long time. The man stuffs a towel down his mouth, then catches sight of Lai-tzu who is watching, a passer-by who happens to have caught the incident. The man runs off.

    Hu Hsueh-chen runs out into the street. Hou appears.

Hou What's happened?

Hsueh-chen This man . . .

Hou It's Chang Chu'er.

Hsueh-chen Has been attacked.

Hou Get a doctor.

Lai-tzu It . . .

Hsueh-chen There's no doctor in the village.

Hou Where's the nearest?

Lai-tzu Lucheng.

Hou What's your name? Can you carry him to Lucheng?

Lai-tzu I can find a stretcher. (*He goes out.*)

Hou His pulse is very weak.

Hsueh-chen Who is he?

Hou He's a member of the work team. What's this?

Hsueh-chen It's a towel.

Hou It says ger oo de morenin. 'Good morning' in English.

    Lai-tzu returns with the stretcher.

Lai-tzu I heard the attack being plotted. A few hours ago. I know who did it.

    Little Li and Ch'i-yun arrive.

Hou Chang Ch'uer has been attacked.

Ch'i-yun Is it the Kuomintang?

Lai-tzu I overheard the planning.

Hou Lift him carefully.

Lai-tzu It was Wang Yu-lai.

Hou Be careful. You're hurting him.

Little Li Yu-lai?

Lai-tzu I overheard Yu-lai talking to his friends. I was listening . . .

Little Li Then why didn't you tell us?

Hou Concentrate.

They lift the body on to the stretcher.

There.

Lai-tzu Don't you want to know who did it?

Hou I've heard what you say. Take him to Lucheng.

Lai-tzu Do I get millet tickets?

Hou Take him.

Lai-tzu It's eight miles.

Hou Little Li. Find someone who will take him.

Little Li and Lai-tzu go off, Lai-tzu whining into the distance.

Lai-tzu I'll take him, it just is a very long way, and if he were a wounded soldier, I'd be entitled to millet tickets, and I just want to know if the same thing applies to . . .

Hou Is he trustworthy?

Hsueh-chen No. He's a Catholic.

A pause. Hou screws the towel up. Cheng-k'uan arrives.

Hu Hsueh-chen, I'm secretary of the Women's Association.

Cheng-k'uan Cheng-k'uan, chairman of the Peasants' Association.

Hou You're both members of the Party, I know. Comrade Hou Pao-pei, leader of the work team.

Hsueh-chen Welcome.

Hou The man he accused . . .

Hsueh-chen Yes . . .

Hou Is a cadre in the Peasants' Association.

Hsueh-chen He's Vice-Chairman.

Hou Yes.

Cheng-k'uan And his son Wen-te is the Head of Police.

Pause.

Hsueh-chen The towels are made by a co-operative in Hantan.

Hou These?

Hsueh-chen I've seen them in Yu-lai's home.

Little Li returns.

Little Li The first day we arrive!

Ch'i-yun Comrade.

Hou Give me time to think. Just give me a moment.

Little Li If the leaders of the village take to attacking the work team . . .

Hou Please. (*He turns to Hsueh-chen.*) Comrades. I am a peasant like you, I come from a village, not that many miles from here. I've lived the same life, so I think you'll understand what I do.

Hsueh-chen Comrade.

Little Li I think we should . . .

Hou Just . . . let me speak. I've only been here a few hours but already the work team has heard a good deal of complaint. Some people who feel that fanshen is not complete. Some who feel they got too little, others who feel that the cadres took most. Whether this is true . . . an attack is made on the life of a member of the work team by a leader of the village on the first day we arrive to investigate.

Pause.

The Vice-Chairman of the Peasants' Association must be taken to jail. His son, Wen-te, the Head of Police, will be taken to jail. His closest friends must be arrested and taken to jail. The work team will be issued with guns. All village leaders are temporarily suspended. The Women's Association. The militia suspended. The village accounts will be examined by the work team. The Party branch will go into secret session to examine its own performance up till now. The work team will take over the affairs of the village. It will root out commandism, hedonism, opportunism. It will re-examine the whole village's fanshen.

Hsueh-chen is staring at Hou.

Comrades, I am not saying you . . . you are thinking of the hours you have all worked, of the days, of the months, of the years, you have given. Don't. Don't think of yourself. Think of the people and how they are led.

Hsueh-chen and Cheng-k'uan go out, saying nothing.

Wipe the slate clean and start again. Is that not right, Little Li?

Little Li Yes.

Hou Ch'i-yun?

Ch'i-yun Yes.

Hou The place is rotten. We must start again.

SECTION SEVEN

I

Little Li addresses the poorest in the village. Lai-tzu, Ting-fu, Yuan-lung, Huan-ch'ao, Old Lady Wang, Hsin-ai, T'ao-yuan. Hou sits beside Little Li as he speaks.

Slogan: THE DRAFT AGRARIAN LAW

Little Li Brothers and sisters, peasants of Long Bow. In the course of the past two years this region has carried out a powerful and enthusiastic land reform programme. Over ten million people have already fanshened. But there are some areas where the peasants have only partially fanshened or not fanshened at all. Now finally everyone must fanshen.

In the past there were mistakes. There was favouritism. People got more because they were soldiers, or because they were cadres. Or because they were highly placed in the movement.

Now the Draft Agrarian Law will correct all such mistakes because it is firmly based on the slogan: 'Depend on the poor peasant, unite with the middle peasant, destroy the feudal system.'

Now what does this mean? It means the feudal system

51

will be finally eliminated and replaced with a new system called 'Land to the Tiller'.

Lands and goods are to be redistributed on one basis and one basis only: how much you have now and how many there are in your family.

So no longer is it a question of what sort of person you are, or whether you are thought to have helped or hindered the movement. This time, those with merit will get some, those without merit will get some. All landlords' property will be divided and everyone will get a fair share. Now how is this to be done?

It is to be done by a rigorous process of classification.

Each head of family in Long Bow will be classified according to what he now has. If he is classified a poor peasant, or hired labourer, he will be given something. If he is classified a middle peasant, he will probably not be touched. If he is classified a rich peasant or landlord, he will have something taken away.

And this time it is you – the poor – the very poorest in the village, who will be in charge of the classification process.

You will run the meetings. Each family head must come before you and reveal his exact wealth and his exact needs.

You will discuss his report and decide his family's class status.

But beware. You – the basic elements – are holding a knife in your hands. We are at war. Class someone now as a rich peasant and he becomes your enemy. Class someone as a middle peasant and he becomes your ally. Class someone as a poor peasant and he becomes one of you. You must take care. For on these classifications will depend what everyone is to get, how they are to live for the rest of their lives.

The peasants applaud.

Slogan: SELF-REPORT, PUBLIC APPRAISAL

Lai-tzu My name is Kuo Lai-tzu. I have two acres, there are four in my family. I have no children. I reap about ten bushels to the acre. And I don't have any kind of draft animals.

Hou Discuss in groups.

> *Lai-tzu before the classification meeting. These are the poorest peasants again: Lai-tzu, Old Lady Wang, Huan-ch'ao, T'ao-yuan, Ting-fu, Yuan-lung and an old woman, Li Hsin-ai. Li and Hou are at the side, writing. The peasants are in distinct groups. The groups go into a huddle.*

Hou Report from your groups.

Ting-fu Poor peasant.

Old Lady Wang Poor peasant.

Yuan-lung Poor peasant.

Hou Poor peasant?

All Yes, yes.

Hsin-ai He hasn't even fanshened.

Hou Poor peasant. I shall write it down. Next.

Lai-tzu Told you.

> *Ting-fu stands up.*

Ting-fu Half an acre.

Hou Name?

Ting-fu My name is Ting-fu. I have half an acre. No livestock, no implements. I have three sections of house.

Yuan-lung Falling down.

Ting-fu And I share a privy, that's it.

Old Lady Wang Everyone knows him, he's a poor peasant.

Lai-tzu He's the hardest worker in the village.

Hou Poor peasant?

All Yes, yes. Poor peasant.

Hou Poor peasant. I shall write it down. Next.

Huan-ch'ao steps up.

Huan-ch'ao My name is Chang Huan-ch'ao.

Old Lady Wang Yes well . . .

Little Li Let him speak.

Huan-ch'ao I'm a blacksmith. I have very little land because I don't farm. I have four sections of house. I have a family of four. That's all.

Hou Discuss in groups.

Old Lady Wang There's no need. He's a middle peasant.

Little Li You must first discuss it in your group.

Old Lady Wang He's a middle peasant because he does so well out of everyone . . .

Yuan-lung How . . .

Old Lady Wang His prices are high and his work's rotten.

Laughter.

Ting-fu He's certainly a terrible blacksmith.

Hou Please.

Huan-ch'ao No, go on. Say what you like, I'm very interested.

Old Lady Wang You . . .

Huan-ch'ao Very happy to hear what you think.

Old Lady Wang We think . . .

Huan-ch'ao Yes?

Old Lady Wang We think you're a disgraceful blacksmith . . .

Huan-ch'ao I see, yes, that's very interesting.

Old Lady Wang And we wouldn't trust you to bang a nail up an elephant's arsehole.

Huan-ch'ao I see. Yes. That's very clear.

Laughter.

Hou Listen, it doesn't matter what sort of a blacksmith he is . . .

Lai-tzu It matters to us.

Old Lady Wang You said a middle peasant is someone who can make their own living . . .

Hou That's not what I said. A middle peasant is someone who himself rarely labours for others. He does. He hires his labour to you. That makes him . . . (*He looks round for an answer.*)

Ting-fu A worker.

Lai-tzu What's a worker?

Hou I don't think . . .

Yuan-lung He's a poor peasant.

Old Lady Wang If we say he's a poor peasant, he'll get

something in the distribution and . . . I don't want him to get anything.

Little Li That really isn't . . .

Old Lady Wang If he were a good blacksmith I'd be happy for him to be a poor peasant.

Hou Good and bad don't come into it.

Yuan-lung Call him a poor peasant.

Old Lady Wang Who must improve his work.

Hou You're a poor peasant who must improve your work.

Little Li Do we all agree?

Ting-fu No.

Little Li Why not?

Ting-fu He's a village worker.

Little Li We don't have that category.

Ting-fu Well, you should. We can't call him a peasant, peasants work on the land.

Little Li Well . . .

Hou He's right.

Ting-fu You can't call him something he's not.

Hou Thank you, Ting-fu. We'll think about it. Huan-ch'ao, we will defer your classification.

Huan-ch'ao Defer?

Hou Yes. The next.

Huan-ch'ao goes back to his seat.

Huan-ch'ao Just wait till it's your turn.

T'ao-yuan steps up.

T'ao-yuan My name is Wang T'ao-yuan. Only two acres. No wife, no animals. My land was given me in the first distribution, two years ago. Before that I had no land at all. I have one nephew to support. That's all.

Hou Discuss in groups.

They do so. T'ao-yuan smiles broadly while he waits.

Each group to report.

A representative stands up from each group.

Lai-tzu Our group wants to ask about the past.

Hou Yes.

Lai-tzu You used to have a lot of money.

T'ao-yuan I have had money, yes.

Lai-tzu I mean, I can remember when you didn't work.

T'ao-yuan Well . . .

Lai-tzu How did you live?

T'ao-yuan This and that.

Lai-tzu You sold heroin.

T'ao-yuan I smoked it myself.

Lai-tzu You sold it . . .

T'ao-yuan In a way.

Lai-tzu What way?

T'ao-yuan Just to make money. I only sold it to make money.

Lai-tzu Well why else . . .

Hou All right.

*Hou nods at the second group whose representative is
Old Lady Wang.*

Old Lady Wang Tell us what happened to your wife.

T'ao-yuan (*to Hou*) Is this . . .

Hou Yes.

T'ao-yuan Well . . . I began smoking heroin in the famine
year and everything I had I spent on heroin. So when I had
nothing left I took my wife to Taiyuan. I was very lucky, I
managed to find a buyer quite quickly. He gave me six
bags of millet, so that sealed the deal.

Old Lady Wang And other people's wives, you sold them?

T'ao-yuan I helped sell them, occasionally.

Old Lady Wang And you got paid for this . . .

T'ao-yuan I was usually given heroin.

Old Lady Wang So your income came either from selling
heroin or selling other people's wives . . .

T'ao-yuan It's . . . one way of looking at it.

Old Lady Wang He should be classed as a landlord's
running dog. (*She sits.*)

Hou Next group.

Huan-ch'ao We want to ask about the donkey. You had a
donkey?

T'ao-yuan Yes, I paid two hundred dollars for it.

Huan-ch'ao What happened to it?

T'ao-yuan It caught a cold, it died.

Huan-ch'ao I see. Thank you. (*He sits.*)

Hou So.

Old Lady Wang May we ask what he now feels about selling his wife?

T'ao-yuan I feel . . . (*He begins to cry bitterly.*)

Old Lady Wang Really it was your own fault. You sold her and now you weep about it.

T'ao-yuan I'm not weeping for her. I'm weeping for my donkey.

Silence.

Hou Classification. From your groups.

Lai-tzu Middle peasant.

Old Lady Wang Rich peasant.

Huan-ch'ao Poor peasant.

Silence.

Hou Discuss again.

3

Little Li working at a desk with a candle on papers. Hou is staring out into the fields.

Little Li I have the results of the classification. Trying to make sense.

Hou What is it?

Little Li One hundred and seventy-four families have been classed poor peasants.

Hou Isn't that what we expected?

Little Li But only seventy-two have so far fanshened. It means there are one hundred families in the village who barely scrape a living. And I've nothing to give them. We found one rich peasant. One. It's not going to go very far. (*Pause.*) It's not land, there's enough land, one acre for every man, woman and child in Long Bow. It's resources. Animals, carts, implements, houses. That's what we need.

Hou I've been over the village accounts to try and see if anything was missed or stolen in the last distribution. Everyone says the cadres took too much, but I can't find anything.

Pause.

Little Li So what do we do next?

Hou Expand the Poor Peasants' League.

Little Li It won't create *things*, comrade. (*Pause.*) I was at college, many years ago. People used to say China is poor, it's poor because it lacks fertilizer, it lacks machinery, it lacks insecticides, it lacks medical care. I used to say no, China is poor because it is unjust. (*Pause. Then he smiles.*)

Hou We must prove it, comrade.

Little Li Yes.

The house lights come up.

Interval

Act Two

During the interval Cheng-k'uan and Hu Hsueh-chen rehearse their speeches for the gate. You watch them prepare the words they will later deliver to the village.

SECTION EIGHT

I

Hou joins the cadres while Little Li sets out the benches and tables.

Hou Are you ready?

Cheng-k'uan I'll never be ready. This is the most frightening day of my life.

Hou Tell the truth and you have nothing to fear.

Cheng-k'uan I know that. But the people . . .

Hou Trust them.

Cheng-k'uan I'd be happy to die tomorrow as long as I pass the gate.

From outside the hall we hear the delegates shout 'Purify the Party'. They are Yuan-lung, Lai-tzu, Hsin-ai, Huan-ch'ao and Tui-chin. They come in and are about to sit opposite the cadres when Hou begins to lead the singing of the Internationale. The cadres all join in. Hou knows it best. Then they sit down.

Hou The Communist Party is the servant of the people.

To prove to you how seriously we take our charge, we have publicly posted the names of our members. It is no longer a secret organization. Now its members will appear before you, the delegates of the people, they will criticize their past actions and invite your grievances. They will then ask you to judge their future suitability for office.

Slogan: THE GATE

Cheng-k'uan Comrades, on behalf of the Party I welcome you, the delegates of the people, and hope that you will speak out clearly and fearlessly what you think. Certainly you need not fear any reprisal. In the past, you made me a cadre, but I am ready to admit that after fanshen I forgot my poor friends.

Yuan-lung gets up nervously to reply.

Yuan-lung I am a poor peasant chosen as a delegate to help purify the Party. I hope every Party member will examine his past honestly. I cannot speak much. We are here because poor peasants do want to help the Party. So we can all fanshen thoroughly. (*He sits down, his ordeal over.*)

Cheng-k'uan So let me start. (*Pause.*) I was born in Long Bow but my family comes from Chih-chou. I grew up a Catholic, I was a hired labourer. I took part in struggle meetings as you know. Because of them I became Chairman of the Peasants' Association. This made me arrogant. For instance, when we had to collect tax grain we never talked it over with the people, we just met among ourselves and decided what each should give, then ordered people to hand over. I think this was wrong, it was obviously unfair. Also, I hit Tui-chin when he made a hurtful remark about my body, sheer bad temper and I have no excuse . . .

Hsin-ai Tell us how much you won out of fanshen.

Cheng-k'uan Ah.

Lai-tzu Yes.

Cheng-k'uan I won . . . more than the masses out of fanshen.

Hsin-ai How much more?

Cheng-k'uan An acre of land. The best. Ten hundredweight of millet. And ten pieces of clothing. Good quality.

Silence.

Then I joined the Party. I thought, I'm on the way up and nothing can stop me. I was working very hard and I thought what's the point of working hard if you don't get a little extra and live better than other people? It was wrong. It was wrong thinking. I've done so much that was wrong. I borrowed a pair of trousers from the public warehouse. They're worn out now. And I would like you to help me. I would like to hear your grievances.

Pause.

Lai-tzu When you took the village tax grain to Hukuan . . .

Cheng-k'uan Yes.

A known scandal.

Lai-tzu Tell us about that.

Cheng-k'uan It was last year. There were two of us, I was with An-ho. We claimed three dollars personal expenses. But in fact I spent the money on cigarettes.

Lai-tzu Why did you do that?

Cheng-k'uan Why?

Lai-tzu Why did you buy cigarettes?

Cheng-k'uan Because my thinking was wrong. I thought I'm a cadre, I'm allowed to loll about and smoke cigarettes. I'm willing to return the money.

Huan-ch'ao How much?

Cheng-k'uan All of it.

Hsin-ai Why?

Cheng-k'uan Why? Because . . .

Hsin-ai You said two of you spent the money.

Cheng-k'uan Yes.

Hsin-ai So why promise to pay it all back yourself? It just proves you're insincere.

Cheng-k'uan Four of us spent the money.

Hsin-ai Then say so.

Huan-ch'ao Tell the truth.

Hsin-ai You don't have to take the blame for what other people did.

Cheng-k'uan No.

Hsin-ai And don't just agree with us.

Cheng-k'uan No.

Hsin-ai Being criticized doesn't mean saying yes to everything.

Cheng-k'uan Yes. No.

Hsin-ai Be objective and then criticize yourself.

Cheng-k'uan Yes.

Pause.

Yuan-lung The candlesticks.

Hsin-ai Yes, the silver candlesticks that were seized from the church . . .

Cheng-k'uan Yes.

Hsin-ai What happened to them?

Cheng-k'uan They were sold.

Huan-ch'ao What happened to the money?

Cheng-k'uan It was distributed, to everyone. It was among the fruits.

Hsin-ai It was a fortune, they were silver candlesticks.

Cheng-k'uan I don't think it was that much.

Hsin-ai Tell the truth.

Cheng-k'uan I really can't remember.

Hsin-ai What do you mean you don't remember – we can find out.

Cheng-k'uan Yes.

Hsin-ai We can ask the landlord's wife, Wang Kuei-ching was business manager for the church. We can ask her.

Huan-ch'ao Well?

Cheng-k'uan Ask her.

Slogan: THEY TALKED FOR SIX HOURS

Hou Are you ready with the list?

Cheng-k'uan All the accusations you have made today. I hit four of you. I failed to consult you. I gave random orders. I took two dollars. Some clothing. I can offer no explanation for the money from the candlesticks. I thought of myself and not of serving the masses. Do you have any further grievances against me?

Pause.

Hou Then you must decide how to deal with him. Cheng-k'uan, you must leave.

Cheng-k'uan I have loved my family. And my home. Now I love . . . the Communist Party. I shall wait patiently for the decision of the masses.

He goes out. A violent argument.

Hsin-ai Suspend him from the Party.

Tui-chin Yes.

Hsin-ai Send him to the People's Court in Lucheng.

Yuan-lung Huan-ch'ao?

Huan-ch'ao I think . . . just make him give everything back.

Lai-tzu I agree, he's admitted his mistakes . . . that's what we wanted.

Hsin-ai How can he give everything back when he says he doesn't remember?

Huan-ch'ao Just give it back.

Hsin-ai We suffered, now he must suffer.

Tui-chin Send him to the Court.

Hsin-ai He must understand pain.

Yuan-lung Why not just ask him to jump down the well?

Hsin-ai Why not? I don't care if he starves to death.

Tui-chin The Party was meant to serve the people . . .

Hsin-ai So long as he gives back what he got during fanshen.

Tui-chin It was meant to lead us to fanshen. But in fact only members of the Party really fanshened . . .

Lai-tzu Then take something away.

Tui-chin They became officials, just like feudal officials . . .

Lai-tzu And now he's sorry.

Tui-chin Cheng-k'uan climbed on our heads . . .

Hsin-ai They all did.

Tui-chin And now we must throw him out.

Lai-tzu You're talking about one of the most popular men in the village.

Tui-chin That just shows you.

Lai-tzu You're talking about two dollars . . .

Tui-chin I'm talking about why, why our leaders are rich, why we're still poor . . .

Lai-tzu The Party . . .

Tui-chin The Party has asked the people to decide, and this is what we decide. Send him to the Court.

Hou The People's Court is for cases you cannot decide yourselves. Is that how you wish to be known? As the village that cannot decide the simplest case?

Yuan-lung All we need to do is suspend him from office, just for a short time, and see if he really wants to reform.

Tui-chin He should be thrown out of the Party.

Yuan-lung No.

Lai-tzu It was only two dollars . . .

Tui-chin It's not what he did. It's what he let others do. How did Yu-lai come to rule this town?

Pause.

Hou (*very quiet*) Yu-lai is in prison.

Tui-chin Yes. Because you came with guns. And threw him in prison. Good. But up till then . . . where were our leaders? Well?

Pause.

Hou So. Do we agree? You suspend him and then see if he corrects his behaviour. Is that what you want?

All Yes.

Hsin-ai He should never be a cadre again.

Huan-ch'ao Be quiet, you old shitbag.

Hsin-ai He should be thrashed with a dogwhip.

Hou Listen. Because you've been beaten you want to see him beaten. All right. Now we oppose beatings and this makes you bitter. You think unless we flay the skin off his back, he'll just carry on as before. But that's feudal behaviour. We are living in a new society. Are we not?

Pause.

Yuan-lung Suspend him from office?

All Yes.

Little Li goes to get Cheng-k'uan.

Hou For how long?

Yuan-lung Six months?

All Yes.

Cheng-k'uan returns.

Yuan-lung We have decided that you have failed the gate, and that you must be suspended from office.

However, in six months you will be given another chance to pass.

Cheng-k'uan I am happy to accept the decision of the masses.

Cheng-k'uan returns to his seat. Hsueh-chen rises.

Hsueh-chen I was a beggar, then a Party member.

Yuan-lung Who are you?

He knows perfectly well. Hsueh-chen smiles.

Hsueh-chen Hu Hsueh-chen, Secretary of the suspended Women's Association. I was a beggar, then a Party member, then in the Association. I have always struggled for equality for women . . .

Yuan-lung Just tell us what you did wrong.

Hsueh-chen Yes.

Yuan-lung We all know what you did right . . .

Hsueh-chen Yes.

Yuan-lung You're always telling us.

Hsueh-chen Yes.

Yuan-lung Outstanding revolutionary cadre. Some cretin even painted you on the wall. So stick to what you did wrong.

Hsueh-chen I think you'll find I've done as you ask. I have a list here. I can name the twenty-three occasions when I feel I may have impeded the revolution.

Yuan-lung We'd like them in alphabetical order.

Hsueh-chen I believe until you make a list, you don't really know yourself. And if you don't know yourself you can't criticize yourself. And if you can't criticize yourself both privately and in front of the masses, you can't be a Communist.

Quiet. The peasants all look at her, taking account.

There is the occasion I shouted at Fa-liang. There is the occasion I called Chuan-e a whore and burnt her best dress because I thought it . . . unsuitable for a woman. There is the occasion I hit Tao-yuan for giving a girl heroin. There is the occasion I tried to get a meeting postponed so I could canvass . . .

Huan-ch'ao This is pointless.

Hsueh-chen There is the occasion . . .

Huan-ch'ao It's pointless reading it out. We know it'll all be there, it'll all be listed, anything we can think of, but it won't . . .

Hou What?

Huan-ch'ao It won't – it won't – it's not what she did, it's that – look on her face . . .

Hsueh-chen Please . . .

Huan-ch'ao Of course she's got her list, it's perfect, but her face . . .

Lai-tzu You can't blame a woman . . .

Huan-ch'ao Look at it, just look at it. She knows she's going to pass, that's what I can't bear, and it shows in her face.

Hsueh-chen I promise you, I don't know.

Huan-ch'ao Look at you. All the time. I have suffered more than you. I know more than you. I'm a better person than you.

Hsueh-chen I don't think that.

Huan-ch'ao Round the lips, just a slight turn at the side, and your head.

Hou We can't pass or fail people's faces . . .

Huan-ch'ao Of course we can. That's just what we should do. Why does everyone bristle the moment she comes in? Because of that look that says she's a leader. That's why the people resent her.

Hou Sit down.

Huan-ch'ao sits. Pause.

Hsueh-chen?

Hsueh-chen I submit to the people. I will try to correct my face.

2

Slogan: THE RESULTS OF THE GATE

Comrade Hou before the people of Long Bow.

Hou We have heard every accusation you have to make against your leaders. Twenty-six members of the Party have appeared before you. Twenty-two have passed the gate, four have failed. Four more still in jail after the attack on a member of the work team have not yet appeared. We have found fifty-five cases of beating. A hundred and three cases of personal selfishness and corrupt practice. Seventeen cases of illicit sexual relations of which half may be called rape. Eleven cases of forgetting one's class. We also found in spite of rumour that the cadres of Long Bow got very little more in fanshen than the people. Tomorrow the work team goes to a regional conference in Lucheng. I shall be able to tell the secretary how we have purged the Party of wrongdoing, and how you have begun the process of purification. I shall be able to say with pride: in Long Bow the Party submits to the People.

SECTION NINE

I

At once the tolling of an enormous temple bell.
Underneath it sitting on a bench the work team in a row.
Sober.

Slogan: THE TRIP TO LUCHENG COUNTY

An Official appears to usher them in.

Official Secretary Ch'en will speak to the Long Bow delegation before the conference begins. He hasn't got very long.

> *The Official leads them through to where Ch'en is at his desk. The team are left standing. Ch'en shakes hands with Hou.*

Ch'en Comrade Hou. Good. Have you prepared your report?

Hou Yes.

Ch'en Good. It will be called . . . as soon as possible. For the moment, the matter of Yu-lai and his friends . . .

Hou Yes.

Ch'en Why was he arrested?

Hou There was an attack . . .

Ch'en I know.

Hou On a member of the work team.

Ch'en The arrest was a mistake.

> *Silence.*

Hou There was evidence . . .

Ch'en I have heard rumours that the four cadres have been tried at a mass meeting and shot.

Hou That's not true.

Ch'en Of course not. The point is I have heard it, peasants throughout Lucheng County have heard it . . .

Hou I can't . . .

Ch'en Let me finish my point. Thirty miles away from Long Bow the rumours are credited. And they lend currency to the belief that the cadres were guilty. And that undermines the work of every cadre in the County. There was not enough evidence for an arrest.

Hou There was a towel.

Ch'en Saying 'good morning'. I know. My own towel says 'good morning'. I doubt if there is a village in all China that does not have twenty towels saying 'good morning'. (*Pause.*) You had no firm evidence. The County police have already decided to release them. (*Pause.*) It seems you made your minds up about the village before you even got there. And then you accepted the worst version of everything you heard. Isn't it true you suspended all the cadres the very first day you were there? Isn't it true you put the whole Party branch under supervision and took control of the village yourselves? Isn't it true that by the second day you were publicly examining the village accounts before you commanded any support among the people? And from what I've heard of the Long Bow gate you countenanced every slur the people could bring against their leaders. Cheng-k'uan failed the gate because he was suspected of misusing money from the sale of candlesticks.

Hou Yes.

Ch'en We've looked into that. The candlesticks weren't

even silver. They were pewter. They were worth very little. And yet you went to Wang's widow for evidence, you went to a class enemy for testimony against a cadre. We have a name for what you did. We call it Left extremism. (*Ch'en picks up a document from his desk.*) Here is a report prepared by the third administrative district of the Taihang subregion. Your mistakes are already listed in that. You have sought support only from the poor peasants, thereby neglecting the middle peasants. You've treated Party members as if they were class enemies. Everything the poor peasants wanted you have believed and tried to give them. You have elevated their point of view to the status of a line. That line is in clear opposition to the official policy of the Party.

Silence.

I shall be using the work of your team as an example to the whole conference of Left deviation. I hope after criticism we shall be able to correct your faults.

Silence.

Shall we go in?

2

Among the ruins of a bell tower. Sitting by a ruined wall is Ch'i-yun cooking soup. Little Li appears quietly.

Ch'i-yun Is he still talking?

Little Li Secretary Ch'en? Yes. He's been talking four hours.

Ch'i-yun What are we to do?

Little Li Work teams throughout the County are to return to their villages. The Secretary feels too many middle peasants have been pushed over to the enemy side. We need all the allies we can get. So he is introducing a new standard in classification. The line between the middle and the rich peasant is to be redefined. We must fix it precisely. It's harder. More complex.

Chang Ch'uer comes in, rubbing his hands.

Chang Ch'uer Is there something to eat?

Ch'i-yun Not yet.

Chang Ch'uer I'm hungry. What were you talking about?

Little Li The new classification.

Chang Ch'uer Ah yes. Classification.

Silence.

Why do you never talk about yourself, Little Li?

Little Li Mmmh.

Chang Ch'uer We think about ourselves. All the time, we all do . . .

Little Li I . . .

Chang Ch'uer I don't know why we always talk about the poor, the poor peasants. Here we are looking miserable as goats, and it's not because we're worried about the poor, it's because Secretary Ch'en has shat all over us.

Ch'i-yun (*smiles*) Yes.

Chang Ch'uer Come on, cabbage. (*Pause.*) I really wouldn't mind being poor. It's a good life when you compare it with being a cadre.

Hou has appeared, confident.

Hou You all heard the Secretary. I have details of the new system here. I don't think it should give us too much trouble. We shall go back to Long Bow tomorrow. What's for supper?

Chang Ch'uer We can't go back.

Pause.

Little Li We must talk.

Hou I think I should decide when we're to talk . . .

Little Li It's a warm night. Look at the stars. I suggest the form is self-criticism, yes?

Hou I don't think . . .

Chang Ch'uer Only if it's honest.

Little Li Of course.

Chang Ch'uer From everybody.

Hou What do you mean?

Chang Ch'uer We can't go back till we've spoken.

Pause. Hou wanders away, serious now, to think what this means. Ch'i-yun speaks very quietly, regretful.

Ch'i-yun You've lost the trust of your team. Sit down.

Pause. Hou sits.

Hou Supper?

Little Li After. Criticism first. Ch'i-Yun?

Ch'i-yun I think most of what Ch'en said is true. When I went to Long Bow I did think poverty was everything. I just looked for rags and fleabites, I thought the smellier the better; lice-ridden, shit-stained old men I thought wonderful, I can't get enough of it, I'm really doing the job. And I believed everything they said, every accusation made against the Party. That was wrong. I lacked objectivity. (*She looks round, handing it on like a baton.*)

Little Li From the very start we persecuted the . . .

Chang Ch'uer Criticize yourself.

Little Li From the very start I persecuted the village cadres. I was over-harsh, I assumed everything was true. I kept telling the village they were poor because the cadres had taken all the fruits. But really, how much did they take? And if it were all divided up, what difference would it make to the whole distribution? (*He looks at Chang Ch'uer.*)

Chang Ch'uer For a long time I've been thinking mostly about myself. After I was attacked I was very ill, the medicine the doctor gave me was very expensive. So I asked my neighbours for help, but they just said, you're a cadre and cadres should serve the people like oxen. Now I'm away from home, from my wife, from my children, and no one is helping me in the mutual aid scheme while I'm away because they refuse to help cadres. All the time, all the time I'm thinking my land is rotting and the people do not trust their leaders . . . I'm a servant of the people but sometimes . . . I find the people very hard to like.

Chang Ch'uer looks up, the baton passed. Hou silent.

Little Li Comrade . . .

Hou I'm not a good leader, I know that. I do try.

Chang Ch'uer Honest, we said, honest.

Hou I know I'm not clever . . .

Chang Ch'uer We said honest. Not humble. Humble isn't honest. Humble's humble. Humble's a way of not being criticized . . .

Hou I do try . . .

Chang Ch'uer Whenever we've tried to criticize you, you just say I know it's terrible, I'm just such a terrible person, you say yes, yes I'm sorry of course I know I'm so weak . . . but that doesn't solve anything.

Hou I lie awake at night . . .

Ch'i-yun That's just what's wrong, don't you see? It's useless lying awake at night. It's no help to anyone, it's subjective. Your work style is undemocratic.

Hou I thought this was to be self-criticism.

Chang Ch'uer We can't go back if you won't talk to us.

Hou I took the job on very proud, very confident, then I began to realize it was more difficult than anything I had done in my life. I lost my nerve.

Chang Ch'uer Why didn't you . . .

Little Li (*stops him*) Ah.

Hou I became afraid to consult you. I felt Little Li was just waiting for me to put a foot wrong. I thought I must be strong or they'll think ill of me. That's what leaders always think. That's what leaders are. Do this. Do that. And at the back of the head . . . what do they think of me? (*He smiles*.) After Ch'en . . . after what Ch'en said to us today I realized I'm not suited to the job, I've led the team badly and I must resign.

Ch'i-yun Oh no.

Little Li No.

Chang Ch'uer Wrong, wrong, wrong.

Little Li Do you understand nothing?

Ch'i-yun What rubbish.

Little Li 'I resign.'

Hou I feel . . .

Chang Ch'uer Always the hero, you . . . always want to be the hero. 'I resign.'

Little Li 'I resign.'

Chang Ch'uer Wonderful.

Hou I'm sure . . .

Little Li I? I? Who is this I? The I who said I don't want my decisions questioned?

Silence.

Hou Yes. That I.

Silence.

Ch'i-yun We have to go back tomorrow and set about reclassifying the village. It will not . . . go down well. No one will light fires for our return. We will have to explain, discuss, report, evaluate, classify, post results, then listen to appeals, explain again, discuss again, classify again, post revised results. How can we do it if we are thinking of ourselves?

Silence.

Right now we are thinking life is easier at home. But that is because we have been badly led.

Hou I . . .

Ch'i-yun Yes.

Silence.

Why do we live in this world? Is it just to eat and sleep and lead a worthless life? That is the landlord and rich peasant point of view. Enjoy life, waste food and clothes,

79

have children. But a Communist works not only for his own life: he has offered everything to the service of his class. If he finds one poor brother suffering from hunger and cold, he has not done his duty. Comrade.

Silence.

You should talk to us more.

Chang Ch'uer It doesn't solve my problem.

Ch'i-yun Nothing will solve your problem.

Chang Ch'uer Thank you.

Ch'i-yun Except working harder.

Chang Ch'uer I work eighteen hours a day.

Ch'i-yun Work twenty. You can if you want to. If we make you want to. But Comrade Hou must give us a lead.

Hou Yes.

Silence. He is at the end of his personality.

What should I do?

Ch'i-yun You have just given us a totally inadequate account of your work as team leader. You must make specific accusations against yourself. Only then will we begin to get at the truth. Only then will we begin to work as a team. You must go back over every event. You must tell us how and where and when you went wrong. When you began not to trust us. You must trace back over everything, every detail, every bad thought.

Hou Yes.

Silence.

I have led the team badly.

Ch'i-yun Be specific.

Hou Once . . .

SECTION TEN

I

Three different households.
Tui-chin is sitting outside his house. Cheng-k'uan is staring into a bucket containing a dead child. And in Wen-te's house Hsien-e is working. Meanwhile the work team try to go about their business.

Slogan: YU-LAI AND WEN-TE RETURN TO LONG BOW

Yu-lai and Wen-te walk down the village street, Tui-chin withdraws indoors and prepares to go to bed. As they look around . . .

Yu-lai What is it?

Wen-te It's called chewing-gum. Someone gave me it in prison.

Yu-lai Ah.

Wen-te gives him the bit he has been chewing. Yu-lai puts it in. Chang Ch'uer goes to Tui-chin's house. Yu-lai smiles at Wen-te.

Yu-lai What a place. Why did we return?

Chang Ch'uer Comrade. There is a meeting tonight. Classification.

Tui-chin I've been classified.

Chang Ch'uer To help classify others.

Tui-chin I have my own classification, that's enough. I'm tired and I'm going to bed.

Chang Ch'uer Tui-chin.

Tui-chin Don't raise your voice, I'll report you.

Yu-lai sits down outside the house and starts to polish his Luger.

Yu-lai Go and find your wife.

Wen-te goes into the house.

Chang Ch'uer We need to form a new Peasants' League.

Tui-chin We've got a Poor Peasants' League.

Chang Ch'uer An official league this time, not a provisional.

Tui-chin Ah.

Chang Ch'uer To carry out a new classification, so we can form a Provisional Peasants' Association.

Tui-chin We've got a Peasants' Association.

Chang Ch'uer A new Peasants' Association . . .

Tui-chin What for?

Chang Ch'uer A new gate.

Pause.

Tui-chin I'm tired.

Tui-chin turns away. Wen-te faces Hsien-e inside the house. Yu-lai still sits outside.

Hsien-e Wen-te.

Yu-lai Tell her we're hungry.

Wen-te My father says we're hungry.

Hsien-e There's corn.

Wen-te She says there's corn.

Yu-lai Rabbit. In a stew. With garlic. And leeks. Pork. Shrimp. Onions. Tell her. Dumplings with herbs. Beancurd. Tell her. Tell her to ask her friends in the village, tell her to visit their homes, suggest . . . they give us . . . their food.

Hsien-e stares at Wen-te.

Hsien-e There's some corn.

Wen-te smashes Hsien-e hard across the face. Then beats her.

Tui-chin It's not as if anyone else'll be there . . .

Chang Ch'uer That's not true.

Tui-chin Nobody obeys orders here any more, what's the point?

Chang Ch'uer Tui-chin.

Tui-chin I was among the keenest, comrade. Among the first. Then when you came, you told us to denounce corrupt leaders. And I did. I denounced Yu-lai while he was in prison. And now he's been released. Do you think he doesn't know? Do you think he isn't waiting for revenge? Feel my back. I'm sweating.

Chang Ch'uer We had no choice.

Tui-chin At least before they would have killed him.

He prepares for bed. Ch'i-yun crosses to Cheng-k'uan's house. Yu-lai calls to Wen-te inside the house.

Yu-lai What does she say?

Wen-te She says yes, certainly, at once, of course, she's just going, sorry to be so long, are you sure that's all you want?

Wen-te thrashes wildly at Hsien-e with his belt. She runs out of the house, at great speed and away.

Ch'i-yun Cheng-k'uan. Why is there no one at the meeting? Cheng-k'uan.

Chang Ch'uer We will organize another gate. To bring Yu-lai and Wen-te before the people. Confront them with their crimes. Sort everything out. Will you testify? Will you denounce them before the gate?

Tui-chin Yu-lai and Wen-te are innocent. Of everything. That's what I'll say.

Wen-te comes out of the house. Stands beside his father.

Wen-te She's gone to get the food.

Tui-chin I trusted you. We all did.

Yu-lai throws the chewing-gum to the ground.

Yu-lai This stuff doesn't taste.

Ch'i-yun I know it's hard. And it's tiring, Cheng-k'uan. But you must never give up.

Cheng-k'uan I buried the cord. I was told to bury the cord.

Chang Ch'uer Are you coming to the meeting?

Silence. Ch'i-yun uncovers the child.

I promise, I promise to try and help.

Ch'i-yun Tell me what happened.

Cheng-k'uan Our child was born in a wash-basin six days ago. None of us knew it was coming so it just fell into a dirty basin at my wife's feet. We had nothing to cut the cord. She was bent forward, the child was filthy, my wife couldn't move. At first I couldn't find the

midwife. Then after an hour she came, with an old pair
of scissors.

*Pause. Chang Ch'uer leaves Tui'chin's house. Tui-chin
goes to bed.*

Cheng-k'uan How can we go on? I'm tired. Everyone says
I've fanshened, but what's changed? Where are the
doctors? How I long for money. Doctors. Scalpels.
Clothes, clean clothes.

Ch'i-yun They'll come.

*Ch'i-yun turns away. Yu-lai looks up smiling at Chang
Ch-uer.*

Yu-lai What's the matter? Can't get anyone to your meetings?

Chang Ch'uer They're frightened.

*Holding the gun with both hands at arms' length, Yu-lai
walks towards Chang Ch'uer.*

Yu-lai Use force.

Chang Ch'uer They're frightened of you.

*Yu-lai steps back. He is genuinely angry. Ch'i-yun has
joined them outside. Yu-lai yells at the top of his lungs,
red, demented.*

Yu-lai Has anyone. In the village. Any charge. Against me.
Will anyone. Speak.

*A silence. Then Yu-lai laughs and fires his gun in the air.
Ch'i-yun turns away. Yu-lai looks up smiling at Chang
Ch'uer.*

Yu-lai Good night.

Wen-te Good night.

They go into the house.

Ch'i-yun Until finally after many months a young bride led the way.

2

Hsien-e crosses the village at night.

Hsien-e I'll give evidence at the gate.

Ch'i-yun Hsien-e.

Hsien-e Against my father-in-law Yu-lai. And against my husband Wen-te.

Ch'i-yun Let me light this lamp.

Hsien-e No. If I testify . . .

Ch'i-yun Yes.

Hsien-e I must never see him again. They'd kill me.

Ch'i-yun Yes.

Hsien-e And I shall want a divorce.

   Pause.

Ch'i-yun You must go to the County . . .

Hsien-e I know. But first I must have the backing of the Women's Association, you must promise me that . . .

Ch'i-yun No one has ever been divorced in Long Bow, the men will be against it.

Hsien-e Of course.

Ch'i-yun And the older women.

Hsien-e Wen-te beat me. And Yu-lai. With a mule-whip. Often to within an inch of my life. I must have the backing of the Association. If I am not given a divorce, I will kill myself. (*Pause.*) What do you say?

Ch'i-yun I say, come in, sleep here, never go home again. We will look after you. Plead your case to the Women's Association, then appear at the gate. I say that women . . . are half of China.

The banner unfurls to read WOMEN ARE HALF OF CHINA. *An embrace. The scene breaks.*

3

Hou To bring before the gate those who have so far avoided it.

Slogan: THE SECOND GATE

This gate is in the church. Present are Wen-te, Hsien-e and Yu-lai. At the side are Comrade Hou and Little Li. Delegates to the gate are Tui-chin, Cheng-k'uan, Hsin-ai and Huan-ch'ao.

Hou Wang Wen-te, son to Wang Yu-lai, suspended Head of Police. You must criticize yourself.

Wen-te I don't want to . . . everything. I'll just list the things. I once beat Hsi-le because he was moaning about fanshen, saying it had been a mistake, so I rapped him about the face a couple of times. That was wrong, I should have talked to him. Also, bitterness. I admit to cursing the work team, when they sent me wrongfully to prison. In public I called them cunts. I said . . . Comrade Hou was a cunt. That was wrong. Also . . .

Yu-lai comes into the meeting late. Walks down the aisle. Sits down. Everyone watches him.

Wen-te I once . . . gave Huan-ch'ao a thrashing because of some silly gossip.

Huan-ch'ao It wasn't gossip, it was true.

Hou Let him speak.

Wen-te I know that was wrong.

Huan-ch'ao Why did you beat me?

Hou Let him finish.

Wen-te I think that's all. I don't think anybody here would have . . . any serious things to add. I would be surprised.

He looks at them all daring them to speak. Huan Ch'ao rises and goes right up to him.

Huan-ch'ao Turtle's egg. Donkey's tool. Your mother's stinking cunt. (*He puts a finger in his face and shouts.*) You beat me because I told the truth. I said you beat your wife. That's why you left me for dead. Because I told the truth.

He tries to strangle him. Hou separates them.

Hou Get him off. Get him off.

Huan-ch'ao (*screaming*) I was left for dead. (*He is dragged off. Then looks round.*) Why? Why have you stopped me? Am I the only one? Am I the only man in Long Bow? I risk my life to accuse them. And you . . . when you find my body in a ditch, you will know everything.

He sits down. Yu-lai speaks very quietly.

Yu-lai The man is mad. There's no case to answer.

Hsien-e stands at once. Her assurance and command are stunning.

Wen-te Not her.

Hsien-e When I was ten, my parents were starving, they sold me to be engaged to Wen-te. In return they got grain and money. I had to go and live in Yu-lai's home. He starved me, I had to go into the fields to find herbs to stay alive. They gave me only water. When I was fourteen, they made me marry him. After the marriage they often locked me in the house for weeks. Wen-te locked the doors and whipped me with a mule-whip. His father was free with me. I have made up my mind to divorce him, I have the backing of the Women's Association. Have I said enough?

Hou Did you beat her?

Wen-te looks at Yu-lai. Yu-lai almost nods.

Wen-te Once or twice.

Hou Why?

Yu-lai Because she used to flirt in the cornfield, with other men. She was late with supper because she'd been whoring . . .

Tui-chin like a barrack-room lawyer.

Tui-chin How old was your wife when you married her?

Wen-te She . . .

Hsien-e Fourteen.

Wen-te Fifteen.

Yu-lai Sixteen.

Wen-te Sixteen.

Tui-chin How did you get a licence at the district office?

Hsien-e He ordered me to say I was sixteen.

Tui-chin Is that true? (*Pause.*) Is that true? (*He turns to Hsien-e.*) Why did you agree to lie?

Wen-te Because she wanted to marry me of course.

Tui-chin Then you admit she lied (*Pause.*) Why did you agree?

Hsien-e Because they threatened my parents.

Tui-chin How?

Hsien-e They threatened to denounce them as Kuomintang agents.

Huan-ch'ao Anyone who disobeyed them was called a spy.

Hsin-ai Yes, that's how they dealt with everyone.

Hou What do you say?

Wen-te It's . . . very hard to remember. I can't remember. I can't remember the answers. (*Pause.*) Criticize me. While I try to remember the answers.

Slogan: THEY TALKED FOR EIGHT HOURS

    Change of pitch. Wen-te is broken, muttering inaudibly. Yu-lai is frozen, a Buddha. The pace is furious.

Tui-chin The opinions of the masses pile up like a mountain.

Cheng-k'uan The list of charges is now five foot long.

Wen-te I can't remember anything.

Tui-chin He doesn't understand, he doesn't even know what's going on. (*He is delighted.*)

Wen-te Criticize me. Please.

Hsin-ai Kick him out of the Party and send him to the County Court.

All Yes.

Hou Do you agree to that, Wen-te?

Wen-te Of course. Yes. Send me to the Court. I deserve it. I have betrayed the masses.

Hsien-e And will you grant me a divorce?

He looks up at her. Then bursts into a fit, banging his head on the ground on each 'Never'.

Wen-te Never. I will never agree to that until the last minute of my life. Never. Never. Never.

Hsien-e You must.

Wen-te I will never beat you again.

Hsien-e He's lying.

Wen-te Never.

Hsien-e What if you beat me to death?

Wen-te I take an oath before the people.

Hou (*quiet*) That's enough, Hsien-e. He won't give you a divorce.

Hsien-e But . . .

Hou We can't help.

Silence. She sits down.

The case demands . . . the severest punishment. Party members have a trust which you have betrayed. The people say you must go to the County Court.

Yu-lai gets up, his patience exhausted.

Yu-lai Bonehead. Plank. Donkey's anus. I coached you for three days and you didn't get one answer right.

Wen-te begins to cry.

Hou Next before the gate. Wang Yu-lai.

The people look glad. Three tableaux of accusation. Then he is thrown down in the cadres' office by Little Li. The rest scatter.

4

Little Li You'll sleep in here. We'll keep you here until your trial.

Yu-lai I want to die. I want to be left to die. There's nothing. Going back to prison, there's nothing.

Little Li You have betrayed the people. And you have failed the gate. There should be nothing.

Yu-lai What can I do?

Little Li You should have told the truth, then you would have had some chance.

Yu-lai If I'd told the truth they would have killed me.

Enter Chang Ch'uer and Ch'i-yun, very up.

Ch'i-yun Where is he?

Chang Ch'uer The people are cheering. The people have just cheered us through the streets.

Ch'i-yun There's a celebration tonight.

Chang Ch'uer The work we can do.

Comrade Hou comes in with Secretary Liu.

Hou Secretary Liu, this is the man. Members of the work team, this is Secretary Liu. He has come from Taihang to check on the progress of the work.

Little Li Comrade.

Ch'i-yun Comrade.

Liu Why is he crying? (*Pause.*) Tell me why you are crying.

Yu-lai I want to die.

Liu Why?

Yu-lai There's nothing.

Liu Nothing?

Yu-lai Nothing for me.

Liu Why?

Yu-lai If I'm sent to the People's Court, I'll be shot.

Liu Who told you that?

Yu-lai If I confess everything, I'll be lynched. Or they'll throw me out of the Party and that's as bad as being shot.

Liu Yes.

Yu-lai People hate me, they want me dead.

Liu You can still decide your fate. It's up to you. I know people who have done much worse than you. They have faced the people honestly and the people have accepted them again as leaders.

Yu-lai I can't face living in this . . .

Liu You can. Everyone can face everything.

Yu-lai The people hate me.

Liu No. They hate what you've done. (*Pause.*) The people have voted to send you to the Court. You are not yet in prison. Walk down the street. Try it.

Yu-lai goes.

How did this happen? You let him lose hope. How could you? Never, never let a man lose hope. It's a waste, to the Party. To the people. It's easy, it's so easy to stamp something out. It's what they do in every country in the world. They cure diseases by killing the patient. But we . . . are going to save the patient.

Chang Ch'uer You're going to let him loose?

Liu Why not?

Little Li He and his son terrorized the village . . .

Liu Ah I see so you thought get them out of the way and everything will be all right . . .

Little Li The people . . .

Liu But it won't, comrade. You can't smooth trouble over, it will come back at you, always it will appear somewhere else unless you dig out the root.

Ch'i-yun The people wanted rid of him.

Liu Of course . . .

Little Li And we proved, we proved today we could remove their fears . . .

Liu Of course you did, that's the easy part . . .

Little Li We proved today the Party is ready to purify its own ranks . . .

Liu No. You proved the Party could be brutal and wasteful. There is a school in Changchih for cadres who cannot pass the gate. A place where they can be re-educated, taken out of their own lives, given a chance to think, to learn, to be objective. He should go there. He should not go to prison. On no account should he be thrown out of the Party. (*Pause.*) It's a practical question, you must say what you think.

Chang Ch'uer Send him to the school. We can use him.

Hou Yes. Our thinking was wrong.

Ch'i-yun Yes.

Little Li No. We said purify the Party, we promised that. Now we mustn't go back. The people need to see him punished.

Liu Or is it you who needs that?

Little Li We worked so hard to organize that meeting.

Liu And you want a reward?

Little Li I want justice.

Liu Well?

Hou The overall feeling of the team is strongly for reforming the man.

Liu Good.

Little Li If men like Yu-lai can remain as Communists then what is the point of the campaign?

Liu There are no breakthroughs in our work. There is no 'just do this one thing and we will be there'. There is only the patient, daily work of re-making people. Over each hill, another hill. Over that hill, a mountain. The Party needs Yu-lai because he is clever and strong, and reformed will be of more value to the people than if he had never been corrupted. We must save him. We can use him. He can be reformed.

SECTION ELEVEN

I

Secretary Ch'en addresses the delegates from the platform.

Slogan: THE SECOND LUCHENG CONFERENCE

Ch'en Comrades. The twenty-year war is almost over. Chiang Kai-shek's armies are doomed. A People's Republic is within our reach. And so we have come to a turning point. And we have called you in today because many wrong ideas have been shared and many wrong actions have been taken.

At our last meeting in Lucheng you were told that land reform was far from complete. We have now discovered, after surveys of the area, that this was wrong, that the feudal system in our County has been fundamentally abolished. The peasants have in the main fanshened. The surveys show that in Lucheng County the poor peasants now farm an average of four-fifths of an acre each, the middle peasants slightly less, the rich peasants one-sixth of an acre each. So there is only one land problem remaining and it is the very opposite of what you imagine: the attack has been overdone.

Think back all of you to the Draft Agrarian Law. Think back to Article 16. 'In places where the land has already been distributed before the announcement of the law, the land need not be further redistributed.'

Is this not such a place? Had we not already spontaneously and in advance of the Party undertaken land reform at the end of the Japanese occupation, BEFORE the law was announced?

Work teams have been applying land reform policy long after land reform has occurred. Because some people still have less, work teams have continued to hunt for non-existent wealth. They have continued to blame and persecute old rank-and-file cadres. And they have frightened and alienated many middle peasants, men who were never exploiters but who have always been our allies and should have been treated as such.

Now how did this wrong line come about? It came about through an excess of zeal. It came about through blind utopianism, because so many work teams were ensnared by the idea of equality, of wanting to give everybody in China equal shares. This idea is dangerous. It encourages wrong standards. It has been condemned by Marx, by Engels, by Lenin, by Stalin. It is Leftism.

Equality cannot be established by decree. Even if we could give everyone an equal share, how long would it last? The strong, the ruthless would soon climb to the top; the weak and the sick would sink to the bottom. Only in the future when all land and productive wealth is finally held in common and we produce in great abundance will equality be possible.

So we have been judging fanshen by the wrong principles.

We have taken absolute equality as our banner. We have tried to be charitable. We have tried to give everyone everything they need. We have tried to be god.

Land reform can have only one standard and it is not equality. It is the abolition of the feudal system. And that we have achieved.

Now we know from history that whenever victory draws near it's easy for cadres to become adventurist, to alienate their allies, to persecute creators of wealth, to make impossible leftist demands. This is counter-revolutionary, because it pits working people against working people and endangers the success of the whole movement.

We must rein ourselves in. Above all in Lucheng County we must begin the work of returning goods and land to those middle peasants from whom we have taken too much.

And we must ensure that landlords are given enough land to make a living.

Little Li gets up and leaves.

How this is to be done we shall discuss in the coming days.

2

Little Li pacing up and down in the square is joined by the rest of the work team.

Little Li It's insane. It's totally insane.

Hou Li . . .

Little Li The policy has changed again.

Slogan: THEY TALKED FOR SIXTEEN HOURS

Little Li We are to go back to the village, we are to tell the people Article 16 has been overlooked, this means the fanshen was finished two years ago, you've had all you're going to get, in fact you're going to have to give some back.

Ch'i-yun You're frightened of the people, Little Li. Frightened to admit you made a mistake.

Little Li I didn't make it. He did.

Ch'i-yun Who?

Little Li Ch'en.

Hou Then tell him.

Little Li They just change the policy whenever it suits them.

Hou I shall go and find Secretary Ch'en and tell him the Long Bow delegation wishes to speak to him.

Little Li Don't be ridiculous. He won't even come.

Hou I shall tell him you have a criticism. I've no doubt he'll come. (*He goes out.*)

Little Li If the Party can make mistakes like that, what is there for us to cling to?

Chang Ch'uer I don't feel that. I feel as if a great rock has been lifted from my back. These last few months I'd come to feel a fool, thrashing around for wealth, trying to level people out, pushing people about. I felt tired and resentful and angry. And now I see my political thinking was

98

wrong, I took a wrong line, I had the wrong objectives, and far from feeling bitter or betrayed, I just feel . . . the knot is untied and I can look at the very same village, the very same people, I can look at the very same facts and I feel happy and hopeful.

A silence. Then noiselessly Hou returns with Ch'en.

Ch'en You wanted to see me.

Little Li Yes. (*Pause.*) I felt . . . the policy had changed.

Ch'en No.

Little Li You changed the policy.

Ch'en No. (*Pause.*) The policy has always been the same. 'Depend on the poor peasants, unite with the middle peasants, destroy the feudal system.' That has always been the policy, is still the policy, and will be the policy in places where the feudal system has not been uprooted. Here it has been uprooted. That we got wrong.

Little Li We?

Ch'en That we got wrong.

Little Li We? We didn't get it wrong. You got it wrong.

Silence.

You got it wrong. I want to hear you say 'I take the blame.' (*Pause.*) Last time we were here you criticized us for arresting Yu-lai. But it was you who approved the arrest in the first place. (*Pause.*) Say the words 'I take the blame.'

Ch'en Each level of leaders does its best to understand overall policy and apply it locally. If you are given a theory you must test it in practice. If it fails in practice it is up to you to send it back. Everyone must be active. Everyone must think all the time.

Little Li 'I take the blame.' Say it.

Pause.

Ch'en Primary responsibility for this last mistake rests with us at County headquarters. I take the blame.

Silence.

Little Li You're just saying it.

Ch'en raises his hands.

You're just saying it to get me back to work.

Hou Li, you're behaving like a child.

Ch'en It's not relevant.

Little Li I thought it was justice, I thought we were interested in justice.

Ch'en Not as an abstract, as a practical thing. We've done what we can. From now on everyone's improvement must depend on production, on their new land, their new tools. If we'd gone on trying to equalize we'd have destroyed even that. Land reform can't be a final solution to men's problems. Land reform is just a step opening the way to socialism. And socialism itself is transitional. All we've done these past few years is give as many people as possible land to work. But our political choices have still to be made. Is each man now to work for himself? Is the pistol fired and the race underway, everyone climbing on each other's back? Or are we to build mutual aid, exchange labour, create property in common, hold the land collectively so we can all prosper together? You see the question has barely been asked. We haven't begun. (*Pause.*) You must go back.

Hou Yes.

Ch'en You must explain our mistakes, the people will be

perfectly happy to listen. Tell the people the truth and they will trust you. One day, some time, this is the hardest thing, they will tell you the truth in return.

Tell them why China must be bold in concept but gentle in execution. Tell them . . . they are makers of the revolution every one.

They have lived already through many mistakes, but these are just ripples on the surface of the broad yellow river. Go back. Tell them.

SECTION TWELVE

I

A musical note, low, sustained.

Village life. Dawn. The village at work. The work team return. They look about the village. People hoeing.

They begin to stop people one by one. Simultaneous dialogue based on the following in each different part of the stage.

You're going to have to give back . . .
Give back?
Yes, it's difficult to explain, let me explain, let me try to explain, there are good reasons.

and

I'm afraid there's been a change of policy. We've been to Lucheng.
I see.
It's best to tell you. I'd like to tell you . . .

and

We think it's best if you know exactly what's happening, there's been a change of policy.
Yes.

A good change, I think, but it sounds . . . hard on the surface anyway let me explain.

and

I'd like to explain to you what happened at Lucheng and then you tell me what you think. It'll need some thinking about.

As they talk the musical note turns into a superb massive groundswell of music that consumes the stage. Banners flood down so that the whole stage is surrounded in red. At the centre the cadres mutter on, gesturing, explaining, trying to hold the peasants' attention, getting a variety of first responses. Just before they are drowned out each cadre gets to the question:

I'd like to know what you think.
What do you think?
Tell me.
Let me know what you think.
What do you think about this?

Then they drown in sound and light.

2

A single peasant. Hoeing in the field, as at the beginning. Hou boxes the compass from the tower: 'There will be a meeting.'

Peasant
There is no Jade Emperor in heaven
There is no Dragon King on earth
I am the Jade Emperor
I am the Dragon King
Make way for me you hills and
     mountains
I'm coming.

He goes to the meeting. The banner round the theatre unfurls the words of the poem.

A MAP OF THE WORLD

For Wallace Shawn and
Deborah Eisenberg

A map of the world that does not include Utopia is not worth even glancing at, for it leaves out the one country at which Humanity is always landing. And when Humanity lands there, it looks out, and, seeing a better country, sets sail.

OSCAR WILDE
'The Soul of Man Under Socialism'

Characters

Elaine le Fanu
Stephen Andrews
Victor Mehta
Peggy Whitton
Angelis
Martinson
M'Bengue

Waiters, Crew, Assistants, Diplomats, *etc.*

A Map of the World was first performed in London at the Lyttelton Theatre on 27 January 1983. The cast was as follows:

Elaine le Fanu Sheila Scott-Wilkinson
Stephen Andrews Bill Nighy
Victor Mehta Roshan Seth
Peggy Whitton Diana Quick
Angelis Stefan Gryff
Martinson Ronald Hines
M'Bengue John Matshikiza
Script Girl Kate Saunders
Make-up Girl Judith Hepburn
Propman Lilla Towner-Jones
Paul Tim Charrington
1st Waiter Bhasker
2nd Waiter Andrew Johnson
3rd Waiter Nizwar Karanj
Diplomats Brian Spink, Jeremy Anthony, Niven Boyd
Boom Operator Bill Moody
Sound Recordist Robert Phillips

Directed by David Hare
Designed by Hayden Griffin
Music by Nick Bicât
Lighting by Rory Dempster

Act One

SCENE ONE. *A hotel lounge. Crumbling grandeur. Cane chairs. A great expanse of black and white checked floor stretching back into the distance. Porticos. Windows at the back and, to one side, oak doors. But the scene must only be sketched in, not realistically complete.*

Stephen is sitting alone, surrounded by international newspapers, which he is reading. He is in his late twenties, but still boyish: tall, thin, dry. He is wearing seersucker trousers, and his jacket is over the chair. He has a now-emptied glass of beer and a bottle beside him. He is English.

Elaine comes through the oak doors, sheets of Gestetnered material in her hand. She is about thirty-five, disarmingly smart and well dressed. Her elegance seems not at all ruffled by the heat. She is a black American.

Elaine The heat.

Stephen I know.

Elaine goes to the back to look in vain for a waiter.

Are they still talking?

Elaine Yes.

Stephen Ah.

Elaine The Senegalese delegate is just about to start. (*She wanders back down, nodding at one of his magazines.*) Is that *Newsweek*?

Stephen Yes. There's nothing about us. (*He has picked it up and now reads from it.*) 'Tracy Underling of Dayton, Ohio, has the rest of her downtown, largely Catholic

Santa Maria College class in thrall with the size of her exceptional IQ, which local psycho-expert Lorne Schlitz claims tops genius level at 175. Says the bearded Schlitz: "Proof of her abundant intelligence is that she has already begun writing her third novel at the age of five." Subject of the novel will be the life of Mary Tyler Moore . . .'

Elaine smiles and walks away.

Elaine America!

Stephen I mean, who actually writes this stuff?

Elaine Is it any worse than ours?

Stephen smiles slightly.

That M'Bengue is appalling.

Stephen Who?

Elaine The Senegalese. He's raising his third point of order.

Stephen It's a compulsion . . .

Elaine Yes.

Stephen . . . I'm afraid.

Elaine, at the back, has a sudden burst of impatience.

Elaine *Why* are there no waiters?

Stephen Because the bar is nowhere near the lounge. In India no bar is anywhere near any lounge in order that five people may be employed to go backwards and forwards between where the drinkers are and where the drink is. Thus the creation of four unnecessary jobs. Thus the creation of what is called a high-labour economy. Thus low wages. Thus the perpetuation of poverty. Thus going screaming out of your head at the incredible obstinacy of the people. (*He shouts.*) Waiter!

Elaine You'll get used to it.

Stephen looks across at Elaine who has sat down and is flicking through a magazine. But she seems unconcerned.

Stephen I had a friend who rang me and said, 'Is your hotel in a bad area?' I said, 'Well, quite bad.' She said, 'Does it have corpses?' I said, 'Well, no.' She said, 'Well, mine actually has corpses.' And she was right. When I went to see her, there are people who sleep on the pavement . . . who have failed to wake . . . who are just lying there with rats running over them . . .

Elaine Bombay's quite prosperous.

Stephen I know. I know. It's a thriving, commercial city of two million people. Only there happen to be seven million people living there, which leaves the extra five million looking pretty stupid every night.

Elaine All right.

Stephen Well.

Elaine If you want to make a speech, go and give it in there.

He looks across at her. She has gone back to reading.

Stephen I would if I could be heard among the clamour of voices. Is there not something ludicrous in holding an international conference on poverty in these spectacular surroundings, when all we would actually have to do is to take one step into the street to see exactly what the problems of poverty are?

Elaine Most of the delegates have.

Stephen Then why is their interest entirely in striking attitudes and making procedural points?

Elaine Because that's politics.

Stephen You accept that?

Elaine Of course.

Stephen (*his voice rising*) When even now out in the streets . . .

Elaine It's the dirt that disgusts you, that's all.

Stephen What?

> *Elaine has put her magazine aside, suddenly deciding to take him on.*

Elaine I've watched you the last couple of days . . .

Stephen I see.

Elaine . . . since we met. You're like everyone. You can't understand why the peasants should choose to leave the countryside, where they can die a nice clean death from starvation, to come and grub around in the filthy gutter, where they do, however, have some small chance of life.

Stephen That's not quite true.

Elaine It shocks you that people prefer to live in cardboard, they prefer to live in excrement, in filth, than go back and die on the land. But they do. And as you want drama, and as this is your third day in India . . .

Stephen Fourth.

Elaine . . . you're determined to find this bad. Because you come from the West and are absolutely set on having an experience, so you find it necessary to dramatize. You come absolutely determined in advance to find India shocking, and so you can't see that underneath it all there is a great deal about the life here which isn't too bad. (*She turns back. Quietly*) At least, if you'd covered Vietnam, that's how you'd feel.

Stephen looks at her for a moment.

Stephen No, well, of course, I'm not an old hand . . .

Elaine No.

Stephen I don't move in your elevated circles. The élite of foreign correspondents . . .

Elaine Quite.

Stephen I'm just a journalist from England on a literary left-wing magazine . . .

Elaine That's right.

Stephen I've never filed stories under fire, or got the natives to shoot my copy in fluted arrows through the jungle, so of course I don't have your lofty overview . . .

Elaine It's just that I can't stand to listen to people making value judgements about other people's ways of life. The hippopotamus may be perfectly happy in the mud.

Stephen And the Indian, I suppose you think, is perfectly happy rolling about in excrement.

Elaine No, I didn't say that.

Stephen Well.

Elaine But it is arrogant to look at the world . . .

Stephen I'm not.

Elaine . . . through one particular perspective . . .

Stephen All right.

Elaine . . . which is always to say 'This is like the West. This is not like the West.' What arrogance!

Stephen No, well, I can't see that . . .

Elaine If I may say . . . I'm sorry. God, this conference.

Stephen I know.

There is a pause.

Waiter!

Elaine smiles.

It makes you so ill-tempered. You think you'll go for a stroll. 'I wouldn't leave the hotel if I were you, sir,' they say. 'The monsoon is coming.' With a great grin appearing on their faces as if the thought of it just suited them fine. 'Ah, good, the monsoon.' And you caught in it the best of all. I suppose it's the only revenge the poor have, that their land is uninhabitable by anyone but themselves. That we can't drink their water, or eat their food, or walk in their streets without getting mobbed, or endure their weather, or even, in fact, if we are truthful, contemplate their lives . . .

Elaine Stephen . . . (*She smiles.*) You exaggerate again.

At the opposite side to the conference hall Victor Mehta has appeared. He is in his early forties. He is wearing a light brown suit and tie and he has thick black hair. He is an Indian, but his manners are distinctly European.

Mehta This is UNESCO?

Stephen Yes. The conference on poverty.

Mehta Ah. (*He turns at once and summons a white-coated boy from off-stage.*) Waiter.

Waiter Sahib?

Mehta Can you see my bags are taken to my room?

Waiter Boy!

Stephen Ah, you found a waiter.

Mehta Certainly. There is no problem, is there?

Two Waiters appear. They argue with the First Waiter in Hindi. The First Waiter dismisses them. Mehta turns back to the Waiter.

And bring me a bottle of white wine. Is there a Pouilly Fuissé?

Waiter Pouilly Fumé, sir.

Mehta Then I will drink champagne.

The Waiter goes. The three of them stand a moment. A chilly smile from Mehta.

So. Off the plane I enjoy refreshments. Will you join me?

Stephen Of course. But I think they may be expecting you in the conference.

Mehta Let them wait.

Stephen is a little surprised, then hastens to introduce Elaine, at whom Mehta is staring.

Stephen I see. Well goodness. This is Elaine le Fanu from CBS Network.

Elaine Very nice to meet you.

Mehta My pleasure.

Stephen Stephen Andrews.

Mehta And somehow I sense you are a journalist as well.

Stephen I work on a small left-wing magazine.

Mehta Yes. I can imagine.

Stephen Mostly it's reviews. And domestic politics. But I'm the youngest, so my brief is the world.

He smiles. There is a pause.

You're very hard on journalists in your books.

Mehta I? (*He thinks about this a moment, as if it had never occurred to him.*) No.

Stephen *The Vermin Class*. It's not a flattering title for a novel on our profession.

Mehta I'm sure Miss le Fanu is not vermin. (*He is looking straight at Elaine, the sustained stare of the philanderer.*)

Stephen No.

Elaine Have you come far?

Mehta I left Heathrow ten hours ago. I left Shropshire –

Elaine Ah, your home?

Mehta Yes – even earlier.

Stephen You're speaking tomorrow?

Mehta Yes. A chore. The necessary prostitution of the intellect. So much is demanded now of the writer which is not writing, which is not the work. The work alone ought to be sufficient. But my publishers plead with me to make myself seen.

Stephen I think you'll find there's great anticipation. I mean, there's some interest as to what you'll say.

Mehta looks away, indifferent.

Particularly the comparison with China. It's impossible here not to compare the two cultures . . .

Mehta Yes?

Stephen I mean, the way the one, China, is so organized, the other, India, so . . . well, this is a theme you have dealt with in your books.

Mehta I suppose.

He is still for a moment, lizard-like. Just as Stephen starts again, he interrupts.

Stephen If . . .

Mehta Of the Chinese leadership the only one I was able to bring myself to admire wholeheartedly was Chou En-lai.

Elaine Ah.

Mehta Because he alone among the leaders had the iron self-control not to use his position to publish his own poetry. Chairman Mao, unhappily, not so.

Elaine Yes. (*She smiles, looks down at the ground, knowingly, having dealt with many such men.*) Do you not admire Mao?

Mehta How can I? Like so many senior statesmen he ruined his credibility by marrying an actress. And what an actress! Madame Mao even claims that she was born beautiful but that in order to identify more closely with the majority of her people, she has managed to will herself ugly. So that even the hideous awfulness of her face is to be marked down as a revolutionary achievement!

Stephen is frowning.

Stephen But there are elements of China . . .

Mehta What?

Stephen . . . elements of the Chinese experiment you admire.

Mehta I admire nothing in the experiment. I admire China itself.

As he speaks, waiters enter in rough formation carrying, one by one, a bucket, a bottle, a bag of ice, and glasses.

Ah, champagne.

As he speaks, the glasses are distributed, the bucket set down.

All old civilizations are superior to younger ones. That is why I have been happiest in Shropshire. They are less subject to crazes. In younger countries there is no culture. The civilization is shallow. Nothing takes root. Even now gangs of crazy youths are sweeping through the streets of Sydney and New York pretending they are homosexual. But do you think they are homosexual really? Of course not. It is the merest fashion. City fashion, that is all. In the old countries, in Paris, in London, when there is a stupid craze, only one person in fifty is affected, but in the young countries there is nothing to hold people back. It is suddenly like the worm factory, everybody fucks everybody, until the next craze, and then everyone will move on and forget and settle down with young women who sell handbags. But meanwhile the damage has been done. The plant has been pulled up at the root and violently plunged back into the earth, so the slow process of growing must begin again. But a worthwhile civilization takes two thousand years to grow.

The waiters have left. Mehta leans forward to pour himself champagne.

Stephen Yes, but . . . (*He gestures at the bottle.*) May I? Surely –

Mehta has taken one sip and puts his glass aside, where he leaves it, untouched.

Mehta It is not good.

Stephen Surely there's a problem, if what you say is true?

Stephen has got up to pour out a glass for himself and Elaine.

Do you say to those young countries, to so many countries represented in that room, countries with no traditions, no institutions, no civilization as we know it, no old ways of ordering themselves – what do you say! 'Sorry, things will take time . . . it may be bloody in your country at first, but this is an inevitable phase in a young civilization. You must endure dictatorship and bloodshed and barbarity . . .

Elaine Mr Mehta wasn't saying that.

Stephen . . . because you are young. There is nothing we can do for you.'

Elaine This is . . .

Stephen No, surely not! They must be helped!

Mehta Nobody can help.

Stephen What do you mean?

Mehta Except by example. By what one is. One is civilized. One is cultured. One is rational. That is how you help other people to live.

He smiles at Elaine, as if only she will understand. Stephen is staring in disbelief.

Stephen You mean you are saying . . . even as someone reaches up to you to be fed . . .

Elaine That isn't . . .

Mehta If I may . . .

Stephen 'Oh, no I can't fill your bowl . . .

Elaine Stephen . . .

Stephen . . . but I would – please – do – like you to admire my civilization: the cut of my suit!'

Mehta is smiling at Elaine, to say he can deal with this.

Mehta What can you do, he proceeds by parody.

Stephen No.

Elaine Stephen's . . .

Stephen No. What you are saying . . .

Elaine (*with sudden violence*) Mr Mehta has written about this.

> *There is a pause. Stephen walks a long way upstage.*
> *Pauses. Turns. Walks back down. Picks the bottle out*
> *and pours himself another glass. Sits down again. Then*
> *Mehta speaks very calmly.*

Mehta It is true that it is hard . . . it is hard to help the poor. Young men like you, who have left the universities, find this sort of talk easy, just as any woman may make a group of men feel guilty with feminist ideas – how easy it is, at dinner tables, to make all the men feel bad, how we do not do our share, how we do not care for their cunts, how their orgasms are not of the right kind, how this, how that, this piece of neglect, this wrong thinking or that – so it is with you, you young men of Europe. You make us all uncomfortable by saying 'The poor! The poor!' But the poor are a convenience only, a prop you use to express your own discontent. Which is with yourself.

> *There is a pause.*

(*darkly*) I have known many men like you.

> *Elaine is slightly shocked by Mehta's cruelty. But*
> *suddenly he seems to relax again.*

The subject was not the poor. I was not speaking of them. The subject was Australia, and why Barry is suddenly in the bed of Bruce. Do you have views on that?

Stephen No.

Mehta No. Because there is no political explanation, so it bores you.

Stephen Did I say?

Mehta I know you. I know it from your look. (*He turns away, shaking his head.*) Politics. It is the disease. Narrow politics. That old bastard Marx . . .

Stephen Well . . .

Mehta The inflammation of the intellect among the young, the distortion. Every idea crammed through this tiny ideology, everything crammed through the eye of Marxism. Tssh! What nonsense it all is. (*He turns back to Stephen. Definitively*) Socialism, a luxury of the wealthy. To the poor, a suicidal creed. (*Then he gets up, smiling pleasantly, as if the day's work were done.*) Well, I am tired of arguing . . .

Stephen Actually, you haven't argued at all.

Mehta What do you mean?

Elaine Stephen.

Stephen I don't call what he does arguing at all. You've attributed to me various views which you say I hold – on what evidence, I have no idea. Marx you mention. I didn't mention him, or universities, or what I'm supposed to think about the poor. I've said nothing. It was you who dragged it in, just as you dragged in all that peculiar and rather distasteful talk about women's orgasms – something, I must say, I rather gather from your books you have the utmost difficulty in coming to terms with . . .

Mehta (*inflamed*) Ah, now I see!

Stephen Yes!

Mehta Underneath all the talk . . .

Stephen Yes!

Mehta . . . all the apparent concern for the poor, now we have the true thing, what we really want to say, what he really has to say: he has read my books! And of course he must hurt me.

Stephen looks down. He answers, still stubborn but also feeble.

Stephen I certainly do think they are not very pro-women.

Mehta glowers at him.

Mehta Ah, well, of course, the ultimate progressive offence among the young men from the universities. In the old days – what was it? – that one must be pro-life; now we must be pro-women . . .

Stephen No.

Mehta Well, ask yourself if your heroes are very pro-women, your Lenin, your Castro . . .

Stephen He is not *my* Castro.

Mehta This ludicrous, long-winded bore who speaks for eight hours on end, who won his battles by speaking whole villages to death – they reeled over, bored in the face of his speeches – this man (we do not say this, it is long forgotten) who was once an extra in an Esther Williams movie.

Stephen There, you're doing it again. I haven't mentioned Castro.

Mehta At a conference on poverty, 'Castro! Castro!' It is the chorus of sheep.

Stephen Why do you come? Why do you come here if it's such torture to you?

Mehta Yes. And why are you here?

There is a sudden pause, after the shouting. Sure of his point, Mehta now formally turns to Elaine.

Miss le Fanu, tonight I am to dine with the Professor of Classical Studies at Delhi University. It is already pre-arranged. He is coming specially, he is flying, as he is keen to hear my views on his new translation of Herodotus.

Stephen speaks quietly as he helps himself, a little drunkenly, to more champagne.

Stephen Oh, shit!

Mehta (*ignoring this*) If our conversation would not be tedious to you, I would be delighted if you would join us for dinner, and afterwards perhaps . . .

Stephen He could fuck your arse ragged in an upstairs room.

An explosion from the others.

Mehta Mr Andrews!

Elaine I must say, Stephen . . .

Mehta I cannot see how that remark is justified.

Stephen smiles, hovering, drunk, magnificent.

Stephen How the right wing always appropriates good manners. Yes? They always have that. Form and decorum. A permanent excuse for not addressing themselves to what people actually say, because they can always turn their heads away if a sentence is not correctly formulated.

Mehta Now it is you who are exaggerating.

Stephen You're like all those people who think that if you say 'Excuse me' at one end of a sentence and 'Thank you' at the other, you are entitled to be as rude as you like in between. English manners!

Mehta Whatever one may think of them, it seems, Andrews, it is only the foreigner who bothers with them any more.

Stephen Yes. How appropriate! That you, an Indian by birth, should be left desperately mimicking the manners of a country that died – died in its heart – over thirty, forty, fifty years ago. (*He gestures to the ceiling of the room.*) This sad, pathetic imitation, this room, this conference, these servants – that all this goes on, like a ghost ship without passengers. The India of the rich! How I despise it!

Mehta Yes. (*Mehta looks at him, watching, not rising to the bait.*)

Elaine You're smiling.

Mehta Yes. It makes me smile suddenly to see the young man . . .

Stephen Stephen.

Mehta . . . to see Stephen gesturing. To hear him argue. In Hindi there is no word for 'eavesdropper'. It is not required. Everyone speaks too loud. When I think of my home, it is of men in rooms arguing. And in the streets, the dying. This is India. Without the will to act. (*His sudden characteristic darkness has come over him. Then he turns to Elaine.*) Miss le Fanu, you are welcome to dine with us.

Elaine Thank you.

Mehta I have asked your Peggy Whitton.

Stephen Who?

Mehta The Peggy Whitton whom I met just now. Do you know her?

Stephen Dark. Attractive.

Mehta She is attractive, yes.

Stephen But she said . . .

Mehta What?

Stephen That she would dine with me.

Mehta moves suddenly and decisively to the door.

Mehta Let her come. Boy!

The Waiter appears.

Waiter Sahib.

Mehta Peggy Whitton, who was on the verandah,
reading, as I came in. Will you ask her to join us?

The Waiter goes.

By chance she was reading one of my books. Then she
looked up. The author was before her. She could not
believe her good fortune.

*At once Peggy Whitton appears. She is in her early
twenties, American, in a plain cotton dress. There is a
pause.*

Peggy Yes?

Mehta Miss Whitton. You are over-extended. You appear
to be eating in two places at once.

Peggy (*looking between them*) Oh, I see. No. I thought
we'd all eat together.

Stephen Mr Mehta is implying this is not on.

Mehta I said nothing.

Stephen He dislikes me. Because I don't just listen when
he speaks. I dispute. He finds this habit offensive. He is the

famous writer. He expects to be allowed to give forth. In his books he makes sure there is no dispute. There are no messy arguments. He writes fiction because in fiction he gets his own way.

There is a pause.

Well, have it tonight. Dine with Peggy Whitton. By all means. (*He turns to Peggy.*) Sit at his table. Lie at his feet. Let him pour gold in your ear.

He goes. Peggy makes to follow him, upset.

Peggy I must follow the boy. And be nice to him. Excuse me, Mr Mehta.

Mehta Of course. Eight o'clock.

Peggy Yes.

There is a pause. She cannot quite leave. Mehta is smiling. They are still.

I better go.

At once music begins to play, quietly. She runs off. Mehta crosses the room towards us. As he does so, the lights go down, dramatically darkening, until they are in two pools only on Elaine and Mehta.

Mehta Why are you smiling?

Elaine Oh . . . men I suppose.

Mehta Children, you mean. Do you know this Peggy Whitton?

Elaine I've met her.

Mehta She's a jazz violinist. Reputedly brilliant.

Elaine Well, I'm sure you will charm her.

Mehta Do you think so?

Elaine Yes, of course. If you want her just ask. Do it. Act. Seize her. Never nurse unrequited desire. (*She gets up from her chair, her acting expanding alarmingly.*)

Mehta You say that?

Elaine Yes! I've lived by it!

At once from the darkness, great cries.

Angelis Lights!

Boom Operator Sound!

Sound Recordist Speed!

Angelis Turn over!

Cameraman Rolling!

Clapperboy Mark it! Scene 86. Take 4.

Huge lights now illuminate Elaine. A 35mm camera has circled on to place. Sound men have edged near her. Elaine steps up into her highlight.

Angelis Action!

Elaine What do you think the purpose of life is? We could be giants. Victor, I swear it's the truth. This mess, this stew of unhappiness. How nobody dares to speak what they feel. There's something inside every human being. Something suppressed. It's got to come out. I tell you, Victor: cut through to it. My friend, I beg you: let that something out.

Angelis Cut! All right, yes, print that.

At once huge lights come on in the studio and the scene fractures. Peggy Whitton, a woman in her early thirties, well dressed in grey cotton trousers and a grey sweater, walks through the chaos. She has been watching the filming of the scene. We are now in SCENE TWO.

Peggy My God, it's terrible. That wasn't the point of the original scene.

Angelis Please, yes, I am with you in a moment, I am most keen to hear what you say.

Stephen Is Paul there?

Angelis Well done, everyone. Monica, all right?

Elaine I don't know. I just don't feel I got her.

Angelis You have her, honestly. That was wonderful. Were you happy, Shashi?

Mehta Yes. I was fine.

Stephen Paul!

Paul Hi. How are you.

Paul is a strikingly good-looking young man, who now embraces the Stephen-actor. He offers him a small punnet of strawberries. Make-up Girl is dealing with the Elaine-actress's face. The Propmen are waiting to know whether to take furniture away.

Make-up That was really great.

Elaine Thank you, Barbara. There's something happening to this eyelash.

Propman Do we take these?

Second Are we going back?

Cameraman Do we need a re-set?

Loader Is it the same shot?

Angelis Look, please, everyone, just give me a moment.

He has raised his voice. There is a silence.

Peggy You've quite destroyed Victor's writing you know.

Angelis Please, everyone, we have a visitor today, who has come to observe our filming. We welcome the real Peggy Whitton, on whom Victor Mehta based his great novel. She made that choice which is at the centre of the book. I am sure she will have all sorts of observations . . . remarks, which will be helpful to us.

She is looking at him. They are quite still.

For that reason I think we may need a moment alone.

A Wardrobe Girl walks on, oblivious of the slight tension.

Wardrobe Girl This hat for Scene Ninety?

Angelis Yes, it's fine.

Then the Martinson-actor.

Martinson Is it me yet?

Script Girl No, your scene's later.

Stephen Angelis, if you need me I'm just slipping out. I'll be in the dressing-room with Paul.

They go.

Sparks Ten minutes, guv?

Angelis Yes, OK.

First & Sparks Ten minutes! Ten minutes everyone!

Everyone disperses. Angelis calls to the Script Girl.

Propman What can I do with ten minutes?

Angelis By the way, Caroline . . .

Script Girl Yes.

Angelis That hat I was shown. It's ridiculous. Please get it changed.

The lights have gone down. The studio is almost empty.

Miss Whitton, be clear. This is not my forte. I am an action director. Cars, fast movement, guns. For motives of tax, my employers are making a more cultural movie. I am told, in order to lose money . . . for reasons it is quite beyond me to understand. Leasebacks, kickbacks, greenbacks, I understand nothing. It was not even meant to be my assignment. Three weeks ago I was about to shoot *Pulveriser 3*. But suddenly instead my business is nuance.

Peggy I want very little. Only that you should stick to the facts.

Angelis (*he calls off*) Get her a chair. Please. Go on.

Peggy For a start, why have you made me a jazz violinist? I was an actress.

Angelis I know. I informed Mr Mehta of the change.

Peggy But what's the point of it?

Angelis It adds colour.

Peggy Apart from anything, it's just so unlikely. All the jazz violinists you meet in Bombay.

Angelis Does it matter?

Peggy Of course. Everything matters. It's a question of tone. For instance, the scene I just saw. The speech 'What do you think the purpose of life is?' Have you heard anyone say anything like that in real life?

Angelis Not in those exact words, no.

Peggy What happened happened purely by accident. It was chance. It was chance that I met him. And in a funny way, it was chance what I did.

There is a pause. Angelis looks steadily at her.

Angelis Perhaps it would be easiest . . . why not tell me the story from your point of view?

A Prop Man arrives with a chair. It is set down immediately in front of an unlit brute. The Man goes. Peggy sits.

Peggy I was staying in that hotel. I was in Bombay. I was making a film. It was a phoney sort of thriller, a heist movie, maharajahs and diamonds and so on. And I was basically a New York actress. Not even that. I was a philosophy major who worked in publishing. Someone wrote a play and asked me to act. And that's what I did. Easy America. The easiest place in the world. (*She smiles.*) Anyway this movie was dumb. It was long and dumb. I was off for a couple of days. Witty and literate people I was pretty short on, and figured that at least if I went along to this conference I'd read about in the papers . . . well, the great thing would be not to have to talk about films. I had briefly met, I guess for ten minutes maybe, this young Englishman . . . well now, there you are, I looked at the script and in your version you have him as a bore. But that's not how he was. The night I first met him he was charming . . . (*She suddenly gives up the struggle.*) Oh look, this is pointless.

Angelis Please, no, say.

Peggy Angelis, you need a decent writer, you know?

Angelis I know.

Peggy I can sit here all day and set you right on everything and you still won't be able to show it. That's what writers do. They make you see it. And on this film the screenwriter is terrible. (*She shakes her head.*) Elaine, for instance. I mean she wasn't direct like that. Not Elaine. She always just insinuated. She was always just there. Oh, and she was so warm!

Angelis (*hurt*) She's warm in this.

Peggy She's understanding, yes.

Angelis She's one of the characters the writer's done best.

Peggy looks at him, as if now realizing how deep the gulf is between them. So it is kindly, as to an invalid, that she now speaks.

Peggy Please, do you think, could you get me a glass of water?

Angelis Yes. I'll get someone . . .

Peggy No . . . if you could . . . get it yourself. I need a moment. Just a moment's clarity. (*She smiles, to try and take the offence out of the request.*) If you would give me a moment, then I'll let you get on with your film.

There's a pause. He turns and goes out. Peggy is alone on the set. The brute behind her slowly begins to burn. She speaks straight to us.

Young. That's the first thing. Young. Unmistakably young. Not even sure or confident. But irreplaceably, indecently young. You never get it back. How can you? Oh God, nothing makes sense. None of it. Unless you understand this one basic fact. How do I put it? (*She smiles.*) That I was so young.

Peggy goes. From the back of the area Victor Mehta is appearing, pursued into the conference hall by men in suits. The Crew transforms the set by laying out rows of chairs to suggest an empty hall. This is as sketchily marked as the previous Indian scene. Martinson, a tall Swede, is pursuing Mehta.

Martinson Mr Mehta, please, I must insist. You must not just walk away from me. I am trying to tell you, it is a simple statement. Mr Mehta, you cannot refuse.

The lights change. The set is by now assembled. SCENE THREE *has begun.*

Mehta You ask me to accept it. I cannot accept it. It's out of the question. I am a free writer. The whole subject of my work is freedom. Now you ask me to give my freedom up. Well, I will not.

Martinson turns despairingly to his colleagues.

Peggy! Where is Peggy?

Peggy Whitton has arrived from the other side.

Peggy Victor, I'm here.

Mehta I am sorry, my dear. I had hoped to have lunch with you. But I am so distressed. There is trouble.

Peggy What kind?

Mehta Why not ask Mr Martinson? He is running the conference. He is the man who invited me to speak.

He gestures at Martinson, who is standing at the centre of a group of suited Diplomats. Martinson is a tall, grave and persistent Swede, whose apparent doggedness turns out to have an iron quality. He is in his forties.

You remember last night . . .

Peggy Yes.

Mehta . . . after our dinner . . . I told you something here made me uneasy from the start . . .

Peggy You enjoyed dinner.

Mehta (*He pauses, thrown by this apparent irrelevance,* *then persists.*) Yes, I did at the time. But that was last night. And now this morning Mr Martinson has come with this evil news.

Martinson Perhaps, perhaps if I were allowed to repeat it to your friend . . .

Mehta Miss Whitton . . .

Martinson It would be a good test. She would be able to judge more dispassionately how serious it is. Miss Whitton?

A pause. Mehta nods.

Peggy Okay.

Martinson turns patiently to Peggy.

Martinson Mr Mehta is upset because there has been an approach from the Mozambique delegation . . .

Mehta Mozambique!

Martinson Yes, you said.

Mehta There is no such place. It is merely a province of China.

Martinson I am not sure they would necessarily agree.

Mehta They are a tongue only. Not even a puppet. They are simply another man's mouth.

Martinson turns back, apparently almost indifferent.

Martinson Well, it is not really central . . .

Mehta It is very 'central'.

Martinson (*ignoring him*) Well, it is not really the point. There is a faction, let us say it, from the socialist countries . . .

Mehta I . . .

Martinson (*holding up a hand to silence him*) Yes. From whatever direction . . . that objects to Mr Mehta's presence at the conference. Because of some things he's written about their countries in the past.

Mehta, justified, looks to Peggy for her reaction.

Mehta You see!

Peggy Well, there are some people –

Mehta Of course, you are right.

Peggy . . . factions that are bound to object to some of Victor's books. I mean, I've only read a couple – sorry, Victor – but what he says doesn't seem to me to read like hostility. He loves the countries; he attacks the regimes. Surely even they can see there's a difference.

Martinson Yes. You're right. But they dislike the implication in some of the novels that anyone who professes Marxist ideas always uses them as a sort of convenience, as if they were justification for whatever terror he wants to commit.

Mehta It's true.

Martinson There's a phrase where you call Marxism 'dictatorship's fashionable dress'.

Mehta That's a very nice phrase.

Martinson Well, they do find that peculiarly insulting.

Peggy Yes. But surely they knew that in advance?

Martinson It still causes great anger.

Peggy It can't be overnight they've started to read.

There is a momentary pause as Peggy waits for the explanation.

So? What are they suggesting? Are you trying to say he's not allowed to speak?

Martinson No, no, goodness, Miss Whitton . . .

He turns round and smiles at the Diplomats, who smile and shake their heads.

Diplomats No! . . .

Martinson No one is suggesting . . . I think that would be terrible. Censorship is something we do not countenance at all.

Mehta Oh, really?

Martinson No.

Peggy frowns, still not understanding.

Peggy So?

Martinson has already begun to take a slip of paper from his pocket.

Martinson A preliminary statement.

Mehta You see!

Martinson That is the suggestion.

Peggy What about?

Martinson Well . . .

Peggy Is that it there?

Martinson Yes. (*He has unfolded it, white, neat, a single page.*) It's been drafted by a committee, just a short statement, that is all.

Peggy Saying what?

Martinson Mr Mehta would read it before going on to give his own talk.

Peggy But what does it say?

Martinson It's about the nature of fiction. (*He smiles again, the quiet incendiarist.*) I suppose it argues all fiction is lies.

Peggy reacts in disbelief.

Peggy Oh, my God . . . I don't believe it.

Mehta Didn't I say?

Martinson Please.

Mehta It is ludicrous.

Martinson No.

Peggy looks at him, lost for a response.

Peggy How long?

Martinson It's brief. As I say, Mr Mehta would read it out before his address, then he would be free to go on and say whatever he likes.

Peggy is about to react, but Martinson carries on, suddenly on the offensive.

Please. I don't like it. I am not easy at suggesting it. It is not the ideal procedure at all. However, bear in mind I am pleading for the survival of my conference. This seems to me a small price to pay.

Mehta I don't accept that.

Martinson looks at him, authoritative.

Martinson We are here to discuss world poverty. The conference has taken many years to assemble, and in a week's time, the reluctant governments of the West will return home and try to forget they have ever attended. It is true. Any excuse they can find to dismiss the whole

occasion as a shambles they will seize on and exploit.
Therefore it is, without question, essential that the
conference is given every chance of life, every chance of
success. If Mr Mehta refuses to read out this little
concoction, then he will make a fine gesture of individual
conscience against the pressures – I will say this and please
do not repeat it – of less than scrupulous groups, and he
will go home to Shropshire, and he will feel proud and
clever and generally excellent. And *Time* magazine will
write of him, yes, and there will be editorials on the
bloody writer's freedom, hurrah! But the conference will
be destroyed. It is a short statement, it is an unimportant
statement, because it is on a subject which is of no
conceivable general interest or importance, namely, what a
novel is, which I can hardly see is a subject of vital and
continuing fascination to the poor. Frankly, who cares? is
my attitude, and I think you will find it is the attitude of
all the non-aligned countries . . .

> *He looks behind him for confirmation, and the*
> *Diplomats all nod.*

Certainly the Scandinavian bloc . . .

Diplomats Yes . . . Indeed, it is our attitude.

Martinson What is your phrase? We do not give a toss
what a novel is. I think I may even say this is Scandinavia's
official position, and if a man stands up at the beginning
of this afternoon's session and lies about what a novel is, I
will just be grateful because then there is a better chance
that aid will flow, because grain will flow, because water
will flow . . .

Mehta This is blackmail!

Martinson No.

Mehta Exploitation of our feelings of guilt! In the West we are always being asked to feel guilty. And so we must pay a price in lies!

Peggy The West?

Mehta Drag us down to their standards! (*He has got up and is now standing in animated argument with himself.*) No, it is wrong!

Martinson turns coolly to Peggy.

Martinson Miss Whitton?

She has been sitting quietly through Martinson's explanation.

Peggy (*very casually*) Well, I mean, we should hear it, shouldn't we?

Mehta What?

Peggy The statement. (*She turns to Mehta.*) Have you read it?

Mehta Are you mad? I did not write it, therefore I shall not read it.

Peggy (*to Martinson*) Read it.

Mehta Don't.

Then, before Mehta can interrupt:

Peggy Victor. Last night, when we went upstairs – to the bedroom.

Mehta Yes, all right, thank you . . .

She then turns and flashes a smile at Martinson.

Peggy We only met last night.

Mehta looks at her beadily. Then, with bitter quiet:

Mehta All right. Very well, yes, let us hear it. Thank you, Peggy.

*He sits down to listen. Peggy smiles. Martinson begins
very formally.*

Martinson 'Fiction, by its very nature, must always be
different from fact, so in a way a man who stands before
you as a writer of fiction is already half-way towards
admitting that a great deal of what he makes up and
invents is as much with an eye to entertainment as it is to
presenting literal historical truth . . .

Mehta gets up, exploding.

Mehta No, no, no, no! It is not to be endured.

Peggy Victor . . .

Mehta It is Nazi.

Peggy It is not Nazi.

Mehta It is Nazi.

*For the first time Peggy starts taking enthusiastic part in
the argument, enjoying herself.*

Peggy 'Nazi' means 'National Socialist'. This is not
National Socialist. It is not German propaganda of the
thirties.

Mehta It is neo-Nazi.

Peggy No, it is a serious proposition.

Mehta Nonsense.

Peggy . . . to which we may listen rationally and calmly
and as adults, and say, 'Yes, mmm, this is so, this is not
so.' Let us therefore . . .

Mehta The woman is driving me crazy.

Peggy . . . exercise our minds and address the real, the
central problem of the day, which is: is all fiction

distortion? Come on, let's examine this. I did a term paper. What do we mean by distortion? Are these good arguments on this piece of paper or are they bad?

Mehta Not enough the moral blackmail of the Third World, but now we have sexual blackmail. A poor man who stumbles into a bed . . . (*He turns to explain to Martinson.*) I have slept with this woman last night; this woman I have embraced . . .

Peggy (*delighted, pretending shock*) Really Victor, you mustn't disclose to the entire UNESCO Secretariat . . .

Mehta I approach this woman, a dinner with friends, a conversation about Greek history, an understanding as between strangers that they will spend a night . . . a civilized arrangement . . .

Peggy (*smiles*) Yes.

Mehta . . . and now she must betray me.

Peggy smiles at him warmly, her mischievousness past.

Peggy Nobody betrays you, Victor. Perhaps Martinson is right. That in the scale of things this doesn't matter very much.

There is a pause as Mehta stands alone, touched. Then he nods.

Mehta Bring me the man who has written this. I will negotiate.

At the back one of the Diplomats goes out.

I do this because she is beautiful. No other reason, yes? Why did Victor Mehta read the statement on the nature of fiction at the UNESCO conference in Bombay in 1978? For thighs, and hair that falls across the face.

At once Stephen Andrews comes in, smiling, talking to

143

the Diplomat. He is followed by M'Bengue, a Senegalese in his thirties, small, bright, elegant. Stephen is gracious, but pleased.

Stephen Ah, well, this is excellent!

Peggy Stephen!

Stephen I hear there is to be a climb-down. Thank goodness. The whole conference is endangered, I heard . . .

Mehta What? Is it him?

Stephen For something so petty, so meaningless . . .

Mehta (*quietly*) Peggy . . .

Peggy I didn't know.

Stephen This is my friend M'Bengue of Senegal. He helped us draft . . .

Mehta Then I will not read it. No, if it is Mr Andrews . . .

He turns away. Stephen smiles.

Stephen . . . these few remarks.

Between them Martinson looks puzzled.

Martinson Are you old enemies?

Mehta No. He insulted me on my arrival here last night, and now I see, yes, it is because of Peggy, because he was to dine with her. That is the motive behind this fine display of principle. She stood him up to dine with me.

Peggy (*looks down*) Oh, lord.

Martinson is still frowning.

Martinson Well, this does not mean . . . surely the person must be separate from the argument?

Mehta No, absolutely not.

Martinson The motive for the argument does not affect its validity. As Miss Whitton said, a thing is true or untrue, worth proposing or not worth proposing . . .

Mehta No!

Martinson . . . no matter who proposes it. As for instance as one might say of Hitler's love of Wagner . . .

Peggy (*groaning*) Oh, my God . . .

Martinson . . . it does not mean . . .

Mehta Let us not . . .

Martinson . . . that Wagner's music is discredited . . .

The Diplomats shake their heads in agreement.

Diplomats No.

Peggy Please.

Martinson And so it is for whatever . . . I cannot say this well . . .

Mehta Indeed.

Martinson . . . reason it is that he comes . . .

Mehta (*exasperated at Martinson's dogged logic*) But you said, you yourself said, less than scrupulous groups were using this argument to threaten . . .

Martinson But you, Mr Mehta, your motives. Only a moment ago you were saying it was not for principle that you would speak; it was for thighs.

M'Bengue (*to Stephen*) Thighs?

Mehta I would give in, yes. Then. But now I will not give in. I am shaken awake.

Elaine comes in, very cheerful.

Elaine Hey, I hear this is getting very interesting.

Martinson I'm not sure.

Mehta (*at once*) Please, no, nothing now, not in front of the press . . .

Elaine Off the record?

Martinson looks across to Mehta, who nods. Martinson takes advantage of the moment to reassert his chairmanship.

Martinson All right. Let us please to put motive aside. Let us examine the true reason for the dispute. You agree?

Mehta looks at him without enthusiasm, but he goes on.

Let us try to understand the feelings of the African countries in particular. Well, M. M'Bengue can explain.

There is a pause. The others look to M'Bengue.

M'Bengue It is true that we have chosen you, Mr Mehta, and it is to a degree arbitrary. There is a greater argument and we are using you as an instrument merely to draw attention to it. It happens that your novels are full of the most provocative observations – I will not linger on them. In particular, what you say of Madame Mao . . .

Martinson (*panicking*) Oh no.

Mehta (*with renewed vigour*) Ah well, yes.

M'Bengue You lack respect . . .

Mehta You ask me to desist from writing of Madame Mao?

M'Bengue No.

Mehta No, I cannot. I am a comic novelist. It would be superhuman to refrain.

Martinson It is not the point.

Mehta You ask me to refrain from writing of a woman who does not dare to make public the date of her birthday because she is afraid it will over-excite the masses? (*He stares insanely at M'Bengue.*) She is a gift. You ask me not to write of her.

Martinson (*quietly leading M'Bengue back*) The greater argument, M. M'Bengue, please.

Stephen Go on.

M'Bengue Very well, it is this. We take aid from the West because we are poor, and in everything we are made to feel our inferiority. The price you ask us to pay is not money but misrepresentation. The way the nations of the West make us pay is by representing us continually in their organs of publicity as bunglers and murderers and fools. I have spent time in England and there the yellow press does not speak of Africa except to report how a nun has been raped, or there has been a tribal massacre, or how we are slaughtering the elephants – the elephants who are so much more suitable for television programmes than the Africans – or how corrupt and incompetent such-and-such a government is. If the crop succeeds, it is not news. If we build a dam, it is called boring. 'Oh, we do not report the building of dams,' say your newspapers. Dam-building is dull. Boring. The white man's word for everything with which he does not wish to come to terms. Yes, he will give us money, but the price we will pay is that he will not seek to understand our point of view. Pro-Moscow, pro-Washington, this is the only way you can see the world. All your terms are political, and your politics is the crude fight between your two great blocs. Is Angola pro-

Russian? Is it pro-American? These are the only questions you ever ask yourselves. As if the whole world could be seen in those terms. In your terms. In the white man's terms and through the white man's media. (*He looks down, as if to hide the strength of feeling behind what he says.*) And so it hurts . . . it begins to hurt that the context of the struggle in Africa is never made clear. It is never explained. Your news agencies report our events, and from a point of view which is eccentric and sensational. All this, day in, day out, we endure and make no protest, and when we come to take part in this conference in Bombay, we find that UNESCO has invited a particular keynote speaker – a black man himself, though of course, because he is Indian, it is not how he sees himself: he thinks himself superior to the black man from the bush – a speaker whose reputation is for wit at the expense of others, whose reporting is not positive, so of course he is called a hero in the West. He is called a bringer of truths because he seeks to discredit those who struggle. And so it is true, yes, in the middle of the night, Mr Andrews and I, walking to the Gateway of India, did say: the greater, the larger misrepresentation we can do nothing about – those who control the money will control the information – but the lesser one, yes, and tonight. A stand is possible. (*He turns to Mehta.*) You distort things in your novels because it is funny to distort, because indeed the surface of things is funny, if you do not understand how that surface comes to be, if you do not look underneath. Just as a funeral may be funny to a small boy who sees it passing in the street and does not know the man who is dead. So also no doubt in Africa it is superficially funny to see us blundering about. But who makes the jokes? The rich nations.

Mehta No.

M'Bengue Jokes, Mr Mehta, are a product of security. If one is secure, one may laugh at others. That is the truth.

Humour, like everything, is something you buy. Free speech? Buy. But what is this freedom? The luxury of the rich who are sure of what they have.

Mehta just looks at him.

Mehta (*quietly*) What would you do? Ban it?

M'Bengue No. I would ask that black men who ascend from their countries do not conspire in the humiliation of those they have left behind.

There is a pause. When Mehta replies it is with a gravity that matches M'Bengue's.

Mehta People are venal and stupid and corrupt, no more so now than at any other time in history. They tell themselves lies. The writer asks no more than the right to point those lies out. What you say of how the press sees you is probably true, and the greater grievance you have I am sure is right. But I will not add to the lies.

There is a pause. And then he gets up.

And that is all I have to say.

Peggy Victor . . .

Mehta No.

Mehta goes out. The whole group is suspended for a moment, and M'Bengue gets up and leaves at the other side. Martinson looks behind him to one of his Aides.

Martinson The educational motion from tomorrow's agenda . . .

Aide Yes.

Martinson We may move it to today?

Aide It's possible.

Martinson Delay Mr Mehta's address until tomorrow. If that's agreeable?

He looks to Stephen.

Stephen Yes.

Martinson The Committee, Mr Andrews, will give us twenty-four hours?

Stephen (*conscious of Peggy's gaze*) Of course.

Martinson gets up and leads his team out silently. Elaine, Peggy and Stephen are left alone.

Stephen Well, there you are.

Elaine I'd thought M'Bengue was a fool . . .

Stephen No.

Elaine When we watched him yesterday, he seemed to be the worst kind of professional politician.

Stephen How wrong can you be? Don't you think? Don't you think, Peggy?

Peggy Oh, yes. He's got a good case. (*She is thoughtful. She starts to move.*)

Stephen Are you off?

Peggy Why?

Stephen I was wondering, no, I'm sorry, it was silly. I wanted to have lunch. Fuck, I shouldn't have mentioned it. Forget I mentioned it.

Elaine Why doesn't everyone just eat their meals on a tray in their room?

Peggy I just don't believe it. Why do people make things so hard? Stephen, last night if you were so upset about dinner, why didn't you say?

Stephen Only slightly. And that's not the whole story.

Peggy I ran down the corridor, I tried to find you after you made that ridiculous scene.

Stephen I'd gone.

Peggy I know.

Stephen I was sickened by Mehta.

Peggy It's so *typical*. If you'd stayed we could have discussed it. But no – throw the whole chess table over. Now we have a problem. Well?

Stephen Well what?

Peggy Well, we've got to get them to sit down and talk.

Stephen Do you mean M'Bengue and Victor?

Peggy Of course.

Stephen Why us?

Elaine Not me, I'm press.

Stephen Anyway, it's hardly likely.

Peggy Why not?

Stephen Well I know this will seem a very minor objection. But they do actually believe different things.

Peggy So what would you do?

Stephen Do?

Peggy Yes, do.

Stephen (*shrugs*) Do nothing. Either Victor agrees his novels are slanted and malicious – which they are – or we can kiss goodbye to the conference.

Peggy And what? What then, Stephen? You would like to

go off and *have lunch*?

Stephen (*stung*) No.

Peggy suddenly smiles.

Peggy Oh God, Stephen, I do understand you. In Westchester County I knew lots of people like you.

Stephen Thank you.

Peggy You know, life can really be quite easy, if you don't always let your emotions get in the way.

He looks at her a moment.

When I was sixteen, I made a resolution. I had a girlfriend, we were walking in the Rockies, and the view, I can tell you, was something as we came over to Boulder, Colorado. And we had a six-pack right there on top of the mountain. And she was a good girl. I mean a really good girl. You could trust your life to her. And there that day we looked over the valley. We thought about our lives and relationships, and said, 'Life can be simple, by will we can make it simple. From now on we are totally free. Let's not ever mess with the bad things at all.' Now what's sad is I saw her six months ago. She's married to a lawyer in DC and he's never there, he's out over-achieving all day, she doesn't like him when he is there, and so she's fucking around, so that one day, she told me, she got this terrible pain here. She was really desperate. Into the hospital. She told me for the first time in her life she prayed. And I said 'Really, what was your prayer, Elise?' And she said 'Oh God, let it not be cervical cancer. God please. God, just do this for me. If it's not cancer, I swear I'll never cheat on Arnold again.' And that . . . (*She laughs delightedly*.) . . . I tell you that, when I come to write my novel about America, that will be its title: *Cheating on Arnold*. That will be its name. Because you see that is not what is going to happen to me. You understand? Because there is no need. (*She says this with the complete conviction of youth. Then smiles.*) Now the two of you, Victor, you, both slightly ridiculous, slightly contemptible, in my view, you see? Elaine will agree. That sort of behaviour, men being jealous, men fighting, it's out of date. Outdated, Stephen. Unnecessary, Stephen. I mean, drop the bad behaviour and you might get somewhere.

Stephen Meaning I will get somewhere?

Peggy Drop the bad behaviour and you will get somewhere.

A silence while this sinks in. Elaine looks down, amused. Stephen cautious, but enjoying his power.

Stephen That's kind of you, but the fact is, I didn't act alone.

Peggy Ah, well.

Stephen There's a committee.

Peggy (*vigorously*) Well, I'm not offering all of them.

Elaine smiles.

Even Westchester County has its limits, you know.

Stephen Yes, but I just helped draft the statement, there are others and they do have views.

Peggy They can be swung.

Stephen Because they're black?

Peggy looks at him with contempt.

Peggy That's when you're really boring, Stephen. The sex drops off you. It's like your prick drops off when you say things like that.

Stephen All right.

Peggy No, not because they're black, you wimp, but because it's a committee of – how many?

Stephen Six.

Peggy Right. And you're on it, that's all. And when you're not apologizing for your own existence, you can actually be quite a plausible human being.

Stephen looks at her, touched.

Stephen Weren't you moved by what M'Bengue said just now?

Peggy Stephen, whose cause does he damage by stopping the conference?

Stephen He doesn't want to stop the conference.

Peggy His own.

Stephen But . . .

Peggy Senegal's. Somalia's. Mozambique's.

Stephen But if Victor could be persuaded.

Peggy Victor was persuaded. I had him persuaded. Until you appeared.

There's a pause. Then Peggy turns, as if finally despairing.

All right, then, make your little stand . . .

Stephen It's not that.

Peggy . . . whatever it is. No one will remember.

Stephen It's principle.

Peggy Principle, indeed! People do what they want to, then afterwards, if it suits them, they call it principle.

Stephen No.

Peggy Rationalization of what you've already decided, that's what principle is.

Stephen is already shaking his head.

Stephen Certain things are important. Certain things are good.

Peggy How can you say, you who are not involved? M'Bengue, sure, he's a member of a government . . .

Stephen He's a civil servant.

Peggy All right, he's a civil servant who represents a government which stands to gain from the successful outcome of this conference – so when he says 'principle', we listen. It's at some cost. It's at some personal expense. But your principles come from a store on the corner and cost you nothing.

Stephen looks down, very hurt.

Stephen No, well, I'm sorry . . .

Peggy Look, Stephen, I don't mean to be unkind to you. I like you.

Elaine (*smiles*) She does.

Peggy You attract unkindness because so often you're not you. You're this ragbag of opinions.

Stephen So are you.

Peggy looks at him, surprised, not understanding.

How is it different? Your freedom you've just told us about, your sexual freedom, what's that if not some contrived and idiotic idea based on some mountaintop experience you've talked yourself into believing was a revelation? And a revelation meaning what? That you may

155

sleep with anyone and not get involved. Gosh, well, thank goodness. What a convenient discovery. Remind me to buy climbing boots next time I'm out.

Elaine Stephen . . .

Stephen The six-pack philosopher. Really! Entitled to patronize. To witter on about freedom. And from what position? From the safety of beauty. From the absolute safety of being beautiful.

He stops, aware of having hurt her. He begins to apologize.

Well, I'm sorry. Something happened to me last night, while you were no doubt with . . .

Peggy Victor.

Stephen Quite. I walked to the Gateway of India with M'Bengue, among the small kerosene stoves, suffocating, the heat, the dope, tripping against beggars, watching boys of ten and eleven with fat joints stuck in their mouths. We walked along Chowpatty Beach, and I listened to a man trying to explain to me what it's like to see the world the other way up. To come – can you imagine – from Dakar, West Africa, to fly through the night and arrive in this conference hall to listen to the well-heeled agents of the West argue that of course aid never gets through, and, when it gets through, how officials rip it off. And how really all it does is create a disease called aid dependency. Aid doesn't really help, the West keeps saying to salve its bloated conscience. Yes, I do feel these things that seem to you affectations only because to believe in anything now in the West, except money or sex or motor cars, is to mark yourself out as foolish. A subject for satire. At which Victor Mehta is adept.

There is a pause. Peggy looks at him, lost. Then suddenly:

Peggy Then you should argue it out.

Stephen What?

Peggy The two of you. Just the two of you on behalf of your committee. Since you believe it so strongly.

Stephen He won't listen.

Elaine He'll listen. If Peggy says . . .

There is a pause.

Stephen I'm not sure.

Peggy Yes. This evening.

Elaine I will adjudicate.

Peggy Brilliant! Elaine will decide. And whoever wins, wins me.

Stephen No!

Peggy Oh yes. Yes. That will be principle. That's what principle is. Having something to lose.

Stephen No.

Peggy That's freedom. I do actually believe in it.

Stephen That's not freedom. My God. That's bartering.

Peggy Elaine?

Stephen It's sick.

Elaine Putting her body where her mouth is, how can that be wrong?

Stephen It's impossible. What would I say to M'Bengue and the others, if I lost, 'Oh, I'm sorry, because of a deal I made we now have to give way to this offensive Indian . . .' No, it's ridiculous!

Peggy Yes, if you lose. But you told me you believed so passionately . . . if you're right after all, if Victor is wrong to say all these things . . .

Stephen He is.

Peggy Very well then. Test it. Test it, Stephen. If you want me, argue it tonight.

She goes out. Elaine and Stephen are left alone.

Stephen Oh, God. Elaine . . .

Elaine looks at him affectionately.

Elaine There's so much passion in you, so much emotion, all the time. This is wrong, that's wrong. Well, tonight you will get the chance to direct that emotion, and in a good cause.

A pause.

What better cause than Peggy Whitton, eh?

There is a moment of warmth between them. Suddenly they both smile at the ludicrousness of the situation.

Come on, I'll buy you lunch.

And at once, Angelis appears from the back of the stage, walking on to the set and calling to his unseen followers. This time the two scenes interweave, one group of people walking right through the other. SCENE THREE *oblivious to* SCENE FOUR's *existence.*

Angelis Lunch, everyone.

Elaine and Stephen are still standing looking at each other.

Elaine I'm fond of you. You're a fool, and I'm fond of you.

Angelis Strike the set!

Elaine Where shall we eat?

Stephen I want to go to the Temple of the Jains. Have you been there?

Elaine No.

Stephen I hear it's beautiful.

The Prop Crew has appeared and is clearing away the chairs. Elaine and Stephen walk upstage.

Elaine And let's go to Doongarwadi, to the Parsee funeral ground.

Stephen Is that where the vultures pick at the bodies of the dead?

Elaine That's the one.

Stephen Good. Let's go there.

The lights lose them as they go.

Lunch before?

Elaine After, I think.

The Assistant has carried on a chair for Angelis's approval.

Assistant Is this the right kind of chair for the bedroom, Mr Angelis?

Angelis Yes, that's fine.

Assistant They want you to look at the bed.

Angelis I will look at the bed later. The bed comes later.

A Crewman walks by with a ghetto-blaster playing Barry Manilow's 'I Am Music'.

Assistant They want to know whether to make the bed soft or hard?

Angelis Soft.

Assistant What colour?

Angelis Blue. Blue spread.

Assistant Really?

Angelis (*panicking now*) White. Oh, God, I don't know. White sheets, white spread too. Sure. What the hell? Who cares? Get the book.

Assistant The book says white.

Angelis Then white. If it's in the book, it must be right.

The set has been cleared. There is only an empty floor. Peggy Whitton runs on, as if the set were still there. She doesn't realize Stephen and Elaine have gone.

Peggy Stephen! Victor agrees. It's on.

She stands triumphant. Angelis does not see or hear her.

Angelis I'm bored.

A great cry.

Lunch! Lunch!

Act Two

At the end of the interval, in the darkness, we hear a recording of Peggy's letter home.

Peggy Dear Sue, Alone but not lonely in Bombay. I have met a man – I cannot tell you – I have met a novelist, Victor Mehta. A man of great gracefulness. Difficult, of course, like the best men. And very proud. In a fit of stupidity, I have agreed – oh, God, how I agreed to this I have no idea – I have agreed to sleep with the winner of an argument. One of the men is Victor. The other . . . not.

SCENE FIVE. *The film studio. There is now a bedroom, which is represented by a bed and a wall behind with a door in it, which leads off to an imaginary bathroom. The room is unnaturally spacious, occupying a large area, detailed but incomplete. Dotted near it are canvas chairs and camera equipment, though the camera itself is missing. The actors are sitting about in casual clothes, waiting for rehearsal. They are not yet in costume. The Elaine-actress is sitting at one side by herself with a magazine. The Martinson-actor is doing* The Times *crossword. He was born an Englishman, but is now a self-consciously international figure in blue jeans, gold medallion and muted Californian T-shirt. The M'Bengue-actor stands in the middle, quite still, looking off into the distance.*

M'Bengue Well, what is happening?

Martinson I don't know. (*He frowns.*) What on earth could be one . . . two . . . three . . . four . . . five . . . six . . . seven letters, begins with Z, and the clue is 'It's the plague of the earth'?

Elaine Zionism.

Martinson What?

The Peggy-actress comes on. She is wearing a band round her head, to push her hair back. She has a dressing-gown on over her shirt and trousers.

Peggy Is there any sign of Angelis?

Elaine No. We're all called, but there's nobody here.

Martinson is staring at Elaine in disbelief.

Martinson What d'you mean, 'Zionism'?

Elaine Well, it's seven letters, beginning with Z.

Martinson But are you just saying it because it's a word?

Elaine It's a word.

Martinson I know it's a word. (*He pauses.*) I know it's a word.

Elaine It's got seven letters and it begins with Z.

Peggy has stood a moment, taking no notice, and now smiles round.

Peggy I want to show you a few bathrobes, and then you can say what's best for the scene, OK?

She disappears through the door in the set and closes it. From the side the Stephen-actor appears, in loose grey flannels and pullover, with a book. He is a pleasant and easy-going man. He sits.

Stephen Hello.

Martinson But are you also saying it's the plague of the earth?

Elaine What?

Martinson Zionism.

Elaine (*frowns*) Well, I don't think it's a very good thing, if that's what you mean.

She goes back to reading, but Martinson looks round to see who else is taking notice, then persists.

Martinson No, that's not actually what I mean. What I mean is, are you actually suggesting that Zionism is the plague of the earth?

Elaine Well, obviously, if it's got seven letters and begins with Z, it scarcely matters what I think about it. What matters is what the compiler thinks, and obviously, I don't know, perhaps *The Times* has Arab crossword compilers these days. Perhaps they have some Libyan on the staff.

Martinson I suppose you think that's funny.

Elaine No, I don't think it's funny. I'm just saying . . .

Peggy has come through the bathroom door in a blue-and-white spotted dressing-gown.

Peggy Well, what d'you think?

Martinson Very nice.

Peggy Monica?

Elaine Fine.

Stephen (*looking up*) Honestly, it's fine.

Peggy goes out smiling. Martinson is still waiting.

Martinson Are you seriously saying . . .

Elaine I'm not saying anything.

Martinson . . . you actually think *The Times* would employ somebody . . .?

Elaine No.

Martinson Do you know the history of the state of Palestine?

Elaine Well, as a matter of fact, yes, I do.

Martinson Do you know what happened to the Jews between 1939 and 1945?

Elaine Yes, I do. They got wiped out.

Martinson It's not funny.

Elaine I know it's not funny, for Christ's sake. I am not for one second saying it is funny. It's you that seems determined to take issue with everything I say.

Martinson I'm not.

Elaine It's just . . . objectively . . . it seems a remarkable fact that a people who once enjoyed the sympathy of the whole world for what they had suffered have, in the space of just thirty-five years, managed to squander that sympathy by creating a vicious, narrow-minded, militarist state.

Martinson (*quietly*) What?

Elaine And as a matter of fact, I think it not funny at all. I think it a tragedy.

There is a pause. Then Martinson turns to appeal to the others.

Martinson Did you hear what she just said?

M'Bengue (*neutrally*) Yes, I did.

Martinson (*turning back to Elaine*) Do you know what Sartre said?

Elaine Yes, I do.

There is a pause.

What did he say?

Martinson Why say you did?

Elaine Well, I mean, I know what Sartre said about various things . . .

Martinson Such as?

Elaine Well, I mean, I can't remember what things he said what about . . . I mean . . . I know he liked actresses very much . . .

Martinson ignores this.

Martinson I will tell you what he said about Israel. That it was a historical exception.

Peggy reappears, in a yellow dressing-gown this time.

Peggy Guys, this one?

Martinson Very nice.

Elaine Sure.

Peggy goes out again.

Martinson That normally the Jews would have no right to the territory of Palestine, but that the crime against them was so great, that it was so out of proportion with anything any people had ever suffered before, that it was necessary to make a historical exception and say, 'Yes, give them the land.'

A pause. Elaine concedes with ill grace.

Elaine OK.

Martinson That's what Sartre said.

Elaine OK.

M'Bengue has leant over casually and is looking down at Martinson's discarded Times.

M'Bengue It's not Z anyway.

Martinson What?

M'Bengue Look, six down is 'evasion'. You don't spell that with a Z. You spell it with an S.

Martinson Are you telling me how to do this?

M'Bengue Which means fourteen across is now a seven-letter word beginning with S.

Martinson looks at him unkindly.

Martinson I suppose you agree with her.

M'Bengue What?

Martinson About the Jews.

Elaine gets up from her chair, suddenly losing her temper.

Elaine For Christ's sake, man . . .

Peggy has reappeared in stripes.

Peggy What do you think?

Elaine (*shouts*) It sucks. (*She throws up her hands in the air, apologizing.*) No, I'm sorry. It's just . . . What are we doing? Where is Angelis?

Peggy I want to do the scene.

Everyone momentarily lost, before Stephen looks up again, mild, oblivious.

Stephen Why are policemen so important in homosexual mythology?

M'Bengue Pardon?

Stephen It's . . . I'm reading about E. M. Forster. What everyone admires in him is not . . . you know . . . books, I mean that's what he wrote, but what everyone really admires him for was having a boyfriend who was a policeman.

M'Bengue Well, it is an achievement.

Stephen I suppose. (*He smiles to himself.*) P. C. Bob Buckingham.

Martinson is frowning, ready to hold forth again.

Martinson But in a sense it's absolutely symbolic in a way, isn't it?

Elaine (*quietly*) Oh, God.

Martinson Surely what he was doing was forcing the authoritarian figure, in a sense, to yield . . . I'm just talking out loud here.

Elaine looks across at Peggy, close to murder. Then goes and lies down on the bed in the fake room.

In some way the father-figure perhaps . . .

Elaine Oh, Jesus, where is Angelis?

Martinson He was seducing him and in some way he was forcing him to admit that his authority was an act, that underneath the social role we all play, we are all . . .

Stephen What?

Martinson Well, you know . . .

Stephen What?

Martinson pauses.

Martinson Gay.

Stephen frowns, mystified. Martinson hastens to qualify.

I mean, not exclusively. We're not, exclusively. Obviously, you would know more about this. If you've seen those films about fish, it's clear. It's been proved biologically. Sometimes it's one thing, sometimes the other . . .

Elaine (*calling from the bed*) And sometimes fuck-all if they're anything like the rest of us.

Martinson explodes.

Martinson Will somebody please tell this woman . . .

Stephen It's all right, honestly. She's just provoking you.

Stephen smiles, placating. Martinson goes on, the air tense.

Martinson We pay a price for suppressing this truth. That we are all bisexual. We hide this fact at enormous expense to ourselves in order to obey some imaginary social norm. But the result of this suppression is great damage inside. Finally . . . yes . . . we implode.

Stephen Yes, well . . .

Martinson Literally!

Stephen (*puzzled*) It's a problem.

Martinson Yes.

At once Angelis sweeps on, followed by Assistants.

Angelis I am sorry, my friends . . .

Peggy Angelis!

Angelis . . . I have been delayed. Crew!

All the actors get up as he calls out.

Elaine Thank God. We were all about to implode.

Angelis Please, we move on, we prepare the scene.

168

Peggy moves on to the set as Elaine and Martinson leave it. Stephen quiet, near Angelis.

Stephen Has there been trouble?

Angelis No. No trouble.

Stephen I thought perhaps . . .

Angelis What?

The furniture in the room is changed round by the Crew, setting it right.

Stephen We had heard that Mehta was coming.

Angelis Mehta is coming, yes.

He moves away, passing Elaine who has collected her script.

Monica, all well?

Elaine Fine, thank you.

Angelis turns, looking at the set.

Angelis Please, now, everyone, we rehearse. It is what? It is the evening. The scene is evening. Peggy at last begins to have her doubts.

Stephen is waiting, refusing to give up.

Stephen Have you spoken to Mehta?

Angelis Only on the phone.

Stephen And?

Angelis It is true there are things he does not like in our production.

Stephen Such as?

Angelis I don't know.

Stephen Angelis. Everyone here has heard rumours that the film is in danger.

A Propman has appeared with an inappropriate pink-feathered fan.

Propman Where do I put this?

There is a sudden quiet. The Elaine-actress speaks with authority.

Elaine Keep going Mike.

There is a moment before Angelis realizes he must square with the actors. Then:

Angelis It is not him. It is Peggy.

Stephen Peggy?

Angelis Peggy came. She visited the set, you remember? Earlier today. She saw the action. It reminds her of the original events – the events, the book, the film. Suddenly she panics. She is now – what? – an older woman, and she sees we are to re-enact a night of which she is no longer proud. Suddenly thinking . . . she realizes she was callous. Her actions seem cruel.

Stephen Right.

Angelis She goes back to Victor Mehta. She tries to stop the film.

Stephen What?

Angelis No, it is fine . . . (*He wanders over to the set.*)

Elaine The film is being stopped?

Angelis There is a contractual argument, that is all, as to whether Victor Mehta has the right to approve the screenplay.

Stephen Does he?

Angelis In theory, perhaps. It is in his contract, yes, but the lawyers . . . you can imagine.

Stephen Angelis –

Angelis His solicitors have notified us of their intention to serve an injunction, and we have notified them of our intention to counterfile. (*He stops, firm.*) It is a game. (*Then smiles, resuming his usual manner.*) So meanwhile, until the resolution, we schedule rehearsal. Yes? Say nothing please.

Stephen All right. (*He walks away, unhappily.*)

Angelis Please, we rehearse. I beg you, let us act.

A Propman has appeared through the 'door' of the 'room' with an enormous bunch of flowers.

Propman You have flowers?

Peggy (*delighted*) For me?

Angelis No, no flowers. The flowers are downstairs.

The Mehta-actor has walked on and has sat down at the desk in the bedroom, taking his jacket off and putting it over the back of the chair. Peggy has for some time been stretched out on the top of the bed in her latest dressing-gown. They are silent, ready to go.

Angelis Madeleine in her place. And Shashi, please . . . to work.

The room is peaceful, ready for action, but the M'Bengue-actor is still standing in the middle.

Angelis Er, John . . .

M'Bengue turns and looks out.

171

M'Bengue 'Slavery'.

Angelis What?

M'Bengue 'Slavery' is the word.

There's a pause. Then he turns and walks silently out of the room.

Angelis OK.

Only Mehta and Peggy remain. The lights change. Peggy, who is staring at the counterpane, now looks up, and SCENE SIX *begins.*

Peggy How do you write a book?

Mehta (*without looking up*) Mmm?

Peggy I mean, when you start out, do you know what you think?

Mehta No.

Peggy I don't mean the plot. I'm sure the plot's easy . . .

Mehta No, the plot's very hard.

Peggy Well, all right, the plot's hard. But what you think . . . do you know what you think?

Mehta No. (*He turns from writing in his notebook and looks at her.*) The act of writing is the act of discovering what you believe. (*He turns back to his work, smiling slightly.*) How do you act?

Peggy (*smiles at once*) Oh, lord . . .

Mehta Well?

Peggy I mean, I don't. Not really. I'm not an actress. I'm too conscious. I'm too self-aware. I stand aside.

Mehta Does that mean you plan to give it up?

Peggy does not answer. She has already picked up a booklet which is beside her on the bed.

Peggy Don't you love this country?

Mehta Why?

Peggy An airline timetable, I was looking . . .

Mehta Were you thinking of leaving?

Peggy No, listen, what I love about India, the only country in the world where they'd print poetry – here, look, at the bottom of the Kuwait-Delhi airline schedule. A poem. 'Some come to India to find themselves, some come to lose themselves . . .' In an airline schedule? Isn't that a pretty frightening admission?

He is about to speak seriously but she interrupts him.

Mehta Peggy . . .

Peggy No, I wasn't leaving. How could I be leaving? I'm here to make a film.

Mehta But?

A pause. Then she looks away.

Peggy But at lunchtime I did something so stupid that the thought of going down those steps . . .

Mehta Ah well, yes.

Peggy . . . into that lobby, along that corridor, past those delegates, into that deserted conference hall, for this appalling contest . . .

Mehta Yes.

Peggy . . . when all I want is to spend my time with you.

A pause. Mehta sets aside his notebook.

Mehta American women, they make me laugh. I am at home.

Peggy Well, good.

Mehta It is like they pick you up in their lovemaking from wherever they last left off. At once, bang! and they're away. No matter with whom it was last time, if it was someone else, no matter, nevertheless, it is go at once. The passion again. Making love to an American woman, it is like climbing aboard an already moving train.

Peggy smiles and gets off the bed to go to the bathroom.

Peggy We have needs.

Mehta I am sure.

Peggy (*calling as she goes out*) We have no guilt. Americans are unashamed of their needs.

Mehta (*smiles*) Yes.

Peggy (*off*) When an Englishman has an emotion, his first instinct is to repress it. When an American has an emotion, his first instinct . . .

Mehta Ah well, yes . . .

Peggy (*off*) They express it!

Mehta Usually at length.

Peggy (*off*) Why not?

Mehta sits smiling, contented, happy with Peggy and able to show it clearly now she is out of the room.

Mehta Always examining their own reactions . . .

Peggy (*off*) Yes.

Mehta Always analysing, always telling you what they

feel – I think, I feel. Hey – let me tell you what I feel . . .

Peggy Sure.

Mehta The endless drama of it all.

Peggy reappears at the bathroom door. She has taken off her dressing-gown and has changed into another loose cotton suit.

Peggy And which is better, tell me, Victor, next to the English? Which is healthier, eh?

He looks at her with great affection.

Mehta You make love like a wounded panther. You are like a paintshop on fire.

She looks at him. Then raises her eyebrows.

Peggy Well, goodness.

Mehta Yes.

Peggy Writer, eh?

He smiles. There is a knock at the door. Peggy goes to answer it.

Mehta It comes in handy.

Peggy Is that what you say to all the girls? 'Thank you, that was wounded-panther-like.'

She opens the door. A Waiter is standing outside.

Yes?

Waiter Mr Andrews. He is waiting downstairs.

Peggy looks at the Waiter a moment, then nods.

Peggy Thank you.

She closes the door, stands a moment, her face turned

away from Mehta. Then she turns, walks across to the
dressing-table and picks up her hairbrush. Then,
casually:

What about you?

Mehta What?

Peggy Are you thinking of leaving?

Mehta No, of course not. I shall stay for this contest
tonight.

There is a slight pause, then both of them speak at once.

Peggy . . .

Peggy I don't know. I can't say which of the two of you
makes more sense to me. I've never had to choose, you see.
Like so many people. I've never made a choice. (*She turns
and smiles at him.*) Sitting at nights with my professors,
eating Angel bars, sure, it was great. Philosophy, that was
my major . . . eight arguments as to whether God exists.

Mehta Does he?

Peggy We never decided.

Mehta There you are.

Peggy But the game was fun. No question. It felt good, it
still feels good, that moment of understanding something.
When you understand an idea for the first time. But
applying it? Well, that's different, the world not offering so
many opportunities for that sort of thing. Arts and
humanities! Philosophy! What's the point in America,
where the only philosophy you'll ever encounter is the
philosophy of making money? In my case taking off T-
shirts. In fact, not even taking them off – I'm too up-scale
for that. I have only to hint there are situations in which I
would show my breasts to certain people, certain *rich*

people, that they do indeed exist under there, but for now it's enough to suggest their shape, hint at their shape in a T-shirt. Often it will have to be wet. By soaking my T-shirts in water I make my living. It's true. Little to do with the life of ideas. (*She smiles.*) Spoiled. Spoiled doesn't say it, though that's what people say about Americans, and spoiled, I suppose, is what I was till lunchtime, till I made this ridiculous offer. A young idiot's suicidal offer with which she is now going to have to learn to live. Yes? (*She turns and looks at Mehta.*) Well, good luck to you. Debate well, Victor, for on your performance depends . . .

Mehta (*smiles*) Don't tell me.

Peggy . . . my future. Tonight.

> *They stand at opposite sides of the room looking at each other.*

Mehta It's your fault.

Peggy Oh, yes.

Mehta You with your 'Oh, it doesn't matter who wins.' It does matter. What we believe matters more than anything. This you must learn.

> *The Waiter knocks on the door. Peggy does not move, just calls out, looking at Victor all the time.*

Peggy Yes!

Waiter Madam, Mr Andrews is asking why you are not downstairs.

Peggy Tell him . . . tell him we are coming. Just one minute. Mr Mehta is preparing his case.

> *Mehta smiles.*

Mehta Kiss me.

Peggy No kisses. I am no longer yours. I belong now to the winner of an argument.

There is another knock at the door.

Peggy Yes!

Elaine opens the door.

Oh, I'm sorry, Elaine, I thought it was the waiter.

Elaine Are you coming down?

A pause.

Mehta Excuse me. (*He goes out.*)

Elaine Do I detect a difference of opinion?

Peggy No, you detect a very harsh man. (*She goes to the bathroom with a glass of water.*)

Elaine Well, you don't have to . . .

Peggy Don't have to what?

Elaine Go through with it. Have a more urgent appointment. Tell them you're busy. Tell them you're working.

Peggy I'm not.

Elaine But just lie.

Peggy Lie?

Elaine Yes, lie. Don't you do that?

Peggy thinks a moment.

Peggy Well, no. (*She goes into the bathroom for her hairbrush.*)

Elaine My God, how do you manage? Lying's the thing which makes life possible. You should work for the networks for a while. I can't imagine a life without lying.

Peggy Why do you pretend to be so hard-boiled?

Elaine I don't pretend. Are you serious? Trying to get my bosses interested in anything which happens abroad, do you think I don't have to threaten and blackmail and *lie*? Ask any journalist. Who cares at all. I do it so's to get something on television about how four-fifths of the planet lives.

Peggy But doesn't it drive you crazy? How can you bear it?

Elaine By 1990 one American in six will at some time in their life have worked for MacDonalds. Put it like that, I'm doing pretty well.

They look at each other.

Tell them you're working.

Peggy No. It's too late.

A pause.

Elaine Are you ready?

Peggy Yes.

Elaine crosses and kisses her.

Elaine Let's go down. (*She turns.*) All right?

Angelis (*off*) Yes. But smile at the end.

Angelis walks thoughtfully on to the set, the lights change and we are into SCENE SEVEN.

Angelis All right. Let's go on. Madeleine?

Peggy Yes?

He turns and sees that the Peggy-actress has turned away as if to cry.

Angelis Are you all right?

Peggy Oh, I'm sorry, I . . .

Angelis holds up a tactful hand at an approaching Crew Member.

Angelis Hold it.

Peggy No.

The Mehta-actor has returned and now goes over to comfort her.

Elaine OK, sweetheart?

Peggy Yes . . . no . . . I'm sorry, it's silly. I just . . . I was doing the scene. I'd never really thought about it. She didn't know what she was doing, Peggy didn't know, she did it unthinkingly . . . I mean she was innocent. (*She looks at them. Then anticlimactically starts to apologize again.*) I don't know, I guess I'd never really thought.

Angelis (*relieved*) OK, right, take the flat out.

Crewman OK, guv.

The wall goes, the bed goes, the furniture is taken out. A Make-up Girl waits with Peggy's shoes. At the very back Stephen is seen going through his lines with the Script Girl.

Stephen Once more.

Script Girl Same line.

Make-up Girl Miss King?

The Peggy-actress goes over to put her shoes on. The Mehta-actor wanders down near her.

Mehta One doesn't think, I know. I'm just as bad. It's ridiculous. One tries so hard when one's acting to make everything real. And yet here we are surrounded by all this apparatus. It's a paradox. You want it to be real. And yet what chance have you? Don't you think?

Peggy Mmm.

Mehta nods, as if the problem is solved, and walks away. He passes the Elaine-actress taking up her seat for the next scene, now with a cup of tea.

Elaine Why doesn't she get on with it?

Mehta I don't know.

Elaine You don't get paid extra for feeling it.

Angelis has gingerly re-approached Peggy, who is standing, seemingly still upset, by herself at the side.

Angelis You *are* all right?

Peggy You want me to go on?

Angelis If you don't mind.

Peggy No, I don't mind.

She sweeps to her place, suddenly bitter, and sits down. Elaine smiles across at her.

Elaine OK, darling?

Angelis stands and surveys the whole scene. He nods at Stephen.

Angelis Michael. Go on.

There is a pause. Then Stephen, with the Script Girl beside him, starts quietly.

Stephen 'The thirst for ideals is at the very heart of things. We may say a people need ideals as they need bread. As great as the need for bread is the need for ideals.'

Stephen walks up to where the other actors are. The Script Girl goes out, like a trainer leaving her athlete.

'The writer serves that need. He should be happy to serve it.'

He sits down opposite Mehta in formal debating position, and at once, as if on cue, Mehta gets up. SCENE EIGHT *begins.*

Mehta What nonsense! I cannot listen to this man.

Peggy Victor, you have agreed.

Mehta I know, I know.

Peggy It was you who insisted.

Mehta I know what I have done . . . (*He stands glowering across the room at Stephen.*) I have tied myself to a night of stupidity. (*He turns and walks away.*) At lunchtime when you came to propose this confrontation, yes, I said, fine, because I knew I would win. As I shall win. Because my case is unarguably correct. But I had not reckoned –

Peggy Victor!

Mehta . . . on the sheer indignity. Even to have to *listen* to such peasant-like ideas.

Stephen just smiles, calm, not rising to the bait.

Stephen You speak all the time as if everything were decided. As if you, Victor Mehta, are a finished human being, and beneath you lies the world with all its intolerable imperfections. As if you were objective and had no part in its emotions. Yet some of its worst emotions you exhibit very clearly.

Mehta Such as?

Stephen Jealousy.

Mehta What do you mean?

Stephen If I mention a novelist, if I mention Graham Greene . . .

Mehta A charlatan. Beneath contempt.

Stephen Ah, well, you see. Exactly.

Mehta What?

Stephen Your views on other writers.

Mehta No! An objective fact! A buffoon! A fool!

Stephen You see! A ribbon of abuse. Pavlovian. At the very mention of the name.

Mehta looks at him mistrustfully, caught out a little.

Mehta So?

Stephen So, in matters which truly concern you, you are far from objective. On the contrary, when things come too near to you, then you fight from your own corner . . .

Mehta Like everyone.

Stephen You fight those things that truly threaten you. In the way Greene threatens you because he is a good writer.

Mehta Balls!

Stephen In the way you will fight tomorrow for the right to make fiction. And why? Why do writers insist on their right to distort reality? You demand it in order to make better jokes.

Mehta looks back at him. Then takes him on, beginning quietly.

Mehta I was born in Bihar, of good family, my father a schoolteacher who died in middle age. My mother died when I was born. A brick-red, hot village on a plain.

Baking in the sun. That was my life for fourteen years, seeking tuition where I could, seeking by the formulation of sentences not to escape from the reality into which I was born, but to set it in order. The setting of things in order, that has always been my aim.

Stephen looks across to Peggy, but she is listening intently.

It never occurred to me from that village that I should not one day seek civilization. The heroes of the world are its engineers, its doctors, its legislators – yes, there are things in the old Empire I admired, that I was bound to admire, because it is clear to any man born into boastful chaos that order is desirable, and the agents of that order must be practical men. I went to London, to the university there, to the country where once medicine, education, the law had been practised *sans pareil*, and found instead a country now full of sloth and complacency – oh yes, on that we'd agree – a deceitful, inward-looking ruling class blundering by its racialism and stupidity into Suez. This was bitter for a boy from an Indian village. (*He shrugs slightly.*) It seems when people become prosperous, they lose the urge to improve themselves. Anyone who comes new to a society, as I did, an immigrant, has his priorities clear: to succeed in that society, to seek practical achievement, to educate his children to the highest level. Yet somehow once one or two generations have established their success, their grandchildren rush the other way, to disown that success, to disown its responsibilities, to seek by dressing as savages and eating brown rice to discredit the very civilization their grandfathers worked so hard to create. This seems to me the ultimate cruelty . . .

Peggy Yes . . .

Mehta . . . the ultimate charade: that the young in the

184

West should dare to turn their faces at this time to the Third World and cast doubt on the value of their own material prosperity. Not content with flaunting its wealth, the West now fashionably pretends that the materialism that has produced this wealth is not a good thing. Well, at least give us a chance to find out, say the poor. For God's sake let us practise this contempt ourselves. Instead of sending the Third World doctors and mechanics, we now send them hippies, and Marxist thinkers, and animal conservationists, and ecologists, and wandering fake Zen Buddhist students, who hasten to reassure the illiterate that theirs is a superior life to that of the West. What hypocrisy! The marriage of the decadent with the primitive, the faithless with the barbarian. Reason overthrown, as it is now overthrown all over the world! An unholy alliance, approved, sanctified and financed by this now futile United Nations.

Stephen Futile? Why futile?

Mehta Futile because it no longer does any good. (*He gets up again, shouting.*) Words! Meaningless words! Documents! So many documents that they boast from New York alone there flow annually United Nations documents which, laid end to end at the Equator, would stretch four times round the world! Yes! Half a billion pages! And this . . . this week one of the year's seven thousand major UN meetings. With working papers, proposals, counter-proposals, records, summaries. A bureaucracy drowning in its own words and suffocating in its own documents. The wastepaper basket is the only instrument of sanity in an otherwise insane organization. Last year a Special Committee on the Rationalization and Organization of the General Assembly was set up to examine the problems of excessive documentation. It produced a report. It was two hundred and nineteen pages long. I ask you, what fiction can there be to compare with this absurdity? What writer could dream up this impossible decadence? (*He stands shaking his head.*) No, there is only one thing I know, and one only: that in this universe of idiocy, the only thing we may rely on is the lone voice – the lone voice of the writer – who speaks only when he has something to say.

Stephen Nonsense!

Mehta A voice that is pledged to individual integrity.

Stephen My God! What delusion!

Elaine It is a bit rich.

Mehta Why? (*He turns. Firmly*) Mankind has one enemy only and it is not poverty. It is self-deception. Yes . . . (*He holds a hand up, anticipating Stephen's objection.*) That finally is my case against you, Stephen. If Miss le Fanu is to adjudicate . . .

Elaine I am.

Mehta Then please remember that my case stands or falls here: that often from the best intentions we tell ourselves lies. Here – my God! – a conference run by the United Nations is a monument built to commemorate self-deception on the grandest scale. We would like it to work and so we pretend it does, but in our hearts – when we are not on our feet, Stephen, not in rooms where words fly up – in our hearts we know the UN is a palace of lies, run by a bureaucracy whose only interest is in the maintenance of its own prosperity. Forty per cent of UNESCO's income is spent in the administration of its own Paris office. A fact. A fact which I have mentioned in my books and for which I am attacked. I am told to point it out is bloody-minded and – what? – 'unhelpful'. And yet to me, I am telling you, not to point it out is worse. (*He stands a moment, nodding.*) Tomorrow I must speak because not to speak is not to be a writer, not to be a man. (*Then he looks away to Stephen, opening his hands as if to say, 'That's it.'*) That, there, is where I yield. I have had the floor.

Stephen Indeed.

Stephen looks at Mehta a moment. Then, when he replies, it is with a new and unsuspected warmth.

We've pretended, you and I, that the debate between us is not to do with personality, only with issues . . .

Mehta That's so.

Stephen But in fact, if I've learnt anything in the last twenty-four hours, it is that no argument is pure, it's always a compound. Partly the situation, partly temper, partly whim . . . sometimes just pulled out of the air and often from the worst motives, Peggy, no offence . . .

Peggy I understand. (*She smiles.*)

Stephen I've grown up here. In this hotel. I came like a boy, a 27-year-old boy, and I can't help feeling whichever way the contest falls, I'm going to leave a man, partly because I've grown fond of you, Victor.

Mehta (*deadpan*) Really?

Stephen And I think I've felt . . . some growing generosity from you, too, especially this evening. You've stopped calling me Andrews. You call me Stephen, perhaps because even if you don't agree with me, you nevertheless now recognize me. Perhaps even as an element in yourself.

Mehta A sentimental line of argument.

Stephen Yes. If I am to win, I must attack the man.

Peggy looks across to Mehta, slightly alarmed. But Mehta does not react.

I am arguing that tomorrow you must go out and denounce your own fiction, because it will be your last remaining chance to rejoin the human race.

A burst of reaction, even Mehta surprised.

Mehta Oh, that's marvellous.

Peggy Gee, I must say.

Mehta Well.

Elaine It's original.

Stephen Everything you say, everything you propose is from a position of superiority and hopelessness. 'What can one do?' you say, grabbing at one depressing piece of information after another, almost – I put it to you – as if you personally were a man now frightened of hope.

Mehta Absurd!

Stephen Oh yes, the gleam that comes into your eye when you have some dismal statistic. 'Sixty-five per cent of people who set out to cross roads get run over,' you say with a satisfied beam, as if their presumption had been justly rewarded. Whereas you, of course . . . The position of the habitual non-road crosser has been wholly vindicated! (*He gestures into the air.*) From way up there you claim to see things clearly. 'The truth,' you say, 'the lone voice.' But in fact your so-called truthfulness is nothing but the projection of your own isolation, and of your own despair. Because you do a job which is lonely and hard, because you spend all day locked in a room, so you project your loneliness on to the world.

Mehta No.

Stephen Partly from anger at your own way of life, you try to discredit the work of other people – out there – a lot of whom have pleasanter jobs than you. (*He pauses. Then, with a smile*) Jealousy . . .

Mehta No.

Stephen There is jealousy there. The jealousy of a man who does not take part, who no longer knows how to take part, but can only write.

Peggy looks across to Mehta, who has turned away.

Oh yes. And the more you write, the more isolated you become. The more frozen.

There is a pause.

Mehta No.

Stephen (*smiles*) You come here to this conference not to publicize your work, or to express your position – what would be the point? Your position is so complete, so closed, there is little point in expounding it. No, you come to scrape around – yes, like the rest of us, to scrape around for contact.

A pause. Then Peggy suddenly seems embarrassed, confused.

Peggy No, please, it's . . .

Stephen What?

Peggy Unfair.

Stephen Why?

Stephen turns back, Mehta himself still impassive.

Your wife, your child, you leave behind in England . . .

He looks quickly to Peggy, who plainly knows nothing of wife or child.

Oh yes. Come here. Five thousand miles. Make love to

Peggy Whitton. Leave. The last emotions left. Jealousy, yes. And lust. What is left in you that is not disdainful, that is not dead? Only jealousy and lust.

There is a silence. Elaine looks between them, warning.

Elaine Look, Stephen . . .

But Stephen is leaning forward to make his main point.

Stephen You will never understand any struggle unless you take part in it. How easy to condemn this organization as absurd. Of course I've sat here and sweated and bitched and argued . . . often with Elaine . . .

Elaine It's true.

Stephen I've run screaming from the points of order and the endless 'I am mandated to ask . . .' But why do you not think that at the centre of the verbiage, often only by hazard but nevertheless at times and unpredictably, crises are averted, aid is directed?

Mehta I dare say.

Stephen Why do you not imagine that if you stopped distancing yourself, if you got rid of your wretched fastidiousness, you could not lend yourself for once not to objection but to getting something done?

Stephen sits back, contemptuous.

Oh, no, it's too hard. Never – the risk of failure too great. Like so many clever men, you move steadily to the right, further, further, distancing, always distancing yourself, building yourself a bunker into which only the odd woman is occasionally allowed, disowning your former ideals . . .

Mehta You know nothing.

Stephen . . . attacking those who still have those ideals with a ferocity which is way out of proportion to their crime.

Mehta is suddenly stirred.

Mehta No!

Stephen Yes! Well, move, move to the right if you wish to. Join the shabby crew if you want to. Go in the way people do. But at least spare us the books, spare us the Stations of the Cross, the public announcements. Make your move in private, do it in private, like a sexual pervert, do it privately. Move with a mac over your knee to the right, but spare us, spare your audience, spare those who have to watch one good man after another go down.

Peggy Stephen, it is too much.

Elaine Please.

Stephen No! (*He has stood up.*) The revenge of the old! All the time! The history of the world is the revenge of the old, as they paint themselves into corners, loveless, removed, relieved occasionally in hotel rooms by the visits of strange women, who come to tell them that, yes, they are doing well and, yes, they may now take revenge on those who are still young. People, countries, the same thing; the world now full of young countries who are trying imperfect, unwieldy new systems of ordering their affairs, watched by the old who are praying that they will not succeed . . . (*He shakes his head. Then suddenly*) If you wish to rejoin us, if you wish to be human, go out tomorrow and parrot whatever rubbish you are handed and at least experience an emotion which is not disdain.

Mehta I would not give you the pleasure.

Stephen I shall not be here.

Mehta What?

Stephen A midnight train leaves for Ahmadabad and on to Jaipur. Frankly . . . (*He smiles and crosses the room.*) . . . my time is being wasted here.

Elaine Stephen . . .

Stephen has collected his abandoned briefcase.

Peggy What are you doing?

Stephen has turned to Peggy.

Stephen Peggy, I'm sorry. Your offer, it was kind, more than tempting. But all afternoon, all evening, I realized . . . also absurd. My own fault. For years I've apologized. A shambler, a neurotic, I've accepted the picture the world has of an idealist as a man who is necessarily a clown. No shortage of people to tell him he's a fool. And we accept this picture. Yes, we betray our instincts. We betray them because we're embarrassed, and we've lost our conviction that we can make what's best in us prevail. (*He smiles, his briefcase closed, and he is now ready to go.*) Well, enough – I'm sorry –

Peggy (*smiles*) Stephen . . .

Stephen . . . of all that. (*He takes her hand a moment.*) No more apology. Hold to my beliefs. (*He turns to Elaine.*) Elaine, I owe you lunch.

Elaine (*getting up to embrace him*) Stephen . . .

Stephen Thank you. Send my best to America. I withdraw from the contest. What you must do only you can decide.

He turns and goes out. The three of them left behind. There is silence. Mehta looks down at the envelope in his hand. Toys with it a moment.

Mehta (*darkly*) I should not have come here. I am going upstairs.

He goes out. The two women are left alone on the stage. Peggy looks down.

Peggy Now I'm going to get drunk.

And as she looks up, the lights fade to darkness, as much like a film fade as possible. There is a pause in the dark. Then the sound of banging at the back. From far away Mehta's voice, a stick beating at the door, and SCENE NINE *has begun.*

Mehta Hello. Please. Is there anyone?

At once, in the darkness, the sound of an Assistant scurrying across the set.

Assistant Coming! Coming!

At the very back of the stage, far further than we realized the stage reached, a door opens, and brilliant light pours through it. Silhouetted in the doorway stands Mehta.

Mehta I am Victor Mehta.

Assistant Ah, yes. You were expected earlier. (*He turns, panicking slightly.*) Everyone! Please! Is there a light there? (*He turns to Mehta.*) Please wait.

Mehta I am waiting.

A single light comes on in the grid and we see the stage is now black. An empty film studio. Angelis is rushing on, in the last stages of pulling his trousers up.

Angelis Ah, my goodness, you are here. We were expecting you earlier.

Mehta has come right down. He is a more formidable man in a camelhair coat, heavier, less dapper. Angelis shakes his hand.

An honour.

Mehta You are pulling on your trousers.

Angelis A friend. (*He elaborates needlessly, embarrassed.*)
In make-up.

Mehta I see.

Angelis A drink?

*An Assistant has brought a chair, but Mehta has
wandered away.*

Mehta Mr Angelis, I cannot pretend I am glad to come
here.

Angelis You have read the script?

Mehta I cannot read five pages.

Angelis (*to his Assistant*) Thank you.

The Assistant goes.

No, well, admittedly . . . there are weaknesses –

Mehta The dialogue. When they open their mouths, dead
frogs fall out.

Angelis Yes, well, certainly . . . it can do with
polishing . . .

Mehta A moral story has been reduced to the status of a
romance, transferred to a vulgar medium and traduced.
Very well. It is what one expects. One looks to the cinema
for money, not for enlightenment. And to be fair, the
money has arrived.

He turns and faces Angelis.

It is in the matter of meaning I have come.

Angelis Meaning?

Mehta Meaning, Mr Angelis.

Angelis Ah, yes.

Mehta looks at him. Then starts afresh.

Mehta There is a balance in the book. Each of the characters is forced to examine the values of his or her life.

Angelis Yes.

Mehta The novelist is accused of dalliance and asked to put a value on what he has seen as a passing affair. The actress questions her easy promiscuity and is made to realize adulthood will involve choice. And Stephen, the journalist, assumes the confidence of his own beliefs.

Angelis And is killed.

Mehta Killed, yes.

There is a pause.

You show this?

Angelis Of course. We have a train.

Mehta looks at him. Another pause.

Mehta In a sense, I care nothing. A book is written. It is left behind you to be misinterpreted by a thousand critics. The reader brings to the book his own preconceptions, prejudices perhaps. He misreads sentences. A tiny incident in the narrative is for one person the key to the book's interpretation; to another it is where he accidentally turns two pages and misses it altogether. So if you come, if you make a film, you reinterpret. And yet, in spite of that, your film is a betrayal unless at the heart it is clear: for all the bitterness, for all the stupidity . . . you must see, we admired this young man.

A pause. Mehta sits back.

Of course, death, death brings him dignity, but also in truth, even at the time . . .

Mehta looks away. Angelis waits tactfully.

Angelis Yes, well, that's clear.

Mehta Clear to you, perhaps. Yes, your intention. But is it there in the script? Peggy didn't see it when she visited this morning.

Angelis I see. Is that all?

Mehta No. The death.

Angelis Ah.

Mehta And the way you tell it.

Angelis I see.

Mehta There is something there. An emotion I had. (*There is a pause. Then, soberly*) Certainly we drove, as you suggest it. Peggy heard first. She was awoken at six and came to my room. We found a taxi-driver. All the way from Bombay he smoked marijuana. Thirty miles out Peggy and I demanded to change cabs. Another drive, the day beginning to get hot. And we knew, long before we reached the disaster, just how close the disaster was. Small groups of people at first; driving further, more people. Now in larger groups, now more excited, finally crowds, in the middle of the valley. A valley like any other but for the crowds. We had expected a corpse. A body on its own, we had thought. It was impossible even to get close to the carriages which had overturned. All one side, people had clung to the framework and been crushed. A single cow had strayed on to the line. Forty more miles to the mortuary . . . to unidentified bodies . . . paperwork . . . hysteria . . . the heat. And the conference itself was suddenly rendered ridiculous. Whatever meaning it once had was now lost. As tomorrow . . . in this barn, the lights will burn, the camera will turn, a predetermined script will be acted out by men and women who know it has been robbed of sense. (*He nods.*) The machine turns of its own volition! Oh, the will that is needed to bring it to a halt! (*He smiles, bitter.*) I was not there, and M'Bengue denounced me. Yes! In savage terms. 'This fascist novelist, this charlatan, who, when the moment comes, ducks the chance to defend his indefensible work . . .'

A pause.

I was not there. I was at the accident.

Angelis Of course.

A silence. Angelis uneasy.

But surely when people realized, I mean, your reason, why you weren't there . . .

Mehta Why should they care? The whole conference was longing for a dogfight. What a disappointment when it did not occur.
    No, the book is clear. I was moved by what happened, and later that day I made a choice. The conference could continue without me. This you do not mention but you must make it clear. I chose to be silent. In memory of Stephen . . . I stayed away.

Angelis I see. Yes. I'd not understood that. If what you're after is this feeling that everything is meaningless, then, of course, we will put that in as well. A slight dialogue adjustment, a page maybe. Then it is clear.

There is a pause. The Stephen-actor has appeared at the back, dressed in baggy trousers and an expensive coat. Soft-spoken. The Peggy-actress is standing behind him, dressed very young in a smart coat and jeans.

Stephen Oh, I'm sorry. Are we interrupting?

Angelis Michael . . .

Stephen We were half-way to Belgravia before I realized I'd forgotten . . .

Mehta is staring at him.

Mehta You are he.

Stephen . . . my script.

Then Stephen makes a formal move towards Mehta, the Peggy-actress following a little nervously behind.

Mr Mehta?

He turns to introduce the Peggy-actress but Mehta, overcome, has turned away, not taking his hand.

Madeleine . . .

Mehta I am sorry.

The other three stand, uncertain. Peggy and Stephen look fresh and scrubbed and absurdly young. Stephen looks nervously to Angelis.

Stephen Angelis, here, said you weren't happy with the text.

Mehta I cannot begin to say. Everything is wrong.

He turns back, recovering. Stephen at his most diffident and charming.

Stephen I can see from the outside it must be discomforting. Film is.

Mehta looks at him with respect. Peggy, emboldened, smiles.

Peggy We can't be doing what you want, Mr Mehta. We're aware of it, ours is bound to be a love story. A commercial picture with, eventually, after the studio, some exotic locations. Sex and death are really the standout features, rather than the arguments in the book, some of which we are filming . . . all of which, I guess, we think, will be cut.

They smile, only Angelis uneasy.

Angelis This is, by any prevailing standard, a picture of integrity.

Peggy Can you imagine?

Stephen Even though they've put in a scene where Elaine bathes topless in the holy river.

Peggy It's true. It's hard to believe.

Stephen Two thousand Indians in dhotis and she takes her top off. A reporter? From CBS?

Angelis looks silently resentful.

Peggy Quite apart from how the holy river . . .

Mehta It is not in Bombay.

Stephen Quite. It's a thousand miles away. That small detail apart . . .

Angelis sulky on his own, as the others smile.

Angelis It is not true. She is to bathe in the tank.

Stephen points to his own forehead.

Stephen We have this book here, however.

Mehta Thank you.

Stephen In our heads. This blunderer . . . (*He gestures amiably at Angelis.*) Me, an actor of limited ability. Madeleine, God bless her, who is reading Herodotus – can you imagine? – to get into the part.

The Peggy-actress blushes and looks at her feet.

'Reading Herodotus?' I said casually one day. 'Oh, you know,' she said, 'just skimming.'

Mehta smiles, touched.

All the warmth, all the kindness we can bring, we will bring.

Mehta Thank you. That is something. I suppose.

He stands a moment, the whole group still. Then, resigned:

For the rest, of course, let it be toplessness.

Stephen What else?

Mehta And bad dialogue. What else?

Peggy No sauna scene so far, but we're expecting one.

Mehta nods slightly, the joke shared. Then Stephen makes to go.

Stephen If you like, I can drive you back to London.

Mehta That will be good.

Stephen I'll just get my things. (*He goes out to the dressing-rooms.*)

Peggy Excuse me. (*Peggy follows him.*)

Mehta Mr Angelis, farewell. Thank you for listening.

Angelis No. (*He shakes Mehta's hand.*) If we can do it as you wish, we shall be pleased.

He goes out. Mehta is left momentarily alone on the huge, empty stage. Then he turns his head and at once Martinson walks on, eerily quiet, and, from the other direction, M'Bengue. SCENE TEN. *The lights change. A sinister calm.*

Martinson Monsieur M'Bengue . . .

The two men stand still opposite each other, formally, in the centre of the stage.

Your speech was excellent.

M'Bengue Yes. I admired this young man. So few whites have any understanding.

Martinson The occasion was perfectly handled. And in a way, although tragic – the tragedy eats into my soul – but also, we must say, the way things fell out has also been elegant.

M'Bengue Elegant?

Martinson Convenient.

M'Bengue looks at him with silent contempt.

M'Bengue I see.

Martinson Mr Mehta's necessary absence certainly removed the problems we had had.

M'Bengue looks at him a moment, still quiet, still calm.

M'Bengue Mr Martinson, overnight I have been reading the conditions, the terms, of the aid you are proposing to give. They are stiff.

Martinson They are exacting, yes. No aid is pure. There is always an element of trade in all such arrangements, and trade, after all, benefits both sides.

M'Bengue Surplus corn, surplus grain from America, at a commercial price.

Martinson Less than the market price.

M'Bengue A considerable price.

Martinson smiles.

Martinson Perhaps.

M'Bengue The other part of the package, the facility of a loan from the World Bank.

Martinson That's right.

M'Bengue At 13 per cent. And not even that is the limit of it. With it a demand for changes in the internal policies of our country . . .

Martinson Adjustments, yes.

M'Bengue . . . deflation of the currency . . .

Martinson Well . . .

M'Bengue . . . high internal interest rates.

Martinson Strict monetary measures. (*He smiles again.*) Good housekeeping, yes.

M'Bengue A recognition that younger countries cannot expect to have social security systems. In sum, the destruction of the policies which brought our government into being. You throw us a lifeline. The lifeline is in the shape of a noose.

Martinson shrugs slightly.

Martinson Well, I think you will find it's not necessarily that sinister. Certainly, over the five-year period the bank is insisting, for its own protection, on certain parameters – is that the word? There may well be some hardship at first. A largely agricultural country like your own, peasant-based, one would expect things to be hard when such measures are introduced. Five years, ten years' belt-tightening. Suffering. Comparative. Then, well, surely . . . you'll be out of the woods. (*He gestures to one side.*) Shall we go through? There's a final dinner. We were going to have pheasant, but it was generally felt, for a symbolic gesture, it being the last night, each one of us will eat a single bowl of rice. I hope it's all right. (*He is about to go.*) Oh, by the way, you will not refuse it?

M'Bengue The loan I cannot. I shan't eat the rice.

M'Bengue turns and goes out. Martinson, left alone, turns and goes out the other way. Mehta stands alone, then the Peggy-actress reappears at the other side of the stage. He smiles absently at her. There is an embarrassed silence between them, Mehta still thinking about the scene which has just passed.

Mehta Do you have children?

Peggy Oh, no. No, I don't. You have a son?

Mehta By my first marriage, yes. I have custody. He lives with Peggy and me. He's sixteen. A boy. He wants to change the world.

Peggy Well, I guess . . . that's the best thing to do with it. (*The actress smiles.*) I'd like to meet him.

Mehta And he no doubt you. (*He stands a moment.*) This feeling, finally, that we may change things – this is at the centre of everything we are. Lose that . . . lose that, lose everything. (*He stands, the man who has.*)

Peggy I'm sorry. I didn't catch what you said.

The Stephen-actor returns, yet more cheerful than before.

Stephen I have an open car. I hope that's all right. It can be a bit cold. It's a steel-grey, 2.4 litre 1954 Alvis. A Grey Lady. With real running-boards. Like this. Not very practical for the English winter. But it is so beautiful. (*He looks at Mehta.*) It's my whole life.

Mehta Yes, I am sure.

*Distantly, music begins to play. Mehta moves a few
paces towards the door, then turns, suddenly cheered.*

Madeleine. Michael. To London. Let's go.

He lifts his arms, the music swells and the lights go out.

SAIGON
Year of the Cat

For Lewis, my son

Characters

At the Bank
Barbara Dean
Mr Haliwell
Quoc
Donald Henderson
Lhan
Phu
Tellers, Customers etc.

At the Embassy
Bob Chesneau
Jack Ockham
Frank Judd
Joan Mackintosh
Colonel Fiedler
Linda
The Ambassador
Secretaries, Officers, GIs etc.

Elsewhere
Van Trang
Nhieu
Brad
Barbara's Maid
Waiters, Bar Girls, People of Saigon

Saigon: Year of the Cat was first shown on Thames Television in November 1983. The principal parts were played as follows:

Barbara Dean Judi Dench
Bob Chesneau Frederic Forrest
Quoc Pitchit Bulkul
The Ambassador E. G. Marshall
Jack Ockham Josef Sommer
Frank Judd Wallace Shawn
Donald Henderson Roger Rees
Mr Haliwell Chic Murray
Colonel Fiedler Manning Redwood
Joan Mackintosh Thomasine Heiner
Nhieu Po Pau Pee
President Thieu Thavisakdi Srimuang

Directed by Stephen Frears
Produced by Verity Lambert and Michael Dunlop

Part One

1. INT. LIVING ROOM. DAY
We are tracking through Barbara's apartment in the largely diplomatic section of Saigon. The blinds are all down against the fierce sun outside. It is dark and quiet and looks cool. There is a little plain furniture in good taste. The living room is bare-floored, tidy, the chairs in plain wood with white cushions. As we move through, we hear Barbara's voice.

Barbara (*voice over*) Afternoons have always hit me the hardest, I don't know why that is, it's always been so . . .

2. INT. BEDROOM. DAY
Into the bedroom, continuous, past the door jamb. We can make out very little, except slits of light across blinds at the end of the room. There is a dim lamp on beside a double bed on which Barbara lies. We track nearer.

Barbara (*voice over*) Mornings are fine, there's something to look forward to, and evenings, yes, I begin to cheer up . . .

In the bed Barbara is lying bunched sideways, not really reading the paperback in her hand. She is in a cream slip, covered by a sheet. She is almost 50 and blonde. She has the quietness and reserve of the genteel English middle class, but in her it has a pleasantness which is definitely erotic. She is sweating slightly as we approach.

(*voice over*) But what would I wish for if I could wish for anything? This would be my wish: abolish afternoons.

3. EXT. TU DO. DAY
Later. After her siesta, Barbara in a linen dress walking

down the busy street at the centre of Saigon. Shops,
cyclists, the low blue taxis. The Vietnamese selling food
and American PX goods on the sidewalk.

Barbara (*voice over*) It was never my intention my life
should be secretive, it came about by accident, I think . . .

She goes into a small newsagent's.

My first affair was with a friend of my father's, so really
the style was adopted from then.

She reappears with the airmail edition of The Times,
and walks on down the street.

People say, 'Barbara, I've never known anyone so
secretive.' But it's only something which has happened
with the years.

4. INT. HALIWELL'S OFFICE. EVENING
A Victorian-seeming office with a fan above. Haliwell
working at a mahogany desk. Behind him, a large old-
fashioned safe and wooden filing cabinets. He is in his late
fifties with some silver hair left. A bachelor, fattening
slightly, in a cotton shirt.

Barbara Mr Haliwell.

Haliwell Barbara. A satisfactory siesta?

Barbara Fine. I collected the paper.

Haliwell Ah thanks.

He looks up. A routine.

Any news of the Arsenal?

Barbara I haven't looked. The sport's on page ten.

5. INT. BANK. EVENING
An old-fashioned commercial bank. Busy. Vaulted

ceilings. Grandeur. Fans. The Vietnamese sitting behind iron grilles, serving a clientele of Asians and whites. Beyond the grilles, a large open area where the desks of the more senior staff are set out. A Client is being ushered in to meet Barbara by Quoc, a tall, thin, grave Vietnamese in his late forties, who wears grey flannel trousers and a short-sleeved shirt. The client is named Trinh.

Barbara Hello.

She shakes Trinh's hand and gestures him to sit opposite her. Quoc brings round documents to her side of the desk and puts them down.

Mr Quoc has explained your application. You have good collateral?

Trinh Yes.

Barbara You're securing the loan with the rest of your cargo fleet?

Quoc Mr Trinh has fifty ships between here and Punan.

Quoc has confirmed this by discreetly referring to a paper which Barbara has in the file in front of her. She smiles warmly at Trinh and begins to write on the file.

Barbara In that case I can't see there'll be any problem.

Quoc (*discreetly again, on Trinh's behalf*) Mr Trinh is only worried about time. How long we may give him for repayment.

Barbara (*quietly, not looking up*) I'm not giving anyone more than a year.

6. INT. BANK. EVENING
The bank now deserted, Barbara tidying her desk. Beyond her the door to Haliwell's office is open and Henderson is packing away the contents of the safe for the night. He is a

*young Scot about 25, with a beard, very lean. He is talking
from the other room.*

Henderson That's the bastard of supporting St Mirren,
they don't always have the result in *The Times*.

Barbara gets up to go.

It's Scotland who go on producing the players, but when
you look for coverage, it's Leeds, Leeds, Leeds. I mean, it's
ridiculous, they're all Scottish players . . .

Barbara Yes, it's tricky I see.

Henderson That and economic misfortune. It's barely
worth reading the thing any more.

*She has gone to the main door and is about to open it to
leave. Henderson has appeared at the door of Haliwell's
office. He speaks from right across the bank.*

Barbara . . .

Barbara Yes?

Henderson Are you free for this evening? I was hoping
we'd be able to go out. It's been some time.

*There's a pause. He looks down, a little embarrassed.
Then with some personal feeling:*

It was wonderful last time.

*She looks at him, straight across the bank, her manners
perfect.*

Barbara Oh Donald, I'm sorry. I'm busy tonight.

7. INT. CERCLE SPORTIF. NIGHT
*The main lounge of the Cercle Sportif. A French colonial
club. A large central room, bamboo armchairs, white-
coated servants with trays. Barbara stands at the main*

*entrance, dressed smartly but lightly for the evening.
Frank Judd, a bespectacled 32-year-old American in
seersuckers and short-sleeved shirt, moves across at once
to greet her.*

Judd Barbara. Hi.

Barbara Frank. How are you?

Judd Come and meet the rest.

*They have arrived next to two men who are sitting
drinking. They now stand up. Colonel Fiedler is a
powerfully built American army officer of 55, in
uniform. Van Trang is a small fat Vietnamese of the
same age, in a shiny black suit.*

Barbara Dean. You know the Foreign Minister, Monsieur
Van Trang?

They smile and shake hands.

Barbara. Colonel Fiedler.

Barbara How do you do?

They also shake hands.

Judd The Colonel's just back this evening from Binh Dinh.

Barbara Oh really? How are things going up there?

Judd I think you'll find him a very good partner.

Barbara Well, I hope so.

Fiedler smiles.

Fiedler Are they ready for us yet?

8. INT. CERCLE SPORTIF. NIGHT
*An annexe of the main lounge. Darker. Green baize tables
have been set out for cards. Barbara, Fiedler, Judd and*

Van Trang sitting as three servants lay out their drinks and unwrap fresh packs of cards for them.

Judd The Foreign Minister plays an orthodox Acol.

Barbara smiles at Fiedler.

Barbara I play a forcing two clubs.

Fiedler No doubt we'll get the hang of each other.

Judd Good. Let's cut for the deal.

A polite cut is silently made. Fiedler starts to deal, as Van Trang makes formal conversation.

Van Trang I have not been in England for too long a time.

Barbara No, well, I haven't been back.

Van Trang Both my daughters are at Cheltenham Ladies' College.

Barbara Ah, well, I'm told it's a very good school.

She smiles and looks away to the main lounge. There a couple of bar girls have appeared, conspicuous in the otherwise discreet surroundings. They wear short slit skirts and heavy make-up. Everyone else ignores them.

Van Trang I wish I got more chance to visit them. I am told Sports Day is the highlight of the year.

Judd smiles, having picked up on the direction of Barbara's look.

Judd We seem to have visitors from Mimi's Flamboyant . . .

Fiedler Well I guess they have nowhere to go. You think there'd be somewhere . . .

Van Trang looks up for the Waiter who appears at once beside him.

Van Trang (*in Vietnamese*) The women.

Waiter (*in Vietnamese*) I'll see to it, sir.

Van Trang turns back. Looks at his cards.

Van Trang It's a shortage of Americans. With so few GIs left the living is hard. What can they do? You created the industry. Now they're fed up because you're no longer here.

Fiedler tries to make light of it.

Fiedler Well I don't know. There are one or two of us . . .

Judd Some of us have friends who keep them in work.

Judd smiles. Van Trang ignores this. The women are led amicably away by waiters. Barbara still watching.

Van Trang One diamond.

Fiedler A spade.

Judd Two hearts.

A pause. Barbara is still staring at the women.

Barbara?

She turns back and, without referring to her cards, shakes her head at Fiedler.

Barbara I'm sorry, partner. I'm no help at all.

9. INT. CERCLE SPORTIF. NIGHT

Later. The game is over. The four of them stroll steadily through the now deserted lounge. Behind them you can see their table being cleared. Fiedler and Van Trang are in front, talking quietly together.

Van Trang Will you be giving us a military briefing?

Fiedler Certainly. There'll be a situation report. Of course, within the terms of the Paris agreement we can no longer give you military advice.

They stroll on. Van Trang makes no reaction.

Van Trang But you have an idea?

Fiedler I see formations. We think the North will make an offensive in the New Year. It's come to be regular . . . like the baseball season.

There is a pause. Then casually:

We'd certainly like to get to see your President Thieu.

He steals a quick glance at Van Trang who does not react.

As for the scale of the offensive and where it might come from, it's a little early to say. There are certainly signs of a build-up. Maybe you should look to Tay Ninh.

There is a slight pause. Van Trang looks at him. Then turns to the others.

Van Trang Thank you, Miss Dean. An excellent evening Colonel.

Fiedler Minister.

Judd Good night.

Van Trang Good night.

He goes. They are by the main entrance. Judd turns casually to Barbara.

Judd Barbara, I'll see you home in my car.

Barbara I arranged for a cab.

10. EXT. CERCLE SPORTIF. NIGHT
Judd and Barbara stand for a moment outside the main entrance to the club. At once there is a giggling noise from

the bushes, brief, sharp in the darkness.

Barbara They're still out there.

Judd Who?

She reaches into her bag for a handful of notes.

Barbara Will you just take some money across?

Before he can answer she anticipates his objections.

Would you do it please? As a favour?

Judd You know it's not . . .

Barbara No. As a favour, Frank?

Judd takes the money reluctantly and goes down the steps. Barbara watches as he crosses the darkened drive and disappears into the bushes. She stands alone in the lit doorway of the Cercle. Judd has now disappeared. Distant voices.

Woman Thank you, Number One. You wanna fuck me?

Judd No. It's all right. It's a gift.

Behind Barbara, Bob Chesneau has silently appeared. He is about 28, very intelligent, in beige cotton trousers and a short-sleeved shirt. His speech is always gentle and gracious, like a polite boy. He stands behind Barbara, looking out also.

Chesneau Hi.

She turns.

Barbara Hello.

Chesneau You waiting for a taxi?

Barbara smiles in reply.

I guess the wheels have finally fallen off.

They both smile.

If you like I could easily help you. I have a car waiting over there.

Judd has returned, his arm outstretched to Chesneau. He is bustling with confidence from a mission accomplished.

Judd Hey, Bob.

Chesneau Frank, how are you?

Judd Do you know Barbara?

Chesneau No. No, I don't.

Barbara turns and smiles warmly at Judd.

Barbara Bob's kindly offered . . . he's going to run me home.

11. INT. CAR. NIGHT
The car. They are side by side in silence. The half-lit streets of Saigon going by. Chesneau driving.

Barbara Where do you work?

Chesneau I work at the Embassy. I'm a minor official. One of many, I'm afraid.

Barbara Why do you drive a Ford Pinto?

He smiles.

Chesneau Oh I see . . .

Barbara I don't understand . . .

Chesneau Neither do we . . .

Barbara The allocation. If the CIA is meant to be so secret, why do you all get issued with the same make of car?

Chesneau Beats me. Perhaps a kind of arrogance. And anyway, let's face it, everyone knows. If all the cultural attachés in Saigon were genuine, this would be the most cultured nation on earth.

A pause.

I'm a spook.

Barbara smiles. She looks out to the streets where the young girls are selling flowers. They hold them out to the cars as they go by.

Barbara Look . . .

Chesneau Yeah.

Barbara They're still out with the jasmine. It's such a beautiful town.

Chesneau Yes it is. I suppose I'd forgotten.

Barbara Well, I know. People do. (*She looks at him. Then away.*)

Chesneau Where do you come from?

Barbara Bournemouth. You wouldn't know it. It's the English version of Vung Tau.

Chesneau By the ocean?

Barbara Exactly. It's where you go when you're planning to die.

Chesneau Oh yeah? Ours is called Florida.

Barbara Yes. Yours has the sun.

12. EXT. APARTMENT BLOCK. NIGHT
The low white apartment block, fronted with palm trees. Chesneau's car stops silently in the deserted street. He gets out of the car to go round and open the car door for her.

She gets out. There is a moment's pause, then casually:

Barbara Yes. Come up. (*She goes on ahead.*)

13. INT. APARTMENT. NIGHT
Chesneau sitting forward on a hard chair with a glass of beer in his hands. He is in the middle of the room. His face is lit by a single warm lamp. Barbara sits on the sofa, her legs tucked under her.

Chesneau It's the ultimate irony really. I joined the CIA to avoid Vietnam. Quite a few of us did the same thing. It was my law professor, he said if you want to avoid a war, the safest place to be is inside the bureaucracy. Tuck yourself away. Join the CIA.

   A pause.

And that was it. They put me in Washington. Strategic analysis, balance of power. I was having a good time. In the way you do. I kept telling myself, well, I don't really work here, I was just avoiding the draft. Till a colleague in the department, as a joke, filled in my name. Like when you order someone *Reader's Digest*, he thought it would be funny if I were sent to Vietnam. (*He looks across at her.*)

Barbara Would you like another beer?

Chesneau Yes, I'll have one more.

   He watches as she gets up and goes to the big old fridge in the kitchen.

You know, I can get you Heineken from the PX.

Barbara No really . . .

Chesneau This stuff has probably killed people.

   She returns with a couple of bottles.

Barbara I like '33'.

Chesneau You must be tough.

She smiles, the old hand. Then settles on the sofa, having given him one.

Barbara What is your view . . . you must tell me . . . will the South be able to hold on?

Chesneau That is my job. To judge that. That is precisely what I'm doing here.

A pause. Then he gets up, putting his beer suddenly to one side.

Thank you for the beer. I've enjoyed talking to you.

She doesn't move, staring up at him.

The days go by. Well, I must thank you.

They look at each other a moment. Then he looks at the floor.

I hope I'll see you again.

14. INT. APARTMENT. NIGHT
The room seen from the bedroom. Barbara sits alone at her desk in her dressing-gown.

Barbara (*voice over*) Dear Mum, I'm sorry it's so long since I've written. To be honest, I've been too busy at work. You'll be pleased with my cheque. A little bit extra. The bank have just come through with my raise.

In close-up her hand as she slips the cheque into the already finished letter.

(*voice over*) Life here continues very much as usual.

Her face, for the first time in close-up, as she licks the envelope.

(*voice over*) The Year of the Tiger will soon be the Year of the Cat.

15. INT. BANK. DAY
Henderson standing at one of the metal grilles opposite a shock-haired young Vietnamese, Phu, of about 25. He is very angry.

Henderson I'm sorry. I have to refuse you. It's simply impossible to take all that money out.

He looks sideways at Quoc who is at a nearby till. Barbara looks up from her desk.

There are government regulations which expressly forbid the export of large sums.

16. INT. HALIWELL'S OFFICE. DAY
Barbara appearing at the door of Haliwell's office. Haliwell is writing at his desk.

Barbara Mr Haliwell . . . I wonder . . . I think Mr Henderson may be needing some assistance out there.

Quoc's face appears in the doorway behind her, still, serious. But Haliwell carries on writing.

Haliwell Right. In a moment.

Barbara Could you come quickly?

Haliwell Yes. (*He carries on writing. He does not look up. Quietly, into his work, without moving*) I'm on my way.

17. INT. BANK. DAY
Haliwell, Quoc and Barbara moving together like a group of floor-walkers, fast, from a great distance towards the incident. Phu takes a small revolver from his pocket. Henderson is standing opposite.

Phu I have a gun.

Henderson Yes.

Phu I demand my money.

Henderson If you'd like to talk to the manager . . .

Haliwell steps forward from the group to stand beside Henderson.

Haliwell Mr . . .

Henderson Phu.

Haliwell Mr Phu, perhaps I can help you.

Phu I want my money.

Haliwell Yes. Yes, of course.

He begins to move across to the grille door between the back and front of the bank.

If you'd like to come into my office . . .

He swings the door open and stands directly opposite Phu who is holding the gun. Haliwell looks him straight in the eye.

Perhaps I might relieve you of that gun.

18. INT. BANK. DAY
The bank closed. Afternoon. Henderson is laughing, sitting on the edge of Barbara's desk. Way behind him the tellers are locking up their drawers.

Henderson Well, I must say, you have to hand it to him. Haliwell really came through.

Barbara He was lucky.

Henderson It was a tactic. I think we should all be grateful it worked.

He laughs again. Quoc comes and sits down near them, quietly resuming his work.

To be honest, I was seriously frightened. (*His tone is suddenly intimate.*) You were bloody great.

Barbara It worked out well.

Henderson smiles a moment, vacantly.

Henderson All right, Quoc?

Quoc Yes thank you, Mr Henderson.

Behind him, a girl who looks to be no more than 14 is getting down from a high stool, picking up her bag, and walking out of frame.

One of the tellers has decided to leave.

19. INT. APARTMENT. NIGHT
Barbara sitting reading a book. Her legs characteristically tucked up under her. Like a quiet animal. She turns a page, silently. Then looks up. Chesneau has appeared at the open door to the living room. He carries his jacket and his shirt is marked with sweat.

Chesneau You should lock the door. I think you're crazy. Do you have any idea of how dangerous it is?

Barbara Nobody wants a white English woman. (*She smiles. She doesn't move from the sofa.*) How are you?

A pause. Then he moves into the room, casually putting a small bunch of flowers down on the table, carelessly, on its side.

Chesneau You've not been at the club.

Barbara Have you been looking?

He nods.

No. I've been reading my books. It's wonderful here in the evenings. The silence, lately. The peace.

He turns at the window and looks at her.

Chesneau I am very emotionally stupid. This is . . . this has always been true. I never know. Even when it's incredibly blatant.

Barbara I think this time you probably have the idea.

He nods slightly.

Chesneau Yeah, I thought I did.

Barbara Yes. You have it.

Chesneau Ah. I came round to check.

Barbara What a relief . . .

Chesneau Yeah . . .

Barbara The embarrassment. If it turned out that you'd got it wrong.

Chesneau Yeah, well, I'd thought of that . . .

He stands, nodding again.

It was a factor. Will you have a cigarette?

Barbara No. No thanks.

He stands a moment, holding the pack out.

Chesneau Hey, I was right. Terrific. CIA! Intelligence, huh?

20. INT. APARTMENT. NIGHT
The bed seen from the living room. They are lying together, still. He has his back against the pillows, she is stretched out across him. Her face is on his chest. A single sheet covers the rest of them. We move in as they talk very quietly.

Barbara And are you there?

Chesneau No, it's done without me.

Barbara What, they're . . .

Chesneau They're beaten, then put back in their cells. Today I went crazy, my best prisoner had been beaten to hell. His shirt fell open, he had scars . . . welts, right across here . . . (*He gestures across his own chest.*)

Barbara It's wrong.

Chesneau Yeah. But it's also just stupid. He's an important enemy source.

There is a pause.

For ten days I've been sitting there. Patiently. A small wooden table. Just leading him on. I get in today, someone's got restless, no point in waiting for Chesneau any more . . . It's stupid. The agents you capture, they're your life-blood. You don't go and hit them in the mouth. Hit people in the mouth, they just go stubborn, or they just tell you what you most want to hear. (*He shakes his head.*) Get the facts first, get things sorted, be sure you've really got hold of the facts. Then later . . . hell, throw him out of a helicopter. But afterwards.

Barbara Does that happen?

He turns and looks at her.

Chesneau (*quietly*) Of course.

21. INT. BATHROOM. NIGHT
Later. Barbara is sitting on a small wooden stool, her back against the wall, with her feet out in front of her on a chair. She is in her dressing-gown. Chesneau's face is below her; he is stretched out in the bath smoking a Marlboro. The only other sound is the occasional ripple of the water.

Barbara The men at the bank, oh, they're quite easygoing.
We've all been here for so long. The Scots are always
bankers. Or else engineers. (*She smiles.*) The funniest is
. . . do you know the British Council?

Chesneau No.

Barbara You don't know, but they still have a library
here. To encourage the spread of English culture. Good
idea, yes? Here in Saigon?

They smile.

I went there. There's now just one girl running it. She's
Vietnamese. She sits at a desk. I went up to her. She
doesn't speak English.

They look at each other. They laugh.

Chesneau Oh yes. Well, sure.

22. INT. APARTMENT. DAWN
*Light beginning to hit the blinds. Barbara sitting on the
sofa, with Chesneau's head on her lap, curled up like a
child pressed against her breasts. The room held.*

23. INT. BANK. DAY
*Morning. Barbara in close-up standing waiting at
Haliwell's office door as Haliwell arrives for work. A well-
defined routine. She is smiling slightly as he goes past her.*

Haliwell Good morning, Barbara. How are you?

Barbara Fine, Mr Haliwell. Thanks.

*She starts to unload the pile of ledgers from her arms.
He picks up* The Times *from his side of the desk and
casually throws it to her.*

Haliwell Look at this. Strikes. Industrial chaos. The whole
country seems to be going to hell.

She unfolds it with one hand, less than curious.

Barbara Good Lord.

Haliwell I mean, it's national insanity. The unions seem to want to run the whole show. I must say, though, one can count one's blessings. (*He is hanging up his coat and now turns, smiling.*) We can all be grateful we're living out here.

24. EXT. OCKHAM'S HOUSE. DAY

The lawn behind Ockham's detached clapboard house. The whole scene gleaming in the sun. There is a party for about fifty people, a mixture of races, all casually dressed. Children are jumping into the portable pool which is next to the house. At the centre a tall, intense man in his early fifties, with sunglasses. He is wearing a shirt and slacks, greeting guests as they arrive. He is Jack Ockham.

Ockham Hi . . . how are you? Nice to see you.

Chesneau appears, Barbara a pace behind.

Bob, how are you?

Chesneau This is Barbara Dean. Jack Ockham.

Ockham smiles slightly and takes her hand.

Ockham I'm very glad you could make it.

Chesneau Barbara works in the bank.

Ockham Good.

He nods slightly. Chesneau unsure of how to introduce her.

Well, Merry Christmas.

Barbara Thank you. And Merry Christmas to you.

Behind them servants are carrying three huge steaming-

hot turkeys to the white tables which are laid out on the lawn. Ockham passes on to greet the next guests, a short Vietnamese General and his taller Wife. They are heard in the background as we follow Barbara and Chesneau, walking into the mass of the party.

Are we a couple?

Chesneau What?

Barbara In public?

Chesneau I don't know. Do you know?

Barbara No.

They both smile.

I enjoy the uncertainty.

Chesneau Yes. Let's not be. For the moment let's stay good friends.

25. EXT. LAWN. DAY
Later. A burst of noise and laughter from a table just behind our group who are Chesneau, Barbara, Fiedler, Judd and Ockham who sits slightly apart. Fiedler has a paper hat. There are streamers and the debris of a good meal. The atmosphere is easy and slightly drunk.

Ockham Bob's never understood the aid allocation. You've never understood it.

Chesneau No, well, that's true.

Fiedler explains, for Barbara's benefit.

Fiedler We want Congress to vote three hundred million dollars to prove they support Thieu's regime.

Ockham Yeah.

Fiedler Now in fact . . . three hundred million, well it's not nearly enough, with the economy as bad as it is. We need more than that. But at least it would be symbolic – a symbol of the American intention to help.

Barbara looks across at Chesneau. He looks down at his hands.

Now back home there's a lot of opposition . . .

Ockham Left-wing elements . . .

Fiedler Liberals, yeah. People who never liked the war in the first place, who are now saying we should just get out, go home, forget about it. Abandon our friends. (*He shrugs slightly, as if suppressing the strong feeling he has.*) Well, I don't think that's a viable option. I don't think that's what Americans should do.

Barbara frowns slightly.

Barbara But isn't the problem . . . (*She pauses.*)

Chesneau What?

Barbara No, I shouldn't say.

There is a pause. Fiedler is looking at Chesneau.

Chesneau Go on.

Barbara No, I really . . . I don't know much about it. (*She smiles and looks away.*)

Ockham (*with characteristic quiet*) Barbara, you must say what you think.

She turns and looks at them.

Barbara I would have thought the problem you have here is the money will go to a particular regime. A regime whose reputation is for corruption. And there are political prisoners as well . . .

Fiedler easy at the familiarity of this charge.

Fiedler Oh well, sure, but . . .

Barbara Please, I'm not saying . . . for all I know Thieu is the best man. It's just that if he goes . . . you will go with him. You may be sitting on a branch that's withered. That's all.

A pause. Chesneau is looking at her.

Fiedler Well, I don't think . . .

Barbara It's . . .

Fiedler There's no sign of that. The regime is hardly threatened from within.

Barbara No?

He is staring at her, frowning.

Fiedler Barbara, there's only one enemy. That's the enemy that's waiting out there.

26. EXT. LAWN. NIGHT
At once, the whole scene seen from the bushes, far away and at night. There is now a barbecue around which people are gathered and others are jumping into the darkened pool. Raised voices and laughter. It is eerie. The shot held.

27. EXT. HOUSE. NIGHT
Barbara and Chesneau left sitting alone on the now deserted lawn, as the party continues indoors. Distant whooping around a lit tree indoors.

Chesneau I decided . . . while you were talking, watching you arguing it out . . . I thought tomorrow I'm going to go in there. It's time I told everyone what I really think.

Barbara is watching him closely.

We're so obsessed with this aid allocation that we pretend that things are much worse than they are. We think that only by exaggerating are we going to get all the money we need. (*He shakes his head.*) All the time we're saying, it's coming, it's coming, quick, give us money, give us aid. But that battle back there in Washington has become more real to us than anything here.

There is a particularly loud whoop from the house, as of a violent party game.

Barbara I must say, from the way they're behaving . . . it doesn't look as if they really think it's the end.

Chesneau No, of course not. Charades. (*He pauses, then moves his glass away.*) But meanwhile the facts get pushed out the way.

28. INT. APARTMENT. NIGHT
The apartment still at night. Barbara in bed. The sound of a very distant explosion, a rumble in the night. Chesneau is seen to be standing at the window, with a towel wrapped round his middle.

Barbara What is it?

Chesneau Oh it's the gas dump. It's always the gas dump when it's that close. (*He holds the blind apart, staring out absently.*) They pretend. They send up rockets. But really the job is done from the inside.

Barbara What d'you mean?

Chesneau Well, they always put up the firecrackers . . . (*He smiles and makes an arc with his arm.*) Great lights in the night. So you think it's being bombed. But in fact there's always an employee working for the VC on the inside, all he's done is slip a detonator in.

He turns and looks at her. The noise has died.

All the rest is show. They like to do it. I don't know why.

Barbara Perhaps because subversion's too easy.

He looks across at her.

Chesneau Something like that.

29. INT. APARTMENT. NIGHT
Barbara in her white dressing-gown sitting directly across from Chesneau at a small table. He is still in his towel. They are sipping tea from small Chinese cups, in the middle of the night.

Chesneau Can you give me an idea of England?

Barbara Well . . . (*She smiles.*) The place is very wet. Which makes its greenness almost iridescent. It is almost indecently green.

They smile.

The people are – odd. They're cruel to each other. Mostly in silent . . . in unexpected ways. It's an emotional cruelty. You feel watched, disapproved of all the time.

Chesneau That's why you got away?

Barbara There's a terrible pressure, all these little hedgerows squeezing you in, tight little lines of upright houses. Everyone spying on everyone else. (*She looks over at him and smiles.*) I'm not even . . . an unconventional woman. I need only that amount of air. But I can't get it in England.

There's a pause. Chesneau is looking at her.

I know what you're thinking. Will I ever go back?

30. INT. BANK. DAY

The hustle of the bank at lunchtime. Shafts of sunlight falling as in a cathedral across the back area, while at the front it is very busy before lunch. Barbara is at her desk, staring hopelessly at a sheaf of papers. Quoc comes over to wait for her verdict.

Barbara Quoc, I'm afraid this isn't possible. Really there's no question of this. (*She looks up at him regretfully.*) It's pointless investing money in transport now the Vietcong are blowing up roads.

Quoc Shall I say this to him?

Barbara Yes. If you want to. I mean . . . yes. It's impossible. How can I possibly defend an investment when we're approaching the worst time of year? I mean of course, yes, when the rains come, I'll consider it again. But until the rains . . . there is uncertainty. Can you tell him?

Quoc Yes. As you say.

> *Henderson has appeared at the desk, hovering. His shirt is cleaner, his beard trimmer than ever. Quoc is putting more papers on Barbara's desk.*

That. Just a signature.

Barbara Hello, Donald.

Henderson I wonder, could I have a word?

Barbara Yes of course. What can I do for you?

Quoc (*discreetly*) And another signature there.

> *Henderson waits for Quoc to finish. Barbara speaks meanwhile.*

Barbara Tell Mr Haliwell about these decisions. If you want my judgement checked against his . . .

Quoc No, it isn't necessary.

He takes the papers and goes. Barbara sighs.

Barbara Oh Lord, do you think it's a personal friend?

Henderson shrugs slightly.

Henderson My point is this. I need to ask you . . . (*He pauses, uncomfortable.*) Do you think I'll ever be promoted in here?

Barbara What are you saying? (*She looks at him, levelly.*) You mean you're leaving?

Henderson Yes, well, possibly. I'm not really sure. (*He looks down, embarrassed.*) I mean, there's you and above you there's Haliwell. Neither of you seem as if you're likely to retire. So the fact is . . . I got round to thinking . . . well, I've been offered a job in Hong Kong.

Barbara Good. You must take it.

Henderson Yes. I would like to. That's right.

They stare at each other.

Barbara Well, that's nice. We'll arrange a party.

He looks at her, then suddenly bursts, like an overflowing sink.

Henderson You know, I am most terribly in love.

She looks panic-stricken round the bank.

Barbara Yes, well, I think this is . . .

Henderson Honestly.

Barbara Hardly the moment . . .

Henderson Just the thought I might not see you again . . .

Barbara turns relieved to Quoc who has returned with
more papers.

Barbara Yes?

Henderson suddenly shouts at the top of his voice.

Henderson Oh God, Quoc, will you never ever leave us?
Can't we have one moment on our own?

There is a pause. All over the bank people stop work
and look up. Quoc is shocked, but looks impassively at
Henderson.

Quoc I'm sorry.

Barbara No . . . You must stay here. Mr Henderson is just
a little upset. (*She looks up at Henderson, quietly furious.*)

Henderson Yes. God, I'm sorry.

Barbara He doesn't mean it. He had no intention of being
so rude.

Henderson shakes his head weakly.

Henderson Really, I'm sorry, it's unforgivable . . .

Quoc looks at them, nods.

Quoc In a few moments, I shall return.

31. INT. BANK. EVENING
The bank, dark now. Among the empty desks Henderson
sits with his head in his hands. Barbara is leaning against a
desk nearby. Beyond them in the distance a young
Vietnamese girl with a long pole closes the shutters on the
high windows.

Henderson Oh my God, Barbara, I can tell you despise
me.

Barbara Have I said anything?

Henderson No. Not at all. It's just . . . your general demeanour. You behave as if I'm doing something wrong.

Barbara looks down at him, as if a little surprised.

I do have to tell you, I've been going crazy . . .

Barbara Well, in that case it's best that you leave. Hong Kong is a good place to forget me. (*She smiles slightly, amused at the ludicrousness of the remark.*) So you'll be much happier there. (*She is looking at the floor.*)

Henderson I would like . . . I feel you disapprove of me.

She does not answer.

You feel I'm cowardly, that's right?

Barbara smiles, this time bitterly, at the inadequacy of what she will say.

Barbara I think that we . . . who were not born here . . . should make sure we go with dignity.

There is a pause.

That's all.

32. INT. BANK. DAY
Morning. The bank is busy again. Tellers moving back and forth. In the middle of the back area, Henderson, turned away from us, is clearing out his desk, like an expelled pupil, as the commerce of the bank goes on.

Barbara (*voice over*) Donald *did* leave with comparative dignity. (*She watches him, from behind her desk.*) Compared with some of the rest of us, I mean.

She turns. Her eye catches camera.

239

Part Two

33. INT. CAR. DAY
Fade-up inside the car. Chesneau's face as he drives through early-morning Saigon. There is a cigarette hanging from his mouth. The cool morning goes by outside. The image holds. Then after a few seconds . . .

Barbara (*voice over*) I used to see Bob whenever it was possible. When we could we met, discreetly, in my room. As time went by it became much harder . . .

34. EXT. EMBASSY. DAY
The great white bulk of the American Embassy in Saigon, cut out against the morning sky. Palm trees and lawns in front of the huge square building. The gates open, the barrier goes up, Chesneau's Pinto goes through, with a greeting from the guard.

Barbara (*voice over*) He could only manage an occasional hour. Anyone who worked in that great white building seemed to vanish inside for the day . . .

35. INT. EMBASSY LOBBY. DAY
Chesneau crosses the guarded lobby of the Embassy, carrying a briefcase. He makes for the elevator, showing his pass as he goes.

Barbara (*voice over*) It was a city inside a city. Always, it seemed, with a life of its own.

The elevator doors close.

36. INT. CORRIDOR. DAY
Chesneau walks along the long neon-lit corridor at the spine of CIA headquarters on the fifth floor of the

Embassy. A jump in sound: typewriters, telexes, shredders, people calling from room to room.

Barbara (*voice over*) On the fifth floor of the Embassy, the New Year had begun much as they'd expected. Offensives from the North had started on time . . .

> *Lines of doors on either side, through which we see desk workers, strategic analysts. The maps, the desks, the charts, the projections, the files. Piles and piles of paperwork. Everyone is in civilian clothing.*

(*voice over*) The town of Phuoc Binh fell at the beginning of January.

> *A cry of 'Hi, Bob' from one of the doors.*

(*voice over*) But then Ban me Thuot followed early in March.

37. INT. OFFICE. DAY
Chesneau standing with his secretary Linda in the communal secretaries' office. She is 24, blonde, big-jawed and plaid-skirted, in the Mid-Western way. He is nodding at some papers she is showing him.

Barbara (*voice over*) Somehow up till then nothing really told them this was going to be the long-awaited end . . .

> *Chesneau nods as the Secretary explains a document to him.*

(*voice over*) They'd lived through so many of these annual readjustments, at first they'd just assumed it was another of the same . . .

38. INT. CORRIDOR. DAY
Chesneau walking on, purposefully, down the corridor towards the far end.

Barbara (*voice over*) Of course, I suppose if they'd just looked around them, if they'd ever just stopped and thought . . .

> *Chesneau reaches the end room. The door is open.*
> *Ockham's office. There are ten people sitting round in*
> *the deep-blue carpeted office, with a pine desk where*
> *Ockham is. Chesneau stops at the open door.*

(*voice over*) But somehow . . . all of us . . . our eye was elsewhere.

> *Ockham looks up from behind his desk.*

(*voice over*) When we realized, it was too late.

39. INT. OFFICE. DAY

At once we join the scene which has plainly already been long in progress. A young Officer lectures from a wall map of Vietnam, pointing with a short stick. Sitting round in the other chairs we see Colonel Fiedler and Judd, among a mixture of analysts and military. Ockham is standing staring ahead, a picture of President Ford behind him. Chesneau sits down, as we pick up the Officer in mid-brief.

Officer . . . hemmed in on the road. The South has lost fifteen hamlets in twenty-four hours. Here. On the road between Quang Tri and Hue. (*He points further down the map.*) Two district towns gone here in Quang Tin. The North heading down towards Tam Ky. (*further down*) Ban me Thuot here, of course, consolidated. And the anticipated push to Tay Ninh . . . (*He points.*) Signs of that are finally happening. This morning they lost the town of Tri Tam. (*He stands a moment, almost apologetic.*)

Fiedler Jesus Christ, they're coming out everywhere . . .

Ockham No, it's not so . . .

He nods at the Officer to sit down.

It's logical, I'm afraid. Once President Thieu decided to abandon the Highlands, everything that's happened makes logical sense.

There is a pause.

Fiedler Do we know more?

Ockham Joan . . .

Ockham, anticipating, has already nodded at Joan Mackintosh, who has got up. She is a CIA analyst, a brisk, well-built woman of about 40, in a pleated summer dress. She goes over to the map.

Mackintosh We have this from Thieu's Cabinet.

Fiedler looks at Ockham, surprised.

Ockham We now have an agent in there.

Mackintosh He explains. He says there is a new strategy. (*With a cloth she wipes the old marks from the laminated map.*) I'm afraid it was only invented this week.

She takes a Pentel and draws a thick line horizontally across South Vietnam from just above Tay Ninh to Nha Trang, so that the country is neatly divided three-quarters of the way down .

That . . . a defensive line . . .

Then she draws three tiny semicircles, way up on the coast in the North, all isolated from the main defensive area. They are around Quang-Nai, Tam-Ky, and Hue and Danang.

Here . . . these enclaves . . . these coastal towns . . . (*She turns back.*) Nothing else. The rest is abandoned.

Fiedler (*quietly*) My God.

Mackintosh (*as quietly*) There we are.

There is a silence. As if to fill it, apologetically, in contrast to her earlier manner, Mackintosh explains.

It isn't . . . we don't think it would be a bad strategy. It's always been an option the South has had. What is disastrous is simply the speed of it. It was intended this option should cover six months. Instead of which it's been three days now since it was implemented and of course . . . (*She looks to Ockham, as if deferring to him, tying herself up slightly as she finishes.*) . . . to do with its suddenness, I think . . . now it's happening, well, we all know . . . it does seem as if it's panic all round.

There is a long pause. Ockham stares ahead. From the back Chesneau speaks quietly.

Chesneau Where's the Ambassador?

Ockham doesn't answer at once.

Still getting his teeth fixed?

Ockham I have it here.

He nods and reaches among the pile of telexes on his desk. He reads from the appropriate wire.

Minor orthodontal surgery was completed in North Carolina last week.

Chesneau And is he coming back?

Ockham Yeah. Eventually. (*He reads from the cable again.*) He says 'No panic.' That's it. 'The situation is not yet serious.' (*He drops it on the desk, then quietly.*) I think that maybe we'd better leave it there.

He nods to dismiss them. People rise uncertainly, Chesneau looking at Judd. Ockham at once starts to talk to Fiedler.

Thank you, everyone. Colonel, if you got a moment . . .

*But we go with Chesneau and Judd, leaving together in
a group of agents, talking under their breath.*

Chesneau It's Loonyville. Land of the Loonies!

Judd That's right.

40. INT. CORRIDOR. DAY
*Continuous. As they come out into the corridor and are
able to raise their voices, the hysteria begins to seep.*

Chesneau Oh my God, the spooks are going *crazy.*

*People around them scatter, still talking, as they go on
down the corridor, Judd already tapping satirically at
his teeth with his fingernail and smiling.*

Judd Teeth!

Chesneau Yeah.

Judd What's he going to do with them? Bite the fucking
VC in the neck?

*They go on down the corridor. Suddenly the remains of
the meeting has broken up and all the other agents and
officers have disappeared, leaving Judd and Chesneau
the last two. Chesneau puts his hand on Judd's arm as
they disappear.*

Chesneau Frank. Suppose it happens. And we
evacuate . . .

*They disappear. The deserted corridor. We catch
Chesneau's voice from round the corner.*

Has anyone thought to look at the plans?

A pause. We look at the empty corridor.

41. EXT. WASTEGROUND. NIGHT

Chesneau's Pinto silently drawing up on a piece of wrecked Saigon suburb. It is so quiet it is as if he has turned the engine off. He comes to a halt. There is just open ground, with some shacks away in the distance, and alone in the wasteground a small tin garage. Chesneau lights a cigarette. He sits a moment in the car. Then he gets out and begins to walk across the silent wasteground.

42. INT. GARAGE. NIGHT

Chesneau opening the corrugated-iron door. The night seen briefly behind him as he slips in. The door closes. At the end a man is sitting on a crate, behind some tyres. He is 40, thin, with exceptionally bad skin. He wears sunglasses. His name is Nhieu. Chesneau speaks quietly.

Chesneau Hi. How are you?

Nhieu I am well, thank you.

Chesneau That's good.

Nhieu I want this to be our final meeting. I don't want money. I want documents out.

Chesneau stands still at the door.

Chesneau Well, if you like. It may not be necessary. I don't think anyone knows what you do.

Nhieu It is a condition.

Chesneau nods slightly, in assent.

When?

Chesneau Your papers? Soon.

Nhieu Tomorrow. And travellers' cheques. American Express.

Nhieu's voice is firm. There is a slight pause.

Chesneau Please tell me first what you have from Hanoi.

Nhieu There was a Cabinet meeting last night. It is now the intention of the Government of the North to press the war as far as it will go.

Chesneau Yes, but is it . . .?

Nhieu It will be military.

Chesneau What makes you say that?

Nhieu They call it blood scent. (*He gestures to his nose.*) The smell of blood in their noses. They will fight, all the way to Saigon.

Chesneau is seen to weigh this up, then decide to go on.

Chesneau You see, the thought was they might stop short of the city . . .

Nhieu shakes his head at once.

Nhieu No.

Chesneau And negotiate for a coalition from strength.

Nhieu Up till last night, yes, there was a faction. But they are defeated. They will fight their way in.

Chesneau looks at him, then goes on.

Chesneau This time, I'm sorry, I will have to ask you how close the source is.

Nhieu Has he ever been wrong? (*He looks straight at him, holding his stare.*)

Chesneau When?

Nhieu Three weeks. The end of April. (*He smiles slightly.*) I am not staying. I will be gone.

43. EXT. WASTEGROUND. NIGHT

The two men pacing together slowly back across the ground. They look small against the vastness of the night, and the tone is of two elder statesmen.

Nhieu I have a cousin in Omaha, Nebraska.

Chesneau Ah.

Nhieu He has a business selling paint.

Chesneau Ah yes. (*He steals a quick glance at him.*) It's very quiet in Nebraska.

Nhieu You are saying I will find no business as a pimp?

> *Chesneau shrugs slightly.*

Chesneau Well, I don't know. It's a land of opportunity.

Nhieu I was hoping also, I might take some girls?

> *They stop, Chesneau registering the request, but not reacting. They have reached the car.*

Chesneau I will try. (*He is about to get in.*) Thank you. You've been a great help to us.

Nhieu The documents.

Chesneau Yes. I will see it's arranged.

44. INT. OFFICES. NIGHT

The deserted CIA offices at dead of night. The secretaries' shared office is completely quiet, and through the open door we see Chesneau at work by a single lamp.

He reaches for a clean yellow legal pad, and quickly writes a few Vietnamese names on it. Then he pulls open a drawer in the side of his desk and takes out a fat, black address book. He opens it. It is thick, bulging, messy. Years of writing in both English and Vietnamese. He flicks

*a couple of times over some pages, then starts
systematically transferring names from the book to his
pad. Crossfade to:*

45. INT. OFFICE. DAWN

*Chesneau sitting back at his desk, the work complete in
front of him, the morning light coming through the blinds.
There's a pause. Then he gets up and picks up the list,
walks off down the corridor.*

46. INT. OCKHAM'S OFFICE. DAY

*Ockham is already at his desk, in shirt-sleeves. He has a
cup of coffee at his side, and he is sitting reading the day's
telexes with his legs up on the table. Chesneau comes in
quietly at the door.*

Chesneau Jack, you're in. (*He nods at a few sheets of
paper he has left on the desk top.*) I left that for you.

Ockham Yeah, I got it.

Chesneau Did you take a look?

Ockham nods slightly.

I've been making a list. (*He approaches the desk with his
yellow legal pad.*) Here's a list of our two hundred most
important local contacts. They should be the first we take
out. (*He settles down to explain.*) I think the way we do it is,
each department draws up a list of its most sensitive men . . .

Ockham Bob, I don't disagree with you. But the
Ambassador has to say when. (*He goes on before
Chesneau can interrupt.*) I've already called him. He
arrived back in the country last night.

Chesneau is looking at him, mistrustfully.

Chesneau Jack, these are the people who've actively
worked for us . . .

Ockham Sure.

Chesneau There's a whole dependent community here. Don't say if the Communists finally get here, we're just going to leave them to be murdered in their beds.

Ockham No question of that. We take them with us. (*He pauses, as calm as ever.*) The question is one of time-scale, that's all.

Chesneau Well, in three weeks . . .

Ockham You don't have to argue. At least you don't have to argue with me. (*He smiles slightly, and looks across at Chesneau.*) The Ambassador's read the report of your agent. He's insisting he sees you himself.

47. INT. AMBASSADOR'S OFFICE. DAY
The Ambassador's office is lined in dark wood. It has a deep-green carpet and fine desk, with flags behind it and photographs of the Ambassador with successive Presidents – Johnson, Nixon, Ford. The Ambassador is a very tall man in his early sixties in a tropical suit. He is sandy-haired, with a disconcerting habit of sometimes seeming neither to see you nor hear you. He gets up as soon as Chesneau and Ockham come into the room, making low murmurs as he settles them in chairs.

Ockham Ambassador.

Ambassador Hi. Good morning. (*He gestures towards a chair.*) Why don't you sit down?

As they settle, the Ambassador wanders, making vague noises.

Bob . . . OK . . . Jack, how you doing? (*Then he settles at his own desk.*) Right. Here we are then . . . (*He looks at Chesneau.*) I read your report. I have to tell you . . . I don't admire it. This is not the sort of thing I like to read.

This war has always been a great test of character . . . at this time more than ever perhaps. (*He now gestures at the report on the desk.*) This simply contradicts all our information. This 'blood scent' theory . . .

Chesneau Yeah.

The Ambassador stops, waiting for Chesneau to say more.

The agent is good.

Ambassador I'm afraid I simply don't accept that. Nothing he says squares with the picture we have. I have read it. Thank you for submitting it. But I shall not credit it when making policy. (*He smiles at Ockham.*)

Ockham I think that's right.

Ambassador I'm telling Washington the North are still keen to negotiate . . . (*He has sat back now, and is off on his own tack.*) This latest round of fighting has been very bracing. It's led to some decisions which were long overdue. President Thieu has succeeded in stripping down the country, he's made it a much more defensible shape. The area we're left with is much more logical, that's the benefit of strategic withdrawal. Now when we fight we're in the right positions. As soon as they see that, the Communists will stop. That's the moment we'll be able to negotiate . . .

Chesneau Sir, I don't think it'll happen like that.

There is a pause. The Ambassador smiles easily.

Ambassador Well, it won't happen if everyone panics . . . if everyone starts spreading depression and alarm . . .

Chesneau No, it's just . . .

He looks for support to Ockham, who gives none.

Our reports from the military indicate a chronic problem of morale.

The Ambassador shifts slightly in his chair.

Ambassador I wonder sometimes if we don't project that. I mean, if the problem isn't more in ourselves. Because we ourselves are a little bit panicky . . . (*He pauses, hanging the sentence in the air.*) So then we kind of see it in the Vietnamese.

Chesneau starts again, calmly, trying to keep to the facts.

Chesneau Sir, I'm worried we corrupt our intelligence. All last year we said things were bad. That was to dramatize, to secure an aid allocation. Now you're asking us to say things are good.

Ambassador Yes well, God, man, I still need money . . .

Chesneau What?

Ambassador That's exactly why your stuff has got to be suppressed. (*He gestures angrily at Chesneau's report.*) Congress is hardly going to vote us more money if they believe that South Vietnam's about to be destroyed.

Chesneau So you're . . .

But the Ambassador has suddenly started raising his voice.

Ambassador And it's *not* going to be! God, how often do I have to say? (*He suddenly starts shouting, with hurt and bewilderment.*) What is this in us? Some kind of *death wish*? Some kind of wishing the whole thing would end?

There is a pause.

Chesneau (*as tactfully as he can*) I think our first duty is to anyone who helped us. It's our job to get those people out . . .

Ambassador Out of the question. No evacuation. I'm not doing anything that smells of defeat.

Chesneau Sir, I can promise it won't be conspicuous . . .

Ambassador Oh yes, that's fine. What? Planes overhead? (*He makes an angry gesture to the sky.*) Great lines at Tan Son Nhut airport? Oh my God, yes, we really need that.

Chesneau interrupts before he finishes.

Chesneau No, I am saying . . . some of the Vietnamese commanders, the men who are out in the field right now, the reason they are fighting so badly is because we've made no plans for their families and friends. Now if we could get that worry removed for them . . .

The Ambassador turns to Ockham.

Ambassador He's saying he would like us to prepare for defeat.

Chesneau insists at once.

Chesneau No, I'm not.

Ambassador There would be chaos.

Chesneau There'll be even greater chaos if we delay. If we leave it to the very last minute, can you imagine what that's going to be like?

There is a pause. The Ambassador looks at him.

Ambassador Chesneau, my aim is exactly to avoid that. There will be no last minute here.

Chesneau Sir . . .

Ambassador The North will stop short and I will

negotiate. But it's essential I do that from strength.

Chesneau is about to interrupt again.

That is why I need a new aid allocation. I've asked for seven hundred million this week. The President has promised he will get it from Congress. (*He sits back.*) Until then we are going to sit tight.

Chesneau (*very quiet now*) But sir . . . with respect . . . you didn't get it last time. In effect you're gambling with thousands of lives.

Ambassador We are going to prove our absolute friendship.

Chesneau Even if it costs our friends their own lives?

There is a pause. The debate is over. The Ambassador speaks, full of sorrow.

Ambassador Bob. I don't like to see you hysterical. I know the work has gotten very hard. I don't like to see you join the conspiracy. (*He looks up at him, a moment.*) You of all people.

His own melancholy is so apparent that Chesneau cannot reply.

Well . . . there we are.

Ockham looks up, shifting as if the meeting is over. But the Ambassador has turned into himself and is staring at his desk.

Ockham Well . . .

The Ambassador looks up.

Ambassador I lost a son.

Chesneau Yes. I'm sorry, sir.

Ambassador My son was killed fighting. He died here. Six years ago. (*He looks at Chesneau.*) No, well, Bob, thanks for the offer. But I don't think we'll be leaving right now.

48. INT. APARTMENT. NIGHT
Darkness. Then Barbara's face, just hit with a streak of light as she unlatches the door. Chesneau is standing outside on the landing.

Chesneau Hi, how are you?

He smiles. She looks at him a moment.

I wanted to see you.

She opens the door.

Barbara Come in. The curfew . . .

Chesneau Oh it's all right.

She closes the door behind him and goes on past him back into the apartment which is darkened, unlit.

I'm afraid I've been drinking. One or two of the Agency . . .

He stands a moment at the door, apologetically, holding a couple of bottles in his hand. She has gone to sit down at the far end of the apartment on a wooden chair.

Have you been sleeping?

Barbara I'm sitting in the dark.

There is a pause. He moves into the darkened room.

Chesneau It's been very bad. Things are bad lately. There's an airlift out of Danang. Hue gone, Danang going . . .

Barbara I heard the World Service tonight.

He stands a moment. She is not looking at him.

Chesneau Listen, I'm sorry . . . I've not been coming to see you. I'm sure . . . you must be angry, I know. It's just . . . it gets to be impossible . . .

Barbara Why do you behave as if I'm your wife?

Chesneau What?

Barbara (*quietly, with no apparent bitterness*) It's unattractive. Pouring out excuses. 'I'm sorry, darling, I'm drunk . . .' I'm your girlfriend, there's no responsibility. And thank goodness, no need to report.

Chesneau looks at her a moment, not understanding her mood.

Chesneau Barbara, I'm sorry, I felt you'd be angry . . .

Barbara Yes, well, I am. Things are coming to an end. That means going into work hasn't been easy. It's not very pleasant, the look people have. Today there was a girl, a teller, she's been working at the bank, I suppose, two years, she came to me to ask if I could help get her out. I said, well, there's a friend of mine . . . (*She looks at him quickly, then away.*) . . . he can get papers, I think.

Chesneau Yeah, it's not . . . it isn't too easy. For the moment we're playing things down.

He pauses, miserably. Barbara is looking down at her hands.

I mean, of course I will for a friend of yours, Barbara. We're trying not to let panic set in.

He goes on, apologetically. She doesn't turn.

That's why the radio doesn't quite come through with things. All the news of the military defeats. We don't want things to get too conspicuous. People might take to the streets.

Barbara Well, I'm sure. You must lie to them. Lying's got you this far.

Chesneau Barbara, you know I have always protested . . .

Barbara Yes of course . . . (*She turns to him at last.*) You've protested to *me*.

> *There is a pause.*

I remember you so many evenings, lying there. A chance to talk about your work. Then you've gone back into the Embassy . . .

Chesneau Barbara . . .

Barbara *Done nothing.* And now you're inventing a fresh set of lies. (*She turns away.*) 'Oh whatever we do we mustn't tell the people. Just get the palefaces out of this mess . . .'

Chesneau That isn't fair. That's not fair to us. The whole thing is just . . . to keep things in hand.

> *There is a miserable silence.*

Barbara (*very quietly*) This girl said to me, 'I know you'll betray us.' I said, 'Oh I don't think that's true.' She said, 'Oh please you mustn't be offended . . .' (*She turns and looks at him.*) '. . . I know what you do is always for the best.'

> *She gets up and goes out of the room. In the distance a light comes on and she passes out of sight. Chesneau alone in the room holding his beer. Then Barbara's voice calling through.*

These people *know*. They know what's happening. The more you lie, the worse it will get.

> *Chesneau turns slightly.*

Chesneau We don't know for sure that everything's over.

Barbara's face reappears in the doorway.

Barbara In that case you're the only people who don't.

49. INT. CORRIDOR. DAY
*The main corridor in the CIA. Empty. The noise of people
at work in the offices. Then after a few seconds the most
almighty explosion not far away. The whole corridor
shakes. At once people come running, Judd first.*

Judd Jesus Christ, what the hell is happening?

50. INT. UPSTAIRS CORRIDOR. DAY
*The Ambassador appears, hands on hips, furious in the
deserted corridor upstairs.*

Ambassador What the hell is going on here?

51. INT. STAIRWELL. DAY
*The enormous stairwell at the centre of the Embassy. The
Ambassador appears on the stairs. Above him, a door is
opened at the very top of the well, and an anxious
American Marine is seen staring up into the sky. The
Ambassador yells up from the railing three floors below.*

Ambassador Soldier, what's happening?

The Marine calls back down.

Marine There's just one fighter, sir. He's bombing the
Presidential Palace, it's like.

*A very loud voice through the whole building,
screaming at full pitch.*

Voice Hey. Get away from the windows. *Everyone.* Get
down on the floor.

52. INT. CORRIDOR. DAY
The corridor now with forty people lying dead-still on the ground, as for a post-nuclear exercise. A pause. Then the whine of an approaching jet and another tremendous explosion. The corridor shakes again. Then the sound of the jet disappearing into the distance. Silence. Nobody moves.

Then the first person sits up.

53. INT. OCKHAM'S OFFICE. DAY
A couple of minutes later. A jump in sound as from outside you can hear people sorting themselves out, calling to one another, as Chesneau comes into the room. Ockham is already on the phone at his desk, apparently as calm as ever.

Ockham (*phone*) OK. All right.

Chesneau What the hell was that about?

Ockham looks up briefly.

Ockham (*phone*) OK. Yeah. I understand.

Chesneau Jack.

Ockham nods and puts down the phone.

Ockham Some mad pilot. A cowboy. Decided to fight the war on his own.

He shrugs slightly and turns back to his desk to sit down. Judd has come in to join them.

What can you do? There's very little damage . . .

Chesneau Nobody knew what the hell was happening. (*He has begun to shout.*) Nobody had any idea how to deal with it.

Ockham No, well, of course.

He looks at him, very quiet, his calm for the first time seeming unnatural, almost pathological.

It was a surprise.

He reaches for a bottle of whisky from a drawer in his desk. Chesneau looks at him, rattled by his elaborate calm.

Chesneau Jack, I thought we had radar defences. This town is meant to be ringed. That maniac came clear through the airspace . . .

Ockham Yes, I know.

Chesneau We're just sitting here. (*He looks up to the ceiling.*) When is that mad bastard in that office going to realize we need to get out?

A pause. Ockham looks at Judd, who is looking at the floor.

Ockham Bob, understand you have my permission. If you're unhappy, you're free to resign.

54. EXT. BASEBALL GROUND. DAY
Chesneau stands in the bleachers watching the lunchtime baseball in the Embassy compound. Judd has followed him out.

Chesneau It's not even me, it's not me I'm thinking of . . .

Judd No . . .

Chesneau I don't give a shit what happens to us.

He sits down on one of the benches and gets out a sandwich. Judd sits beside him.

It's those thousands of people who helped us. We made them a promise. And it's getting too late. The Ambassador

dreams of some personal triumph. Ockham moves his
furniture out . . .

Judd I didn't know that.

Chesneau Sure. *Things*. Joan's cat . . .

He nods at Joan who is approaching them.

Objects. Money. Everything but the *people* can go.

*Joan opens her handbag to give a note to Judd. Inside
Chesneau sees a .45 pistol.*

New gun, Joan.

Mackintosh I got it in case we ever get caught. (*She smiles
at Judd.*) Frank and I . . . we have an agreement. We're
going to shoot each other in the head.

*She goes. Chesneau watches her leave, but Judd has
turned and is looking at Chesneau, as if preparing to say
something difficult.*

Judd Bob, I've been wanting to say to you, you don't get
anywhere by being awkward.

Chesneau Awkward?

Judd Lately you've become very loud. Whether you're
right or wrong, it's not very effective. You're not going to
make anyone want to change their mind. Jack Ockham,
for God's sake, he's as eager to start the evacuation as you
are. More eager. But he also knows the way to persuade
the Ambassador is never going to be by raising his voice.
I'm not quite sure why you do it. What your motives are
for this bitterness, Bob. It's self-indulgent. And it doesn't
have the effect you require.

There is a pause.

I say this from personal friendship.

Chesneau (*quietly*) Is this what everyone feels?

55. INT. BANK. DAY
The bank besieged with people desperate to trade their piastres. Much argument with tellers. People behind the counters working flat out. A Teller brings a packet to Barbara's desk where she is working.

Teller This has been delivered by hand.

Barbara Thank you.

> *The Teller goes. Barbara looks at the packet, opens its top, takes the merest second's glance, then gets up and goes over to another of the tellers, a girl of 17 on a high stool. At once Lhan gets up and follows Barbara to a small filing office at the side of the main hall.*

Lhan, come in here . . .

56. INT. FILING OFFICE. DAY
Continuous. They go in, Barbara closing the door, then she takes the packet and empties it out on a small table.

Lhan Thank you.

> *Inside the packet are an air ticket and a passport which Barbara hands across, as she looks in the ticket.*

Barbara Here's your passport as well.

Lhan Thank you, Miss Dean. (*Lhan is delighted. She gestures outside.*) I have the dollars.

Barbara That's all right. You'll need them where you're going. The flight is today. You must leave the bank early.

Lhan All right. (*She takes the ticket from Barbara. Then pauses.*) Miss Dean, I have an aunt. Also . . . she has two brothers.

Barbara looks at her a moment, then leans across and kisses her with great affection. Then she leaves the room, but not encouragingly.

Barbara Leave their names. I'll see what I can do.

57. INT. SHREDDING ROOM. DAY
At once a great noise as Ockham moves down a line of eight paper-shredders which are being fed continuously with thousands of documents, which are being unloaded by teams of assistants. We are in a large filing room, almost like a steel vault, whose contents have been ransacked and poured out on to the floor. As Ockham moves down the line, assistants come up to him with individual bundles for his personal approval.

Ockham Yeah, all that. (*He looks briefly at the next bundle.*) Get rid of it. (*The next.*) Yeah. Yeah. Sure, that as well. Anything with names we got to get rid of it. (*He speaks even before the next assistant has reached him.*) If it's got names, then it must go.

58. INT. INCINERATOR ROOM. DAY
An inferno of heat and noise. A terrible whine from the machines. Three men dressed only in trousers are shovelling piles of shredded paper into the incinerators. There are carts of shredded paper waiting to go. The fire inside is fierce. Ockham stands near the men, shouting at the top of his voice to be heard.

Ockham It's hot.

Man Yeah. Ventilation. (*He points up to the ceiling.*) I don't think it's working.

Ockham nods. Then gestures at the great piles of paper.

Ockham I'm afraid this is only the beginning. Just keep going as long as you can.

59. INT. OCKHAM'S OFFICE. DAY
Ockham is now sitting at his desk downstairs. Round the door appears a very Ivy League State Department Young Man, nervous, in a suit. Ockham looks up.

Young Man I'm sorry, sir. It's the Ambassador. He says can you turn the incinerators off?

Ockham frowns.

He says he's sorry, but please can you do it?

The Young Man looks nervously at Ockham.

He says the ash is falling on the pool.

60. INT. BANK. NIGHT
Quoc is sitting alone with the ledgers in the deserted bank. He is at his desk, in the back area. Barbara appears in front of him, very still.

Barbara Quoc. I'm afraid I sent Lhan off today.

Quoc Yes, that's all right. She told me she would go.

Barbara nods slightly.

Barbara I wanted to ask . . . if you would like me to help you.

Quoc No.

There is a pause. Quoc stares at her impassively.

Barbara I felt I must ask.

Quoc Whatever happens, I am staying in my country. My family, my life is here.

Barbara But you hate the Communists.

Quoc No, I don't hate them, I fear them, that's all.

She looks at him as if about to say something important.

Barbara The bank will trade until the last moment.

Quoc Yes, of course.

Barbara I needed to say . . .

She stops, unable to express herself. She puts her hand suddenly over her mouth. Quoc seems simply to wait. She sees this and turns away.

Well, I'm sorry, I shouldn't have disturbed you. (*She turns to go.*) Good night, Quoc.

Quoc Good night, Miss Dean.

61. INT. SITUATION ROOM. NIGHT
A group of senior Embassy men in the situation room. In the DAO's office inside the Embassy. It is late at night. The maps on the walls are dramatically lit by neon. At the centre of the room, surrounded by senior military, the Ambassador sits in deep gloom. Chesneau sits near Ockham. The Officer at the wall has just finished reporting from a large map of Military Region Three.

Officer I'm sorry, sir. There is nothing in the military situation which gives any grounds for hope. I would say . . . Saigon is encircled. At any moment the attack can be pressed home. (*He waits a moment, then tries to go on.*) In a way, I don't quite know why they're waiting . . .

Ambassador They're waiting because they still want to talk. (*His voice is barely raised.*) Why fight your way in when you can negotiate? They don't want to see this city destroyed.

There is silence. He is plainly on his own, yet no one wants to speak. Ockham leads quietly.

Ockham Well, in that case, there's a precondition.

Something we've discussed here before. For many years. It is a condition that the North will not negotiate unless President Thieu is removed.

Ambassador And it is of course I who must do it.

There is a pause.

Oh yes, Jack. *I* must hold the knife.

Everyone looks at him in concealed astonishment. The military stare as he goes on.

This man who's been loyal to us. A cup of bitterness. And you are all so keen I should drink.

Ockham looks down, embarrassed.

Ockham Well, it does seem . . . if we want to negotiate . . .

Ambassador Oh yes, of course, sound reasons I'm sure. (*He gets up from the chair and moves across the room, muttering. Then he turns and faces them.*) Well, so be it. It's what you've always wanted. All of you. Well . . . you have your way.

He looks down to the floor. There is a silence.

Chesneau (*neutrally, not intimidated*) Does that mean, sir, we can start to evacuate?

The Ambassador turns and looks at him.

Ambassador Oh yes, Chesneau. Let hell come down.

62. INT. BAR. NIGHT
A rundown bar in the centre of town. Behind the bar the TV is on and Thieu is addressing the nation in obviously historic terms. At the bar in a line sit Chesneau, Joan Mackintosh, Frank Judd and Brad, a middle-aged American industrialist. Chesneau gets down from his

stool and passes the television as he goes to the phone.
He dials.

Chesneau Barbara. It's Bob.

Barbara (*voice over*) Hello.

Chesneau Are you watching?

63. INT. APARTMENT. NIGHT
In Barbara's darkened apartment the trunks have been
pulled to the centre of the room, and her belongings are
half packed into them. She is sitting on the edge of the bed
and in the room distantly you can see the same flickering
image on the TV behind her – Thieu in black and white.

Barbara Yes. The television's on.

Chesneau (*voice over*) The Ambassador went to get rid of
him this morning. He still seems to think it's going to help
him get talks.

   Barbara is staring ahead, detached.

Barbara Does that mean . . .?

Chesneau (*voice over*) Yeah. We start the big evacuation.
All our effort's now to get people out.

   Barbara does not react. He goes on with false
   enthusiasm.

(*voice over*) The wraps are really off. It's really beginning.

Barbara Ah well, good.

Chesneau (*voice over*) Yes. Well, we're pleased.

   Pause. Barbara waiting. Chesneau's voice changes tone.

(*voice over*) Barbara, are you planning . . . are you going
to leave yet?

Barbara No. (*She looks down.*) I've nothing. I've no life out there. Also . . . Bob . . . (*Her need is suddenly naked.*) I miss you . . . can we meet?

64. INT. BAR. NIGHT
Continuous. Chesneau stands by the bar, turned away from the others, phone in hand, listening. He pauses a moment.

Chesneau I'd like to see you. But I have to go to the airport tonight.

65. EXT. OCKHAM'S HOUSE. NIGHT
Ockham's house seen from the front in the near darkness, late at night. Just a glint of light on the front steps and into it at once steps a short, beautifully dressed dandy. He stops a moment. It is Thieu. Then Chesneau's voice from the dark, tactful.

Chesneau Sir.

> *Behind Thieu, unseen in the dark, a couple of bodyguards whisper quietly but urgently. Thieu nods and moves down the steps, out of the light. At once we see a black car drawn up in the driveway. Judd holding the back door open. The small figure gets silently into the car. Judd goes round the back and closes the trunk, which is crammed with many fine leather suitcases. Chesneau is waiting at the passenger door and the two of them get into the seats, slipping in like French gangsters. Chesneau starts the engine. Then looks in his rear mirror where he can see Thieu's face staring straight ahead.*

Sir, if you could . . . if you could just keep down.

66. EXT. STREET. NIGHT
The black car moving smoothly through the now silent

*curfewed streets. The only moving object on a still
landscape. As it goes by we see Judd and Chesneau, but
the back is apparently empty.*

67. INT. CAR. NIGHT
*Chesneau intent on driving, looking around. Judd beside
him looks in the mirror, shifts slightly.*

Judd (*quietly*) Are you, em . . . are you going to join your
family, sir?

Thieu's voice from the floor of the back of the car.

Thieu No. They are buying antiques. (*He nods
judiciously, then looks quickly at Chesneau, alert for
trouble from outside.*) They have already gone to London.

*We see Thieu for the first time. He is sitting on the floor
of the car, right down at the back. His two bodyguards
are squeezed beside him. Judd's voice.*

Judd (*voice over*) London's nice at this time of year.

68. INT. GYMNASIUM. DAY
*A wide shot of the huge empty gymnasium which the
DOA will use as evacuation headquarters. It is almost
empty but for some trestle tables which stand waiting,
stacked at the side of the building. Old basketball nets
hang from the ceiling.*

Barbara (*voice over*) So it began, the delayed evacuation . . .

69. INT. GYMNASIUM. DAY
*Fiedler at the centre of the gym. Now teams of marines all
around as he describes how he wants everything laid out.*

Fiedler Tables . . . Lines of applications . . . Vietnamese
exit papers over there . . . (*With each instruction he
gestures hugely.*)

70. INT. GYMNASIUM. DAY
The scene being transformed. Tables being set up. Men arriving with temporary office equipment. Catering equipment passed hand to hand along a human chain. Fiedler on the move, pointing to where everything is to go, receiving attendant soldiers as they come to him for instruction.

Barbara (*voice over*) Out at the airport they transformed the gym . . .

Fiedler points to one corner.

Fiedler Kitchens. (*Then to a pile of equipment.*) Gas burners. (*He points again.*) Toilet facilities . . .

A Soldier has come up to him, pointing to a fresh mound of PX goods.

Soldier Sir, this is three hundredweight of franks and beans.

They stand, laughing easily.

71. INT. GYMNASIUM. DAY
The scene transformed completely. Tables set out in immaculate rows. Men waiting behind them to receive the lines. Ropes set out to define the lines. Kitchen staff waiting with gleaming equipment. In the space of a few hours, a perfect logistical operation has been finished, and the team for the job now stands waiting.

Barbara (*voice over*) They built a facility they called Dodge City.

Fiedler at the centre of the room turns to an attendant officer.

Fiedler OK, everyone. Open the doors.

Part Three

72. INT. TAXI. DAY
Fade-up. Barbara in the back of a taxi going through the streets of Saigon. They are very crowded. On the sidewalks people are gathering round the street traders, who have huge piles of goods stacked around them.

Barbara (*voice over*) The last few days the streets were always busy . . . all the objects people needed to unload . . .

Watching the sidewalks going by from behind the glass.

Wherever you went, air-conditioning units . . . fridges . . . televisions . . . stoves . . .

73. INT. APARTMENT. DAY
Barbara's apartment now cleared out. The luggage neatly stacked at the centre of the room. Around the walls and shelves have been cleared. On a rail in the corner of the room there are still a few dresses and Barbara is now handing one to her Maid.

Barbara Have this, OK?

Maid Yes, thank you. (*She holds it up delightedly against her body.*) Hey, it's good, it really looks good . . .

Barbara looks at her a moment.

Barbara You know it means that soon I'll be leaving?

Maid Oh yes. (*The Maid turns with unconcern, and stands delightedly with a mirror.*) Hey, I'm going to look good.

74. INT. CERCLE SPORTIF. DAY
Barbara in the women's locker room at the Cercle Sportif. It is deserted. Grey ranks of closets. She has opened her

locker and is pouring old tennis gear on to the floor.

Barbara (*voice over*) Suddenly at last the Cercle Sportif was deserted . . .

75. EXT. CERCLE SPORTIF. DAY
A few solitary Frenchmen in chic costumes sit by the large, slightly green pool with Doric pillars behind. The odd servant brings them iced drinks. They read Le Monde.

Barbara (*voice over*) Only the French still sit by the pool . . . As if the Americans had only come briefly and the French had never expected they would stay.

76. INT. CERCLE SPORTIF. DAY
Barbara sitting alone with a drink, staring out, in the part where we earlier saw them playing cards. A waiter comes across with a bunch of roses. She is suddenly beginning to look old.

Barbara (*voice over*) The Foreign Minister I'd played bridge with sent me roses. Later I found out he'd already gone . . . (*She smiles up at the waiter, puts the flowers carelessly aside. Voice over*) Like so many . . . without any warning. The Americans got him away in the night.

77. INT. GYMNASIUM. DAY
The gym, transformed again. Now crammed with evacuees in long lines, some of whom have been sleeping on the spot, waiting for their turn for their applications to be processed. The place is patrolled at the side by GIs in olive drab. Judd is pushing his way through the crowd with a short Vietnamese of about 45, who has an overstuffed suitcase. He is trying to reach Colonel Fiedler who is still at the centre of things, but by now worn down, frazzled. Judd has to shout to make himself heard.

Judd Colonel, I'm wondering . . . This is a friend of mine.

Fiedler Everyone seems to have so many friends.

Judd He's a tailor. He made shirts for the Embassy.

Fiedler looks at him a moment, then turns to Judd.

Fiedler Any idea why he's decided to go?

Judd turns to the tailor and speaks to him in Vietnamese. As he answers, Judd translates.

Judd Everyone else is going . . . all his friends have already left.

Fiedler Yeah, OK . . . (*He looks at the tailor hopelessly.*) Well, why not then? (*He reaches across for a couple of exit papers from an officer's pile on a nearby table.*) Tell him he may have to wait for a while.

78. INT. BANK. DAY
The bank as normal, peaceful now, in contrast to the airport. Everything in its familiar place. Barbara working at her desk. Quoc appears beside her.

Quoc Miss Dean, I'm afraid we have lost Mr Haliwell.

Barbara What?

He reaches out with an envelope.

Quoc He asked to pass you on this. (*She looks up, then goes and opens the door of Haliwell's office.*)

79. INT. OFFICE. DAY
The office is empty. The desk cleared. The ledgers in a tidy pile at the side of the desk. The Times still in its place. A coat hangs on the coat rack. Barbara moves into the office, reading the letter. Quoc follows her in.

Quoc He went for lunch and he left you this message.

Barbara Yes.

She has opened it. Inside there is a note and an airline ticket. She looks at the ticket, then turns as if to resume normality.

Well, thank you, Quoc.

Quoc lingers, surprised he is being dismissed.

Quoc Are you leaving?

Barbara What?

Quoc Will you follow him?

She looks at him a moment.

Barbara What do you think I should do?

Quoc raises his eyebrows slightly.

Quoc I would say yes. It will come anyway. Better you do it as soon as you can.

80. INT. BANK. DAY
The back area. Everyone diligently at work, as Quoc and Barbara come out of Haliwell's office. She makes for the desk, pauses a moment, reaches for the cardigan which is draped round the back of the chair.

Quoc No, leave that. It is less suspicious.

She nods and begins to move away.

Barbara Yes.

Quoc But your handbag . . . if you want cigarettes . . .

He is pointing to the bag which is left on the chair. Barbara realizes and dips down to pick it up.

Barbara Yes. Thank you.

Quoc No. You are welcome.

They stand looking at each other.

Barbara Goodbye, Quoc.

Quoc Goodbye, Miss Dean.

81. INT. BANK. DAY
At once a high shot of the bank at work. Barbara walking quickly down the stairs and out the main door.

82. INT. CORRIDOR. DAY
The busy corridor at the CIA Headquarters, fifth floor. Chesneau is coming down the corridor. He is wearing a helmet, and his hand is stuffed with papers. Judd is coming from the other direction, also in a helmet.

Chesneau What's the news?

Judd There's been a second ultimatum. It says all US personnel must withdraw . . .

They keep on moving together towards the office.

If we don't get out there's going to be bloodshed . . . (*He turns back ironically.*) The Ambassador says they still want to talk.

83. INT. OFFICE. DAY
The office is as busy as ever, but all the secretaries who are otherwise dressed normally are wearing helmets. The effect is very odd. As soon as she sees him coming through, Linda gets up to talk to Chesneau, who is coming in talking to Judd.

Chesneau And we're expecting an attack on the airport . . .

Linda Bob . . .

Chesneau nods to Judd that he'll join him in a minute,

*recognizing the seriousness of Linda's tone. She silently
nods him over to the quiet corner of the office. They go
to a filing cabinet which has a Thomson sub-machine-
gun lying incongruously on top of it.*

There's a woman downstairs.

Chesneau frowns.

The woman who came with you . . .

Chesneau Ah yes. (*He stands a moment, not knowing
what to do.*)

Linda . . . last Christmas . . .

He nods.

Chesneau Put her in a room. I'll be down when I can.

84. INT. EMBASSY. DAY
*Barbara is walked down the ground-floor passage of the
Embassy by two Marines. They open a door, and inside is
a deserted office, which has been cleared. It is empty.
Barbara goes in. The walls are decorated by pictures of
America, posters of the Rockies, Manhattan, etc.*

Barbara Thank you.

*The two men go, closing the door. She sits down,
alone.*

85. INT. BANK. DAY
*Quoc sitting at his desk, as usual. The work of the bank
going on. A couple of tellers laughing, during the slack
period. Then a third teller signals to Quoc to come over. A
young American Woman is at the other side of the
counter.*

Woman I'm so sorry. I need my credit cleared. Is the
manager here?

Quoc Yes of course. I'll just speak to him. (*He reaches through the guichet and takes her cheque book.*) Will you hold on a moment, please?

> *We see him walk into the manager's office, having tapped three times on the door. He goes in. A pause. The tellers chatter, oblivious. Then after a few moments he comes out again, closing the door behind him. He rejoins the tellers and customer.*

The manager says, yes, we can pay on this. (*He pushes the book back.*) Would you like to make out your cheque?

86. EXT. EMBASSY. NIGHT
The American Embassy seen from outside. The huge white building. The night is silent around it, but high in the building lights burn.

87. INT. OCKHAM'S OFFICE. NIGHT
A very low-key briefing, dead of night. Ockham at his desk, the few trusted analysts around the room. Ockham tired. There are cans of Heineken on his desk.

Ockham The North is going to give us twenty-four hours. It's been negotiated. That's how long they're willing to hold off. Washington is insisting no phoney heroics. We are only to take essential locals with us at the end.

Chesneau What does that mean?

Ockham It means what we want it to, Bob. (*He smiles, bitterly.*) They've never known anything of what it's like here. (*He looks down, uncharacteristically emotional.*) Meanwhile please . . . your work is nearly over. I'd advise you all to try and get some sleep.

88. INT. EMBASSY. NIGHT
Barbara asleep in a chair in the Embassy office. Chesneau

standing over her in the near dark. She looks abandoned. Chesneau speaks to her asleep.

Chesneau I'm sorry, I was working.

She wakes. Looks at him. Smiles.

Barbara What?

Chesneau I didn't forget you.

Barbara I couldn't face leaving.

Chesneau No, it's all right.

Barbara Haliwell went . . .

Chesneau In that case he must have caught the last plane. (*He moves away.*) The airport's gone.

Barbara in real panic looks across at him.

Barbara Oh Bob, have I been very stupid?

Chesneau No. You can helicopter out. The Jolly Green Giants. We're bringing them into downtown Saigon.

Barbara looks at him, puzzled.

Barbara But how do you know . . .?

Chesneau There's an agreement. They're giving us exactly twenty-four hours. And everyone's ready. All American citizens have been issued with assembly points. (*He smiles.*) They're waiting for a signal.

Barbara smiles also, in anticipation.

Barbara You play 'White Christmas'?

Chesneau Yes. They're serious.

Barbara I thought it was a joke.

Chesneau It's a joke. It's serious as well.

They smile at each other, the old humour between them,
the old tone of voice.

The radio station plays Bing Crosby, and all Americans
know it's the end.

89. EXT. EMBASSY COMPOUND. NIGHT
The empty compound outside the Embassy streaked with
searchlights which are now on for the night. The noise of
gunfire has now died. From the dark, running very lightly,
come two GIs and an Officer, making for a huge tree
which dominates the compound. One GI stumbles slightly
as he reaches it.

First GI Shit.

Officer Keep it quiet.

Second GI How the hell . . .? (*He gestures despairingly at*
the huge chainsaw he is carrying.) There's no way he ain't
going to hear it.

Officer It's the Ambassador's favourite tree.

The First GI makes a signal of despair and looks up at
the great branches of the tamarind. The Officer shrugs.

We've gotta do it. We need the landing space. (*He nods at*
the Second GI.) Nothing for it. Let's go.

The two men start the chainsaw. The petrol motor is
deafening.

Jesus.

It bites into the trunk. At once, at a high window, way
up on the top floor of the Embassy, the stricken figure
of the Ambassador appears, like a prisoner shouting
from behind his bullet-proof glass.

Ambassador What the hell is going on here?

90. INT. APARTMENT. DAY

There are some bags, packed, in the centre of the room. Chesneau stands alone in the living room. He is looking at his watch. It says 7:45. Barbara is out of sight, gathering stuff from the bedroom. She calls to him from there.

Barbara (*voice over*) Nearly ready.

Chesneau It's OK.

Barbara (*voice over*) I'm sorry, I'm taking your time up.

Chesneau No. (*He stands, patient. Then almost to himself*) Go your own speed.

For the first time Barbara appears, by the door jamb. She holds a few random objects she is planning to pack.

Barbara Do you want to go?

Chesneau Yeah, there'll be choppers at the Embassy.

Barbara And what . . . you think I should get on?

Chesneau Well sure, I mean . . .

Barbara No I meant . . . you mean *now*? Or can't I hang on for you?

A pause, he does not reply.

I've never even asked where the helicopter takes me.

Chesneau To the Philippines.

He smiles slightly, but already she is going on with a new urgency.

Barbara Listen, I have a friend. A terrific girl. She used to bring me laundry. Put her on. She's a wonderful girl. Let her go in my place.

He is still looking at her.

Why not? Just the chance to be with you. (*She turns away*.) It's the waste. All the time we've wasted.

Chesneau Yes, I know. That was my fault.

He moves across the room. She is in his arms.

When I first came here, Barbara, I thought I could do this job decently. I thought it was honourable work. And even now I'm not ashamed, all the work we've done, this week, all the people I've managed to get out. But also it's the nature of the thing. It's been left to us. 'Hey, you guys, go and make us look good.' Well, we didn't. We weren't any better at losing the war than we were at winning it. And Barbara . . . you made it worse for me. Every time I saw you, you made me feel guilty. I couldn't take that after a while. That's why I stopped coming to see you. (*tenderly*) Now it seems stupid. Now that we're here.

They embrace. There is a pause.

Barbara It's so strange. Everywhere you go you hear people saying 'Oh I loved this country.' That's what they say. They usually say it just as they're leaving. 'Oh I loved this country so much . . .' I realized when I was in the bank one evening. This was . . . oh some time ago. I tried to say something affectionate to Quoc. Well, that's what you're left with. Gestures of affection. Which you then find mean nothing at all.

Chesneau (*moved*) Barbara, please . . .

But she at once moves past him, leaving the room.

Barbara Put me on a helicopter!

Chesneau Barbara . . .

Barbara Shut up! Put me on!

*She leaves the room. A silence. Chesneau, left alone,
stunned by this sudden change.*

*We cut to Barbara in the bathroom. She is putting her
toilet things into a sponge bag. Chesneau appears
behind her at the door.*

Chesneau What will you do? Will you go back to
England?

Barbara My mother.

Chesneau May I come and see you there?

*She turns and looks at him as if the idea were self-
evidently absurd. Then she quietly tips the cosmetics
into the sink and leaves them behind.*

Barbara I think let's leave the place to be looted. Don't
you think so? (*She goes from the bathroom. She goes from
the main room, leaving her bag behind on the floor.*)

Chesneau Sure, if you want.

91. EXT. STREET. DAY
*Chesneau comes quickly down the stairs carrying
Barbara's luggage urgently now to the car. As he puts it
down he looks up into the sky, and we cut to the
helicopters arriving overhead. Marine helicopters are now
flying overhead into the city. Chesneau and Barbara drive
together through the streets. As they pass along a shopping
street, they see the old South Vietnamese flags being pulled
down, and the flags of the new regime being put up.*

*As their car draws closer to the Embassy, they overtake
straggling lines of Americans who are walking with their
suitcases down the road towards the compound.*

92. INT. CAR. DAY
*Inside the car the radio is playing 'White Christmas' as
Barbara watches the stragglers in the street.*

Barbara Look! Coming in on signal . . .

Chesneau smiles. The crowd begins to thicken as they approach the Embassy. They pass burning and wrecked-out cars. As they get near the gate they see a huge crowd. Barbara points to the thickest part.

Look! Over there!

93. EXT. EMBASSY GATE. DAY
Outside the Embassy in the huge crowd, Haliwell is desperately trying to push his way through. He is carrying a suitcase, lost in a hostile crowd.

Haliwell English! English! Please I'm English! English! Please let me through!

94. INT. CAR. DAY
Barbara desperately trying to catch sight of him through the crowd. Chesneau trying to edge the car towards him through the crowd, who are now beginning to turn ugly. They bang on the roof. They hit the side of the car with their fists.

Barbara He must have got caught at the airport.

Chesneau Hold on. Let me try . . .

95. EXT. STREET. DAY
The first great helicopter hovers over the Embassy to make its way down into the compound. At once the crowd begins to push even harder, packing in a press towards the gate.

Haliwell English! English!

In the excitement he is pushed to the ground. Some random rifle shots are fired in the air. People scream. Chesneau draws alongside Haliwell.

Chesneau Quick. Get him in.

*Barbara reaches for the door and opens it, as Chesneau
stretches right across the seats and pulls Haliwell like a
beached whale into the car. He turns back to the wheel,
while Barbara closes the door.*

Haliwell My God!

Chesneau Close the door!

Barbara slams it as the car is inched towards the gates.

Haliwell Oh God, for a moment out there . . .

*He stops, checking himself. Barbara looks at him. He
tries to smile and shake his head. The gate is opened
fractionally to allow Chesneau's car into the compound.*

Chesneau Right, OK. We're getting there.

*We watch the crowd surging against the gate, the GIs
holding them back with rifles.*

Barbara For a moment you felt what it's like to be them.

96. EXT. COMPOUND. DAY
*The tremendous circular cloud of dust going up as the first
helicopter comes down with a great roar by the tree
stump. Marines jump from the helicopter with guns as it
lands. The crowd inside the compound, half white, half
Asian, gathers round to get on. The GI is shouting above
the noise.*

First GI It's all right. Everyone's going. Please. Everyone.
Just hold on.

*By the gate the far greater crowd is pressing much more
urgently to get in. A man now flings himself at the gate
in an attempt to climb over. At once a GI brings his rifle
butt crashing down on his head.*

284

We cut back to the GI inside the compound.

Everyone OK. There will be a place for you. Everyone inside is going to get on.

97. INT. CORRIDOR. DAY
Colonel Fiedler walking along the main corridor in fatigues and helmet. It is absolute chaos. The place has been ransacked as fast as possible to destroy as much equipment and papers as possible. People are running back and forth with stuff for the incinerators. The Colonel is simply opening the door of each room and shouting inside.

Fiedler All right, please, let's get on with it. Everyone out. We're all going home.

> *He comes into the communal office, now ravaged by the speed of the exit. Linda and the others are still working in helmets, piling stuff out of cabinets on to the floor.*

All women first. Hey –

> *He smiles at Linda. The mood is good-hearted.*

Out please. (*then a military joke*) Everyone, please, in orderly lines.

98. INT. PASSAGEWAY. DAY
At the end of a concrete passageway you can see teams of people, about forty in all, feeding papers into the burners in the distance. They are scorched with effort. At the front there is a Soldier hauling a bag along, single-handed. He is stopped by an Officer.

Officer Soldier, what's that?

Soldier It's two million dollars, sir.

> *The Officer looks at him.*

It's the Ambassador's emergency fund.

Officer Where's it going?

Soldier I've orders to burn it.

The Officer nods, and casually reaches into the bag, takes out a handful of dollars and stuffs them into his hand.

Officer All right, soldier. I'll see to that.

99. EXT. COMPOUND. DAY
The crowd gathered at the helicopter. We watch the Commanding Officer at work, striding round the area.

Commanding Officer OK here, please. Yeah. You here. OK, yeah.

The Marine inside the helicopter yells across.

Marine That's all we can take.

Chesneau appears at the Officer's side.

Chesneau Bill, I've two friends.

Officer Sure, put 'em on then.

Chesneau turns back. At the front of the crowd, Barbara and Haliwell are standing together.

Chesneau Barbara!

They make their way past the crowd to the helicopter. Haliwell gets on. Chesneau holds a moment with Barbara.

Good luck, OK?

As they stand looking, the Officer passes them impatiently.

Officer Come on, please.

And Chesneau steps back, yells to the helicopter.

Chesneau Goodbye, Mr Haliwell.

Barbara God, have I really got to get on to this thing?

She is muttering to herself as she makes her way. Chesneau waves to Haliwell inside.

Officer OK, everyone, please – let's lift it.

The crowd falls back.

Stand by. Everyone clear.

She is sitting opposite the open main door of the helicopter, next to Haliwell, as it begins to go up. She is wearing a panama hat. She is an old English spinster. The image rises into the air and out of the frame as we hear the voice of the Officer.

Next lot, OK? Right. Get ready. You. You and you, right? Right. Over here.

100. INT. OFFICE. DAY
Chesneau with an axe is now attacking the laminated maps on the walls of his office. They are absolutely covered with the red scrawls of the advancing army. He is making wild swings to cut the wood they are mounted on. Systematically taking his own anger out. Judd arrives, alarmed by the noise.

Judd God almighty, what the hell are you doing?

Chesneau turns smiling.

Chesneau How do you suggest I get rid of these things?

Judd If we had any sense, we'd just set fire to it, we'd burn the whole place down.

He turns hopelessly to survey the amount of paper still left in the office. Chesneau has pulled the drawer out of a filing cabinet. It is full of plastic individual name cards, several thousand. Each with a person's name on it.

Chesneau What about these? People's name plates . . .
agents who worked for us . . . (*From the drawer he also
takes duplicated foolscap sheets, all with lists of names.*)
Lists. All the people we promised to get out . . .

Ockham appears at the door.

Ockham Oh Bob, could you come?

Chesneau Yeah . . .

Ockham waves airily as he goes.

Ockham Just leave that . . .

*As he goes out the main office, Chesneau sets the drawer
full of names and lists down on a desk.*

We've got problems with helicopter sites.

*They go out. We pause a moment on the drawer
Chesneau has abandoned on the desktop.*

101. EXT. EMBASSY. DAY
*A line of people being passed hand to hand up a dangerous
chain that leads to the very top of the Embassy where a
Compound Officer then handles them into the helicopter
on top. Next to him is the Officer with two million dollars.
They shout.*

Bag Officer This doesn't look good.

Commanding Officer The ground's too dangerous.

*He points down to the compound where the crowd are
now looking up towards the roof. Around them the
gates are still besieged.*

We got frightened of killing the gooks.

*Bag Officer nods. And then he puts his hand on the
Compound Officer's shoulder, as he steps into the line*

to leave. *The Compound Officer frowns slightly at the size of his bag.*

You taking that?

Bag Officer Yeah, I have to.

The Compound Officer moves round to signal to the pilot.

Compound Officer OK. Right. Lift away.

He holds both thumbs up. In an immensely precarious movement, the Green Giant lifts off. As it does, it tilts to one side. We just catch sight of the Bag Officer, desperately grabbing at the bag as it slides across the floor. As the helicopter gains height, the bag falls. Thousands and thousands of dollars flutter out of the air.
  The crowd in the compound looks up as the money flutters down on them and into the pool.

102. INT. SCHOOL. EVENING
A Vietnamese schoolroom. Two hundred people sitting patiently on the classroom floor with their baggage, while in the headmaster's small office off the main room, an American in late middle age is sitting on the table with a telephone. We recognize him from the Tu Do bar earlier. He has a saddlebag. As he speaks he looks to the crowds, cramped and patient on the floor.

Brad Jack, it's Brad.

Ockham (*voice over*) Yeah.

Brad Brad at Forbes Chemicals.

Ockham (*voice over*) Yeah, I know who you are.

Brad I'm with my designated employees. Jack, we've been waiting six hours. (*He looks out to the playground which is cleared and empty, as if waiting for a landing.*) We're at our assembly point, but nobody's come for us. All the choppers are flying right by.

There's a slight pause at the other end.

Ockham Yeah, that's right. They're on their way to you.

Brad We've decided to make it through town. I'm going to lead them across to the Embassy . . .

Ockham (*voice over*) No, please, Brad . . .

103. INT. OCKHAM'S OFFICE. EVENING
Continuous. Ockham exhausted at his desk. His office is ravaged. The contents have been cleared by Marines who are still working to take things out. The remains of the CIA corps, who number about eight, are working around him on the phones ringing in the offices. There is a great deal of drink – a crate of Heineken at the centre of the room.

Ockham It's not a good idea.

Brad (*voice over*) But, Jack . . .

Ockham If you just hold on, we will come and get you . . .

He turns and looks at Judd who is talking on another phone.

The crowd's getting ugly, you must stay where you are.

Judd (*simultaneously*) No, they're coming, I promise you . . .

Chesneau drops a scrawled note across the desk to Judd.

Chesneau Another two hundred waiting in Cholon.

Judd sees it but does not acknowledge it. Instead he

*picks up in his other hand a phone which is ringing and,
while he talks to the first source, cuts the second phone
off by pressing down on the cradle.*

Judd It's OK. You will be collected. (*Then he drops the
newly dead line into the waste-paper basket.*) Nobody is
going to get left behind.

104. INT. BANK. NIGHT
*Quoc alone in the bank, closing the shutters with the long
pole. It is eerily dark and quiet. Then he walks back across
the deserted bank and picks up his briefcase which he puts
under his arm. Then he goes to the door and, without
looking back, goes out.*

105. INT. WASHROOM. NIGHT
*The Ambassador stands washing his hands, then dries
them carefully and walks out of the washroom into the
deserted corridor.*

106. INT. CORRIDOR. NIGHT
*He walks along the corridor and goes into his office. The
corridor is deserted.*

107. INT. OFFICE. NIGHT
*He walks through his outer office which is now unmanned
and goes into his own inner office. It is similarly deserted.
He goes to the American flag which is pinned on the wall
and now unpins it. He takes it from the wall and folds it
into the shape of a tea towel. Then he puts it in a plastic
bag which he has left on his desk. He then picks up a cable
from his desk and with the bag and the cable leaves the
room.*

108. INT. CORRIDOR. NIGHT
The corridor which only a moment ago was deserted is

*now full of the remaining staff who number twelve in all.
They have appeared while the Ambassador has been in his
office and are now waiting for him in the corridor. He is
haggard, he has flu, he looks terrible. He reads them the
cable.*

Ambassador Gentlemen. This is from the President. The
Ambassador is ordered to leave. (*He looks down.*) We are
withdrawing the American presence under orders. (*He
nods slightly and looks at them.*) Thanks very much.

109. INT. CORRIDOR. NIGHT
*The whole group seemingly driven along the corridor by
the stricken giant at their head. They keep close together
as they walk through the darkened building. Ockham and
Chesneau are at the back like straggling schoolboys who
can't keep up on the walk. They whisper furiously to one
another.*

Chesneau What's going to happen to all those people?

Ockham Bob, there's nothing . . .

Chesneau There are thousands of them still at the
assembly points. I tell you, they've been waiting all day.

Ockham We can't, there's nothing . . .

There is a strange bump and clink in their progress.

Shit.

Chesneau What's that?

Ockham Whisky bottle.

*A bottle has rolled out on to the floor from Ockham's
pocket, but they do not stop to pick it up. It is left there.*

Face it, Bob. There's nothing we can do.

110. INT. CHESNEAU'S OFFICE. NIGHT
*The group go past the open office door. We just catch
their voices as they do.*

Chesneau But Jack . . . listen . . .

  *A pause. The office ransacked, deserted. Then we adjust
  to settle in the foreground on the drawer full of agents'
  name plates, forgotten on the desk.
    We hold on that.*

111. INT. STAIRWELL. NIGHT
*At the top landing as the group all reach it, the military are
waiting already by the exit door at the top of the building
to take the Ambassador out on the last flight.
  As the group reaches the small landing, the Ambassador
turns to speak to the assembled company. He still holds
his bag.*

Ambassador Gentlemen, before I leave I would like
to . . .

  A great cry from the bottom of the stairwell.

Soldier Sir. Sir. Let's get the hell out.

  *The Ambassador shocked by the voice of the panicking
  Soldier.*

They're breaking into the Embassy.

Ambassador What?

Soldier They've heard this is going to be the last flight.

  *There is a second's indecision on the Ambassador's face,
  then suddenly he gestures at the door.*

Ambassador All right – out!

112. INT. EMBASSY. NIGHT
*At once the mad scramble is shown going on downstairs
as the two GIs on guard desperately close the main doors
to the Embassy against the crowd. Then they run across
the lobby to where a third GI is waiting holding the door
to the stairway open.*

First GI OK, for fuck's sake lock it.

*The main doors being smashed open and the crowd
pouring into the Embassy.*

113. INT. STAIRWELL. NIGHT
*At the top of the stairwell, the military and CIA scramble
desperately out of the tiny exit door on the landing out to
the waiting helicopter.*

114. INT. STAIRWELL. NIGHT
*One GI slamming the stairwell door and locking it while
the other two run for the stairs.*

115. EXT. ROOF. NIGHT
*The waiting helicopters now loaded, waiting, blades
turning. The door to the stairwell held open by the last
Officer.*

116. INT. STAIRWELL. NIGHT
*The last Soldiers running up the stairs. Reaching the top.
There are sounds of people coming up from below, but at
once the GIs open gas canisters and throw them down the
stairs at the approaching crowd. You catch a glimpse of
them scampering through the door and it closing as the
screen smokes out.*

117. EXT. STREETS. NIGHT
The streets of Saigon. Night. Quiet. Nothing moves. Eerie.

The sound of the helicopters has gone. The cathedral. The opera house. Tu Do deserted.

118. EXT. COMPOUND. NIGHT
The two hundred Vietnamese and Brad in the school compound, waiting, scanning the empty sky.

119. EXT. STREETS. NIGHT
A side street. Round the corner, jogging in a small group, come eight soldiers in formation. They are in army uniform, with guns, in full battledress. As they turn into the street, the group suddenly breaks up and they stop. They put down their guns, and start to undress. They put down their boots, guns, clothes, in small heaps on the pavement. They stand a moment in their boxer shorts. Then turn, as casually as they can, and disappear down the street. The little puddles of clothes left behind them.

120. INT. HELICOPTER. NIGHT
Inside the helicopter the group has settled, cheerful. A false exhilaration. Chesneau is sitting next to Judd, on one side. Suddenly he remembers.

Chesneau Shit.

Judd What?

Chesneau I've remembered . . .

Judd puzzled.

Judd What?

Chesneau looks down, appalled, disturbed. Avoids the question.

Chesneau Something.

Judd (*a joke*) Do you want to go back?

Chesneau turns, looks back, the truth dawning on him of what he has done.

Chesneau (*under his breath*) God forgive us.

Suddenly the Pilot turns and yells back from the controls, as a can of Heineken is opened in front of him.

Pilot Hey, you guys. We're all going home!

Fast fade.

THE BAY AT NICE

For Blair

Characters

Valentina Nrovka
Sophia Yepileva
Assistant Curator
Peter Linitsky

The Bay at Nice was first performed at the Cottesloe Theatre, London, on 4 September 1986. The cast was as follows:

Valentina Nrovka Irene Worth
Sophia Yepileva Zoë Wanamaker
Assistant Curator Colin Stinton
Peter Linitsky Philip Locke

Designed by John Gunter
Lighting by Rory Dempster
Directed by David Hare

The scene is set in Leningrad, 1956.

A large room with a gilt ceiling and a beautiful parquet floor. At the back hangs Guérin's huge oil painting of 'Iris and Morpheus', a triumphant nude sitting on a cloud over the body of the King of Sleep. The room is airy and decaying. It is almost empty but for some tables pushed to the back and some gilt and red plush hard chairs. Sitting on one of these is Valentina Nrovka. She is a lively woman, probably in her sixties but it's hard to tell. She is dressed in black. Her daughter Sophia is standing right at the far end of the room looking out of the main door. She is in her early thirties, much more plainly dressed in a coat and pullover and plain skirt.

Valentina You don't want to leave an old woman.

Sophia You're not old.

   Valentina looks round disapprovingly.

Valentina This graveyard! I'm not going to speak to all those old idiots.

Sophia They expect it.

Valentina Nonsense! I'll sit by myself.

   Sophia is still looking anxiously out of the door.

Sophia I'm afraid we've offended the Curator.

Valentina Don't say *we*. I offended him. He was shabbily dressed.

Sophia He wanted you to see the new extension.

Valentina What for? He insults the walls by hanging them with all that socialist realism. Whirlpools of mud. I'd rather look at bare walls. At least they are cleanly painted. I'm tired of looking anyway. 'Look, look . . .' (*She smiles, anticipating her own story.*) Picasso lived in a house so ugly – a great champagne millionaire's Gothic mansion with turrets – that all his friends said 'My God, how can you abide such a place?' He said, 'You are all prisoners of taste. Great artists love everything. There is no such thing as ugliness.' He would kick the walls with his little sandalled foot and say, 'They're solid. What more do you want?'

Sophia By that argument, if everything's beautiful, then that includes socialist realism.

Valentina Please. You know nothing of such things. Don't speak of them. Especially in front of other people. It's embarrassing. (*Valentina has got up from her seat and is walking to the other side of the room.*) What rubbish do they want me to look at?

Sophia They think they have a Matisse.

There is a silence. Valentina shows no apparent reaction.

Valentina You haven't been to see me.

Sophia No. I've been busy.

Valentina Ah well.

Sophia The work has been very hard. And the children. At the end of the day I'm too tired to do anything. I've said to my employers, as a woman I resent it.

Valentina 'As a woman'?

Sophia Yes.

Valentina What does that mean?

Sophia Well . . .

Valentina This fashion for calling people women. Now always 'as a *woman*', they say. It was so much more fun when I was young and you could just be a person. Now everyone speaks 'on behalf'. 'On behalf of Soviet women . . .'

Sophia I only meant that I have a family. I also have a job. That's all. And at the school I am taken advantage of.

Valentina They take you for a fool. They know you can never say no.

Sophia is looking across at her back, trying to judge her mood.

Sophia Who visits you?

Valentina No one. The Troyanofskis of course. They are terrible people. Madam Troyanofski wants to start a salon. I've told her it's too late. All the artists are dead. The poets are moaners. And the playwrights are worse. Because they're exhausting. People run round the stage. It tires me. In their stories the minute hand is going round like crazy. But the hour hand never turns at all. (*She smiles.*) 'Ah well,' she said, 'if there are no artists worth asking, we can always talk philosophy.' No thank you!

Sophia She likes ideas.

Valentina Yes, well, they're Jews. (*She shrugs.*) Tell me, who do you think I should be seeing? Name anyone in Leningrad who's worth an hour. A full hour.

Sophia Well, of course I enjoy everybody's company. I find something good or interesting in everyone.

Valentina looks at her mistrustfully.

Valentina Yes?

Sophia Shall I get you something to drink?

Valentina Where is this man?

Sophia You frightened him.

Valentina What? So much he's thinking of not showing me the painting?

Sophia I'll go and see.

Valentina No, stay. I want to talk to you.

Sophia stays, but Valentina makes no effort to talk.

Sophia The twins both asked me to send you their love.

Valentina How old are they?

Sophia Eight.

Valentina Then plainly you're lying. No eight-year-old asks after adults. Or if they do, they're faking. Why should your children fake?

Sophia I said I would be seeing you and I suggested . . .

Valentina Ah well, yes.

Sophia . . . they send you their love.

Valentina Now we get the truth of it. Their love was solicited. Like a confession.

Sophia If you insist.

Valentina And Grigor . . . what?

Sophia Grigor is working. He would be here today.

Valentina But?

Sophia But he is working. And he's not interested in art.

Valentina No.

There is a pause. Sophia looks away, as if anxious to say more, but not daring.

Where is the painting?

Sophia They're getting it now. It's in a vault at the bottom of the building.

Valentina Have you seen it?

Sophia Not yet.

Valentina What does it show?

Sophia A window. The sea. A piece of wall.

Valentina It sounds like a forgery.

Sophia They think you will be able to tell.

Valentina How can I tell? I don't know everything he painted. Nobody does. He got up every morning. He set up his easel and he started to paint. If at midday he was pleased, then he signed it. If not, then he threw it away and began fresh the next morning. It was said, like a dandy who throws white ties into the laundry basket until he ties one which pleases him. (*She smiles.*) Matisse was profligate.

Sophia So there may be lost work?

Valentina Well, of course. (*She turns away, contemptuously.*) And if there is, what will happen to it? They will put it on the walls of this hideous building. And the state will boast that they own it. And people will gawp at it and say 'What does it mean?' Or 'Well, I don't like it.' I am told that in the West now people only look at paintings when they are holding cubes of cheese on the end of toothpicks. To me, that says everything of what art has become. (*She smiles.*) Yes, indeed, I sympathize with Grigor. Why be interested in all this gossip and hoopla?

Sophia No, you're wrong. It is painting itself which Grigor dislikes.

Valentina Because you paint?

Sophia looks at her angrily.

Sophia I shall look for the Curator.

Valentina I have heard all these rumours. Even I. Who have no contact with life except through the Troyanofskis. They are my inadequate means of access to what is happening in the world. Through them everything is admittedly made mean. And yet. I have heard of your behaviour with Grigor.

Sophia Mother, I don't want to speak about it now.

Valentina Why?

Sophia You will learn in a moment. Soon I shall talk to you.

Valentina When?

Sophia When I have your whole attention.

Valentina Are you choosing your moment?

Sophia No.

Valentina It sums you up. You think everything is a matter of mood.

Sophia I know you better than that.

Valentina You think attitudes are all to do with whim. You understand nothing. Attitudes are all to do with character.

Sophia Please don't lecture me. (*She is turning red with the effort of having to say this.*) If we are to speak we must speak as equals.

Valentina is looking across at her with sudden kindness and love.

Valentina Little Sophia, you've used up all your courage already. Come here and tell me what's going on.

Sophia, trembling, doesn't move as Valentina opens her arms to her.

Sophia No, I won't come. I mustn't. I'm determined to be strong with you.

Valentina You've come to make a speech?

Sophia Well, yes.

Valentina Well, make it.

Sophia What, now?

Valentina Yes.

There is an agonizing pause.

Sophia No, I can't.

Valentina Why not?

Sophia Because I have rehearsed but now I'm frightened. I've said these things to no one.

Valentina And yet everyone knows.

Sophia does not move.

Sophia I work. I am sober. I am honest. All day at that school. As you say, always extra duty. I stay long after class. Then I go and stand in line in the shops. I look after the children. I offend no one. And yet if I even have a thought – a *thought* even – it's a crime. Everyone is waiting. Everyone stands ready to condemn me. (*She turns and suddenly rushes to the far side of the room.*) No, it's too cruel.

She is overwhelmed. She stands facing away from the room. Her mother does not turn. Then in the silence the Assistant Curator comes in carrying a canvas which is facing towards him. He is in his mid-thirties. He wears a blue suit. He is nervous.

Assistant The painting is here.

Valentina Where?

Assistant I have it. Madame Nrovka. (*He holds it out, a little puzzled, from the far side of the room.*)

Valentina Put it down.

Assistant Where?

Valentina Well, over there.

She gestures at a distant chair. He leans it on the chair, face turned away.

Assistant Will you view it?

Valentina I will look at it later. I'm talking to my daughter.

Sophia Forgive me. I'm appallingly rude. (*She wakes up to his embarrassment and walks over to shake his hand.*) I'm Sophia Yepileva.

Assistant I'm the Assistant Curator.

Valentina No doubt your boss has sent you. He is too frightened himself.

Assistant I'm sorry?

Valentina If he is frightened, why did he ask me? Why do you need me? Surely you have experts?

Assistant We do. Of all kinds.

Valentina What do they say?

Assistant There is a slight problem. (*He looks nervously to Sophia, as if not liking them both to be there.*) How shall I put it? There are shades of a dispute. The scientific experts are used to handling *older* paintings.

Valentina Yes, of course.

Assistant We know a great deal about pigment chronology. We have radio carbon. We have X-ray crystallography. We have wet chemistry. All these are invaluable if the painting is old enough. Because dating is what usually gives the forger away.

Valentina But Matisse is too recent.

Assistant That's right. (*He smiles, nervous again.*) That is what we – who help run the museum – we are saying this to the scientists, you see. Who do not work for us. They work for the Ministry.

Valentina Ah, well.

There is a pause as the Assistant appreciates she has understood the problem, then he hurries on.

Assistant Their work is very useful. It is respected. Within certain limits. They have proved that if the canvas was forged, it was forged some time ago. Almost certainly in France. They can establish that. Where and when. That is useful work. But it does – in this case – we believe – stop short of *who*.

Valentina Which you mean is much more a matter of taste.

Assistant Oh no . . . not entirely . . . (*He smiles reassuringly at her.*) There is circumstantial evidence. We can guess at motive. We are very suspicious. Obviously. Because Matisse is so recently dead. Only two years ago. If someone were trying – what? – to test the water, this would be an ideal moment. A forger usually offers a cycle of work.

Valentina This would be the first.

Assistant Exactly. (*He looks to Sophia.*) Forgers usually can't resist. Once they have acquired a style, they're reluctant to let go of it.

Valentina No different from painters. Except the very greatest.

Assistant Vrain Lucas forged manuscripts in the hands of Julius Caesar, the Apostle Paul and Joan of Arc. A bewildering diversity. But mercifully for us, exceptional.

Valentina And what about the art critics?

Assistant Yes, a couple have also had a look.

Valentina Well?

The Assistant looks hopelessly.

Assistant Adjectives are so subjective, isn't that the problem? 'Over-decorative'. 'Too plastic', they say. 'Too cold'. 'Not fluid'. They mean one thing to one man, something quite different to another. (*He pauses a moment.*) So we thought to ask someone who knew the man himself.

Valentina shrugs this off.

Valentina Surely many people knew him. He even visited this museum, I think.

Assistant I gather, yes. We were honoured. Some time before the war.

Valentina So?

Assistant It was felt you understand his spirit.

312

Valentina The experts concede that?

Assistant Well, no, actually . . .

Valentina smiles, her judgement confirmed.

Professor Satayev expressly forbade your being asked. He was against it. He has authenticated the painting, he insists. By scientific methods.

Valentina (*ironically*) Well then?

Assistant But if he were wrong it would be a major embarrassment.

Valentina For whom?

There is a slight pause.

For whom?

The Assistant looks nervously to Sophia.

You mean for the authorities?

Assistant Well, perhaps. Yes. For everyone.

Valentina So the white witch is called in.

She smiles. Sophia looks uneasily at the Assistant.

Assistant As you know, Matisse himself was fanatic. In his own lifetime. He would always go round to check the work being sold under his name. By an irony the letters of authentication he then wrote are in themselves incredibly valuable. They change hands at three thousand roubles. One or two, we think, have already been forged. (*He smiles.*) The whole business is way out of hand.

Valentina He would be appalled.

Sophia (*frowns*) How do you decide? Finally?

Assistant There are tests. But these are all negative by nature. They tell you if it cannot be Matisse. Dating, pigment, brushwork, so on. If the negative tests are all passed you are forced to conclude the work must be real. The absence of disproof is finally proof. No one ever says 'Oh yes, this is his . . .' Except . . . (*He pauses.*)

Sophia When?

Assistant Except when there's someone. I don't know . . . when there's someone who knew him quite well.

There is a pause. Valentina seems uninterested, with thoughts of her own.

Sophia I see.

Valentina My daughter is a painter.

Assistant Oh really? I'm afraid I don't know your work.

Sophia My mother is exaggerating. I'm an amateur only.

Valentina She tried to paint the sun.

Sophia Yes, Mother.

Valentina The sun can't be painted. Cézanne said, it can be represented but it can't be reproduced. She tries to prove Cézanne wrong.

Sophia Yes, Mother, but I do it for pleasure.

Valentina Pleasure!

Sophia Yes. I sketch for myself. Not to be in competition with great artists. You think we all want to be Cézanne. Why?

Valentina You should want to be Cézanne. Or else why paint?

Sophia For enjoyment.

Valentina That's nonsense. Painting must be learnt. Like

314

any other discipline. Why go in with no sense of what others have achieved?

Sophia I don't think like that. To me, that's not the point of it.

Valentina Then what is the point of it?

Sophia I paint simply in order . . . (*She stops. Then rather feebly, as if knowing how lame it sounds*) . . . to show what is there.

   Valentina gestures, her case proved.

Valentina That is why she can never be good. What you do is called photography. They said of Picasso that he couldn't paint a tree. They were wrong. He was painting trees when he was eight. It quickly came to bore him. He had no interest in trees after that. But he could paint the feeling you had when you looked at a tree. And that is more valuable. Painting is ultimately to do with the quality of feeling. That is why you will never be able to paint.

   The Assistant looks between the two women, embarrassed. But Sophia seems unfazed.

Sophia (*quietly*) I don't know.

Assistant I can't tell. I'm an Academician. My heart is in the catalogue.

Sophia Ah, yes.

Assistant Matisse is a dauntingly complex subject. To be honest, I haven't lately looked at his paintings. I like them. I love them, in fact.

Sophia Well then, marry them.

Assistant What?

Sophia No, it's just . . .

Sophia is smiling. So is Valentina. A joke shared.

It's what my son says. I have twins. When my daughter's eating, say, chocolate cake, when she says 'I love this cake' . . . 'Well then, marry it.' That's what my son says.

There's a pause. The Assistant seems bewildered, the women both amused.

Assistant If . . .

Valentina What . . .

Assistant No . . .

Sophia I'm sorry.

Assistant No, if . . .

Sophia I'm just being silly.

Valentina To get back to the subject.

Assistant Yes.

Valentina Where was this found?

The Assistant looks anxiously between them.

Assistant It belongs to a Count. A Tsarist.

Valentina I see.

Assistant He left his home in 1919. He went to live in the South of France. He claims the canvas had been discarded in Matisse's hotel.

Valentina In Nice?

Assistant Yes. In the Hotel de la Méditerranée. He was a friend of the manager's. The painting had been literally thrown out. I know it's hard to believe.

Valentina I don't think so.

Assistant He never had it catalogued or valued because of the irregular way in which it was acquired. He was frightened his ownership would then be challenged.

Valentina And how do you come to have it?

Assistant It's a bequest. The Count died earlier this year. In fact of a disease which has hitherto been diagnosed only in horses. A kind of horse flu, it turned out. The doctors thought he was medically unique.

Valentina My goodness.

Assistant I mean, he raced a great deal. That's what he did in France all the time . . . all the time the rest of us were here. So to speak. The Count bred horses in the Midi.

There is a pause.

Valentina I see.

Assistant The puzzling thing of course is, since he fled Russia, why he chose to leave us a painting of such value in his will.

Valentina That puzzles you?

Assistant Yes. Not you?

Valentina No. (*She is suddenly very quiet.*) You've not lived abroad.

Assistant Well, no . . .

Valentina I was some time in Paris. Oh, many years ago. Before the revolution.

Assistant Yes, I know.

Valentina It can pall. Being away. Believe me.

Assistant Yes, I'm sure.

Valentina We must all make our peace.

Assistant You mean the Count has made his? By an act of generosity?

Sophia Yes. Or else he's sold you a pup.

The women smile. The Assistant looks discomfited.

Valentina Well, that's right.

Sophia I don't understand the legal position. If the Count stole it.

Assistant 'Stole'? I wouldn't say 'stole'.

Sophia Picked it up.

Assistant He acquired it.

Sophia Legitimately?

Assistant Oh, well, really . . . (*He suddenly becomes expansive.*) Apart from anything, so much time has gone by. All art is loot. Who should own it? I shouldn't say this, but there isn't much justice in these things. If we examined the process whereby everything on these walls was acquired . . . we should have bare walls.

Sophia My mother was just saying how much she would prefer that.

Valentina Come, what does it show?

The Assistant makes as if to go and pick it up.

No, tell me.

Assistant Well, it's like a sketch – I'm not speaking technically . . .

Valentina No, I understand.

Assistant I mean a kind of dry-run. For everything that follows. Except the foreground is bare. There is no woman. There is no violin. There is no chair. (*He shrugs.*)

There is just a wall. A pair of curtains. Wallpaper. Open windows. The sea. (*There is a sudden silence. Then he shrugs again.*) It is either a copy. Or a beginning.

Valentina Yes. (*She pauses a moment, then she speaks with great finality, as if finishing a poem.*) He did them. Then he threw them away. (*She gets up from her chair and walks to the far side of the room, where she addresses the Assistant.*) You may bring me some tea.

Assistant Well, I will. I shall leave you some time with the painting. Alone.

He looks a moment to Sophia who does not move.

I am very grateful. And the Curator, I think, would be grateful too for your subsequent discretion. Our scientists must not be upset.

The Assistant smiles and goes out. The women do not move.

Valentina He's a weak man.

Sophia Yes.

Valentina He doesn't give a fig about painting.

Sophia Do you need time?

Valentina turns and looks her straight in the eye, level. Then she turns away.

Valentina No. I already know.

There is a pause. Valentina deep in thought, Sophia watching her.

Make your speech.

Sophia What?

Valentina I am ready.

Sophia Now?

Valentina Yes. Isn't that why you're here?

Sophia No. I wanted to come with you. I was interested.

Valentina You want to leave Grigor.

Sophia hesitates a moment.

Sophia How do you know?

Valentina You've wanted to leave since the moment you were married.

Sophia That's not true.

Valentina What else could it be? But now I can see you are hardening. You have the will. It's there. I sense it in you. You have become determined.

Sophia First I want to talk to you.

Valentina Don't lie. Please don't lie. I can tell you've made up your mind. Haven't you?

Sophia does not answer.

Sophia, please. Talk to me properly.

Sophia Yes.

There's a pause. Valentina is very quiet.

Valentina Then I am sure you've met another man.

Sophia looks down.

Sophia Yes.

Valentina You're in love.

Sophia I think less and less of love. What does love have to do with it? What matters is not love, but what the other person makes you. (*Sophia turns and walks away to the* *far side of the room.*) When I stand next to Grigor, it's clear, he is a dutiful man. He's a model servant of the State. Next to him, I look only like a fortunate woman who must struggle every day to deserve the luck she's had in marrying someone so worthwhile. That is my role. In marriages everyone gets cast. The strong one, the weak. The quick one, the slow. The steady, the giddy. It's set. Almost from the moment you meet. You don't notice it, you take it for granted, you think you're just *you*. Fixed, unchangeable. But you're not. You're what you've been cast as with the other person. And it's all got nothing to do with who you really are.

Valentina Nothing?

Sophia With Grigor, I'm dowdy, I'm scatterbrained. I'm trying to prove myself. All the standards are his. Grigor, of course, has nothing to prove. He's a headmaster at thirty-seven, the Party approves of him. He can always find his shirts in the drawer. I usually can. But Usually is no good next to Always. 'Usually' becomes a great effort of will. All I can do . . . no, all I can *be* is an inadequate, minor commentary on Grigor's far more finished character. Grigor and Sophia. After ten years we each have our part. Whereas when I'm with . . . this other man . . . then suddenly I'm quite someone else.

There is a pause.

Valentina He is a less good man, I assume from what you're saying . . .

Sophia Oh no, it's not as easy as that.

Valentina He is less of a challenge, is that right?

Sophia No!

Valentina You've found yourself a mediocrity, so you suffer less by comparison. Is that what you mean?

Sophia Not at all.

Valentina Well, is it? (*She asks this with sudden emphasis. She waits, then getting no reply, laughs.*) What does he do, this other person with no name?

Sophia He works for the Sanitation Board.

Valentina Well, exactly!

Sophia is pointing at her, bright red with anger.

Sophia Mother, if you prevent me, I will never forgive you.

Valentina Me? What can I do?

Sophia Withhold your approval.

Valentina My approval?

Sophia Yes.

Valentina From an empty room you never visit?

Sophia I visit you.

Valentina You visit occasionally. Would you really miss that?

Sophia is exasperated.

Sophia You don't even like Grigor.

Valentina Well . . .

Sophia It's true. You never did. From the start. You said he was a prig.

Valentina What do I matter? It's not me you have to fear. If you don't know by now, you must face your own conscience. Your children.

Sophia Do you think I've not thought of them? Mother, it's hard. But I have the right to live my own life.

Valentina turns away, smiling.

Valentina Oh, rights.

Sophia No doubt by will . . . by some great effort of will our marriage may be saved. By will, we may grow old together. But I remember once you said to me: nothing's worth having by will.

Valentina Did I say that?

Sophia looks at her, then moves away, shaking her head.

Sophia And anyway, it's wrong. There's a principle.

Valentina Oh, really?

Sophia Yes.

Valentina You still believe in that?

Sophia Of course. What do you mean? In their private life, a person must be free to live as they choose.

Valentina raises her eyebrows.

Valentina My goodness me, your principles are convenient. You call that an ideal?

Sophia Forgive me but I'm afraid . . . yes, well I do.

Valentina How convenient. Goodness. An ideal. Which also coincides with what you want. How perfect. What perfect luck. Run off with this man. Call it 'living my own life'. 'I must be myself, I must do what I want . . .' (*She smiles.*) I have heard these words before. On boulevards. In cafés. I used to hear them in Paris. I associate them with zinc tables and the gushing of beer. Everyone talking about their entitlements. 'I must be allowed to realize myself.' For me, it had a different name. I never called it principle. I called it selfishness.

Sophia How can you say that to me?

Valentina Oh yes. Men – your father's friends – used these very same words. Many times. When I was pregnant they said 'Get rid of it. You must live your own life. A child will burden you. You have a right to be happy. Get on with your painting, and realize yourself.' You owe your very existence to the fact I did not choose to live my own life.

Sophia Yes, but that's different . . .

Valentina No, not at all. It's what's involved in facing up to being an adult. Sacrifice and discipline and giving yourself to others, not always thinking of yourself, and sometimes . . . yes . . . being harsh. As I am being harsh . . .

Sophia Oh, how you love that harshness. Nothing can ever be harsh enough for you.

Valentina turns away, but Sophia does not relent.

Well, that's not my fault. It's your fault. You like responsibility? I give it you. It was your fault. It was your life you ruined. You did it. All by yourself. Without consultation. (*She turns away.*) Well, I'm not going to let you now ruin mine.

Standing at the open door of the room now is Peter Linitsky. He is in his mid-sixties, he is bald, he has an unremarkable blue overcoat and carries his hat in his hand. His manner is apologetic.

Peter Excuse me.

Sophia Oh God.

Peter Am I interrupting?

Sophia No, no, come in.

Valentina Please go away. Who is this?

Sophia It's him.

Valentina What do you mean?

Valentina is genuinely taken aback by Peter's age and his appearance.

Sophia It's Peter.

Valentina Peter?

Sophia Yes, Peter, for God's sake. Wake up, Mother. The man with no name.

Valentina It's him?

Sophia Yes.

Peter What?

Sophia Yes. Goodness. How many times?

Peter What do you mean, no name?

Sophia Forget it.

Valentina Are you with the Sanitation Board?

Peter Well, I . . .

Sophia Leave it. You know he is. Don't answer, Peter.

Peter I didn't get the chance.

Sophia Don't play her game. She contrives to make the words sound like an insult.

Peter If you . . .

Valentina What words?

Sophia Sanitation Board.

Valentina Did I?

Sophia suddenly turns to her mother with surprising force.

Sophia Down here below you, people are forced to be ridiculous. Yes. We lead ridiculous lives. Doing ridiculous things, which lack taste. Like working for a living. For organizations which have ridiculous names. 'Oh, I'm from the Department of Highway Cleansing.' 'Oh, I'm Vegetation Officer in Minsk.' That's work. It's called making a living, Mother, it involves silly names and unspeakable people – the mathematics teacher, for me to work beside her, to have lunch, to watch her pick her dirty grey hair from the soup, it's torture, I'd rather lodge beside an open drain. But that's how people live. We have to. We scrabble about in the real world. Because we don't sit thinking all day about art.

Valentina turns bitterly to Peter.

Valentina Is she like this with you?

Sophia Don't answer.

Valentina Peter?

Peter Like what?

Valentina Self-righteous.

Peter Er, no.

Sophia Would you two like to be introduced?

Valentina Not specially.

Peter Good afternoon.

Sophia His name is Peter Linitsky. My mother.

Peter At last.

Valentina I feel I already know you. Do you have a wife?

Sophia Say nothing.

Peter I did.

There is a pause. Finally Peter feels compelled to fill it in.

She is an extraordinary woman.

Valentina I'm sure. Now you're rid of her. Leningrad is full of ageing men praising their wives. Whom they have invariably left. If you hear a man praise his wife in Russia, it means they are no longer together.

Sophia Peter left six years ago.

Valentina Peter left?

Peter No, seven.

Valentina Oh, seven is one better, of course. Don't miss one. Each one counts. Doesn't each one make it more respectable?

Peter I have a divorce.

Valentina Well done. It's hard.

Sophia Divorce is possible.

Valentina Yes.

There is a pause. Nobody moves.

Sophia Mother, it's possible.

Valentina Yes.

Valentina looks at her a moment, with the calm of someone who suddenly knows they have an unanswerable argument.

Peter, I know nothing about you. For all I know, you're a kind and decent man. I'm sure you managed a divorce. But I am sure . . . I would stake my life . . . you are not in the Party.

There is a silence.

Peter No.

*Valentina nods very slightly, acknowledging the
admission. Sophia looks between them. Quietly:*

Sophia Mother, neither am I.

Valentina looks at her steadily.

I have already written to the paper. To place an
advertisement.

Valentina Does Grigor know?

Sophia No.

Valentina It means nothing. When did you write?

She doesn't answer.

Peter She wrote a week ago.

Valentina How long will it take?

Peter The waiting-list is nine months, to get your item in.
At the moment. Some people have waited a year.

Valentina Nine months for the advertisement?

Peter That's right. Unless . . .

Valentina What?

Sophia (*finishing for him*) . . . it can be brought forward.

Valentina What? Are you thinking of moving out of
Leningrad?

Peter and Sophia look at one another.

Sophia No . . .

Peter We . . .

Sophia No, there are towns, we know of towns . . . not
far away . . . where the queue is not so long for the local

paper. And the papers there give more space. A month.
Two months. But you must prove residency. You must
room there. And . . . there's no question . . . Peter can't
leave his job.

Peter (*smiles*) No money.

Sophia And I can't leave mine. I can't take the children.

Valentina Well, here they won't print it. They will ask
Grigor first.

Sophia That's not the law.

Valentina They will ask him. He won't agree to
publication. Let alone to all the Court procedures which
follow.

Sophia It doesn't matter. I still have the right.

Valentina suddenly gets angry.

Valentina Don't use that word. You have the *right*? What
does it mean? It doesn't mean anything. Be a person. Do
what you have to. Don't prattle about rights.

Sophia looks to Peter for support.

Sophia Mother, there are ways. It can be speeded.

Valentina I've never heard of it.

Sophia If you spoke to Grigor.

Valentina If *I* spoke?

Sophia Yes.

Valentina Is this what you came here to ask me?

Sophia If you said you'd seen me . . . and you knew how
deeply I felt. You know what the legal criterion is for
divorce? It's quite simple. The criterion for divorce is
necessity.

There is a pause.

Mother, I need to be free.

Valentina smiles. Lightly:

Valentina Grigor's not free. You're not free. Child, you've lived thirty-six years. How can you be so naïve?

Sophia Is it naïve?

Valentina Of course. There's no freedom.

Sophia Oh, really? That's not what I've heard.

Valentina Where? Where do you think there is freedom?

Sophia Well, I've always heard . . . from what you say of Paris . . .

Valentina Don't be ridiculous.

Sophia Your life there.

Valentina I was seventeen!

Sophia With . . . how many lovers? My mother always told me . . . (*She turns to Peter.*)

Peter Goodness.

Sophia While she was meant to be learning to draw.

Valentina That was Paris. (*She pauses, as if protecting a memory.*) Paris was different.

Sophia Oh, I see. And is Paris the only place where people may be happy? (*She waits a moment. Then quietly*) Or is it just you who wants it that way?

There is a silence. Sophia waits. But Valentina just seems amused.

Valentina I see. And you think freedom is happiness, do you?

Sophia doesn't answer.

You think it's the same thing? Do you, Peter?

Peter Well I . . . I don't know. I'm pressed to make a living. Half goes to my ex-wife. My children are grown-up. They work in a factory making bottles. One's doing quite well. The other was born a bit slow. So I am always thinking of him. Most days. Most hours. (*He smiles thinly.*) I'm not an expert on freedom.

Valentina Yes, well, you're wiser than her.

Peter looks a little nervously to Sophia.

Peter I only know I've not had much luck in things. I find myself nearly sixty-three. And . . . never really had the chance to take a risk in my life. What else is there now for me but Sophia? I don't mean it unkindly but . . . well, I live alone, I have a room, I'm a great lover of walking, I meet in the park with other model aircraft collectors . . .

Sophia His aircraft are beautiful.

Peter No, they're . . . quite average. But without Sophia I might as well die. (*He takes another look at her.*)

Valentina You didn't think that before?

Peter What do you mean?

Valentina Before you met her?

Peter No. I mean, no. Hardly. How could I? But I think it now.

Valentina Well, that's love for you, isn't it? Before you met her you were happy.

Peter Not happy, no.

Valentina But not 'Oh, I'll die'. (*She suddenly raises her voice.*) You're Stravinsky's grandfather.

331

Peter I don't understand.

Valentina Stravinsky's grandfather died trying to scale the garden fence on his way to an assignation with his mistress. He was a hundred and eleven years old at the time.

Peter smiles. Valentina laughs. Only Sophia is not amused.

Sophia Don't say that of Peter.

Valentina And what . . . what anyway . . . (*She moves suddenly and decisively on to the attack.*) What if you succeeded? What if she uses you to get her a divorce?

Sophia I'm not doing that.

Valentina What then?

Peter What do you mean?

Valentina Love is pain. Am I right?

He looks mistrustfully, fearing a trap.

Peter Not entirely.

Valentina Look at you now. You're in torture. You shift from one foot to another . . .

Peter Well, I . . .

Valentina You're forever taking sidelong glances at her, checking up on her, seeing she approves of everything you say. Thinking all the time, how does this go down with Sophia? In fiction it makes me laugh when books end with two people coming together. Curtain! At last they fall into one another's arms! The reader applauds. But that's where books should really begin. (*She smiles.*) This fantasy that love solves problems! Love makes you raw. It strips the skin from you. Am I right?

Peter In part.

Valentina Suddenly everything has to matter so much.
Really, who cares? Suddenly to be aware, to be prey to
every exaggerated detail, every nuance of someone else's
feelings. How demeaning! What possible point? And then
what? What in the future? What will you do? Spend two
years in the courts? Two years of little sidelong glances,
and oh, is it all right? Is she weakening? Do I love her?
Does she love me? And at the end, what? You'll suddenly
realize – not a plateau. Oh no. Not safety. Not if it's love.
Really love. Just as likely agony. Oh yes. A pure gambler's
throw. And for this? For *this*? Chuck out everything.
Husband. Jobs. Children. Grigor. Yes. Destroy Grigor's
life. For a bet placed by two shivering tramps at the
racetrack. (*She leans forward.*) And there's nothing
guaranteed at the end. (*She gets up, her case proved.*)
People should stick. They should stick with what they
have. With what they know. That's character.

Sophia You think so?

Valentina Certainly. But these days people just can't wait
to give up.

> *Sophia smiles, as if not threatened by any of this.*

You make such a fuss about everything. I just get on with
it. I know what life is. And what it cannot be.

> *Peter is puzzled by Sophia's calm. Now Valentina*
> *insults him aimlessly, with no real feeling.*

You're a silly bald man. You're old and you're bald. Your
shirt is too young for you. Your trousers are absurd. Is
there anything worse than men who can't grow old with
dignity? (*She sits at the side of the room, the storm blown
out.*) I was promised tea. (*She suddenly shouts, as if she
can't think of anything else to say.*) They promised me tea.

Peter I will get it for you.

Sophia No. Let me go.

She smiles and goes out. Peter is left standing near the canvas, Valentina sitting.

Valentina She's a good girl. There's no harm in her. She's just weak. And talentless. Her father was a soldier. I knew him three weeks. He claimed there was a war. What did I know? He said his battalion had to move. Perhaps it was true. I never saw his battalion. He said the French had a war to go to in Abyssinia. I've never checked. Was there such a thing?

Peter I've never heard of it.

Valentina There's no way to tell.

Peter This was in Paris?

Valentina Yes. Paris and Leningrad. It's all I've known.

Peter waits a moment.

Peter You must have met everyone. I mean, the famous.

Valentina Certainly not. It wasn't like that. I had no interest. I once was asked to a party to meet Ford Madox Ford.

Peter There you are.

Valentina Him I had heard of. Because they said he was the least frequently washed of all modern novelists. So I didn't go. (*She shakes her head.*) People get it wrong. They have no idea of it. Remember, we were poor. We had no ambitions for ourselves. At school we were a strange group. All penniless. Hungarians, a Chinese, some Americans. Well, Americans have money, but no one else. One boy wanted to pose in the life class. He was one of us. He needed to make money. He said 'Well, why not?' All

334

day we looked at naked people. Men, women. 'You're not embarrassed,' he said, 'people come in, take their clothes off. It's fine. Why not me? Why not give me the money?' But we all had a meeting. We said no. A line would be crossed. (*She pauses, deep in thought.*) A naked stranger is one thing. But one of us naked – no. It's all wrong.

Peter waits respectfully.

Peter This was an art school?

Valentina School of painting. At the Sacred Heart Convent. In the Boulevard des Invalides.

Peter Who taught you?

Valentina A man who said he wanted to turn his lambs into lions.

Peter Who was that?

Valentina Henri Matisse.

There is a pause.

Peter Matisse?

Valentina Yes.

Peter You mean Matisse?

Valentina I said Matisse.

Peter Yes, I know.

Valentina Why, you admire him?

Peter Just the idea that he was alive. And he taught you. It seems unbelievable.

Valentina Well, it's a fact.

Peter I didn't know he taught.

Valentina He taught for three years.

335

Peter Then?

She turns and looks at him.

Valentina Then he didn't teach any more.

Peter looks down a moment.

Peter You mean . . . look, I know nothing – art! – but I've seen some things he's done . . . but what I mean, did he feel there was no point in teaching?

Valentina How would I know? He taught us rules. He believed in them. Not Renaissance rules. Those he was very against. He disliked Leonardo. Because of all that measuring. He said that was when art began to go wrong. When it became obsessed with measuring. Trying to establish how things work. It doesn't matter how they work. You can't *see* with a caliper. (*She smiles.*) Of course there were rules. He was a classicist. This is what no one understood. He disliked in modern painting the way one part is emphasized – the nose, or the foot, or the breast. He hated this distortion. He said you should always aim for the whole. Remember your first impression and stick to it. Balance nature and your view. Don't let your view run away of its own accord. For everything he did there was always a reason. No one saw this to begin with. On the walls of Paris, people painted slogans: Matisse is absinthe, Matisse drives you mad. But to meet, he was a German schoolmaster with little gold-rimmed glasses.

Peter I've seen those drawings he did of himself. I like him in the mirror when he's drawing a nude.

Valentina Yes, it's witty.

There is a pause.

Even with colour . . . the colours were so striking, people thought, why is this face blue? This is modern. But it wasn't.

Each colour depends on what is placed next to it. One tone
is just a colour. Two tones are a chord, which is life. (*She
turns a moment, thoughtfully.*) It was the same with the
body. No line exists on its own. Only with its relation to
another do you create volume. He said you should think of
the body as an architect does. The foot is a bridge. Arms are
like rolls of clay. Forearms are like ropes, since they can be
knotted and twisted. In drawing a head never leave out the
ear. Adjust the different parts to each other. Each is
dissimilar and yet must add to the whole. A tree is like a
human body. A body is like a cathedral. (*She smiles.*) His
models were always very beautiful. Sometimes he worked
with the same model for years. No one drew the body better
than him. The lines of a woman's stomach. The pudenda. A
few curls. He could make you think of bed. And yet when he
was working he said, he took a woman's clothes off and put
them back on as if he were arranging a vase of flowers.

There is a pause.

He loved going to the mountains. When he was tired, he
said it was a relief. Because it's impossible to paint them.
You can't paint a mountain. The scale is all wrong.

Peter That's funny.

*She looks at him, suddenly resuming her original
answers.*

Valentina As to teaching, yes, of course, his teaching was
inspiring. But it was as if Shakespeare had taught. It gave
you an idea. But then when you pick up your own brush,
you're faced with the reality of your own talent.

Peter Frustrating?

Valentina Not always. But how do I say? It's a very
different thing. Talking is easy. Oh yes, and Matisse could
talk. But genius is different.

Peter frowns a moment.

Peter Did it depress you?

Valentina No. I went on painting. Although I knew my limitations. I painted by will.

Peter By will?

Valentina Yes.

Peter It's odd.

Valentina What?

Peter Last night, now, Sophia used that same phrase. 'By will.'

Valentina Yes. She used it to me. (*She looks at him a moment.*) He taught a few years, then he went travelling. He went to Italy, Algeria, Tangiers. By then he was yet more famous. He'd given Picasso one of his paintings. Picasso's friends, who were all very stupid and malicious, used it as a dartboard. But it didn't matter. Matisse's reputation was made. He bought a house in Clamart. People mocked him because it had such a big bathroom. On the ground floor. Too much contact with Americans, that's what people said. He'd developed an interest in personal hygiene. But it wasn't true. Matisse was always clean. (*She smiles.*) I went there a couple of times. Madame Matisse used to cook. She served a jugged hare which was better than anything in Europe. And with it, a wine called Rančio. It's a sort of Madeira. Heavy but excellent. I've never had it since.

Peter I don't know it.

Valentina Years later in Berlin, he went for a great exhibition of his work. And waiting for him was the most enormous laurel wreath. 'To Henri Matisse, *cher maître* . . .' or whatever. He said, 'Why do you give me a wreath?

I'm not dead.' But Madame Matisse plucked a leaf and tasted it. She said, 'This will make the most wonderful soup.'

There is a pause.

Peter Yes.

Valentina It was all one progress. I can't explain. I lost touch with him. I think everyone did. He simply moved out of all our lives. Yet whenever I heard later stories, they fitted. With him, everything belonged.

Peter I can see that.

Valentina I've seen photographs of him when he was dying. He's painting on his walls with a brush tied to the end of a long stick. He's too frail to move from his pillows. It's the same man I knew almost fifty years ago. (*She smiles.*) There was only one little – oh – what? – one tiny denial. Which was love. He told me he was too busy. To think of love properly. I mean, to explore it. No, he said. I have no time for that.

Peter I find that strange.

Valentina He was asked by an American journalist how many children he had. Four, he said. What are their names? Let me see. There's Marguerite. And Jean. And Pierre. He said suddenly, 'No, I have three.'

Peter But isn't that . . .

Valentina What?

Peter A bit callous?

Valentina I think it's admirable.

Peter Why?

Valentina Priorities!

Peter smiles.

Peter It seems a bit chilly to me.

Valentina He loved his family. He painted faces above his bed. He said he slept badly, but he always felt better if he could imagine his grandchildren. So he put them on the ceiling above him. That way he said, 'I feel less alone.'

Peter But what did they feel?

Valentina Does it matter? Marguerite was tortured by the Gestapo. She was in the Resistance. When she came home and told him, he couldn't paint for two weeks. Then he abandoned the work he'd been doing when he heard. Her pain was real to him. He was in anguish. But he could not incorporate her suffering. He didn't want to. He went on painting in just the same way.

There is a pause.

Peter What about you?

Valentina Me?

Peter Were you like that? Disciplined?

Valentina Good Lord, no. No. I wasted my time. Love was *all* I had time for. At least until the twenties.

Peter Sophia said . . . (*He pauses.*)

Valentina Yes?

Peter She suggested . . . that for some reason you decided to come home.

Valentina That's right. (*She waits.*) What else did she say?

Peter No, nothing, just . . . she said, you didn't have to.

Valentina I didn't have to. It was a choice of my own.

There is a pause. Peter waits.

I didn't know Matisse well. But I understood him. I understood what's called his handwriting. I love this phrase. Do you know what it is?

Peter No.

Valentina It's a painting term. Which is indefinable. It's not quite even signature. It's more than that. It's spirit.

She looks at him a moment, then Sophia returns, silently, with tea in a pot and cups on a tray. She moves round.

Sophia Here's tea.

Valentina Well, thank you.

Sophia Everyone's vanished. The museum's closed.

Valentina Already?

Sophia It's dark now.

Valentina I didn't notice. What have you done with the Assistant Curator?

Sophia I told him to wait. (*Sophia gives her tea.*)

Valentina Thank you. You've been talking of me, I gather, to Peter here.

Sophia Not in particular. Do you want tea?

Peter No, thank you.

Sophia We're always short of time. Me and Linitsky. (*She smiles affectionately at him.*) We meet in a café far from our homes. Most of the time we talk about how to meet next. Then when we meet next, how to meet next. And so on.

Valentina It sounds most exhausting.

Sophia In China they say if you want to be taught by a

particular professor, you must go to his door every day and ask to be a pupil. And every day for a year, two years, three years, he will close the door in your face. Then one day he will suddenly accept you. He's been testing your endurance. To see if you want the thing badly enough.

Valentina What a sentimental notion.

Sophia It's true.

Valentina I'm sure it's true. (*The hardness of her tone suddenly returns.*) And meanwhile your life has gone by.

Sophia looks a moment to Peter.

Sophia So what did you decide?

Peter Sorry?

Sophia The two of you.

Peter Oh. (*He pauses.*) About what?

Sophia Peter . . .

Peter Oh, I see.

Sophia I'm asking, will my mother help us?

Peter I don't know. She didn't say.

Valentina smiles to herself.

We didn't get on to the subject. To be honest, we were talking about art.

Sophia Oh God.

Peter I know.

Sophia Really, Peter. I asked you . . .

Peter I know. I'm ashamed.

Valentina Did you give him a mission?

342

Peter I got distracted, that's all.

Valentina What was he meant to be asking me?

Sophia (*to Valentina*) Nothing. Mind your own business. (*to Peter*) Really! Do I have to do everything myself? (*She is at once contrite.*) Oh God, I'm sorry.

Peter No, no . . .

Sophia Forgive me, I didn't mean to be unpleasant.

Peter You're not being unpleasant. Really.

Sophia I'm sorry, Peter.

Peter No, it's my fault.

Valentina Is this how your home life will be? God help us. I think you'd both be better off on your own.

Sophia Well, perhaps. (*She turns to Peter.*) What do you say?

Peter No, I don't think so. For me it's an adventure, you see. At last something's happening. Even if, as you say, its unbelievably uncomfortable. It uncovers feelings I didn't know I had. (*He smiles, nervously.*) For a start, I'm jealous. It's illogical. Jealous of the past. Of the life Sophia had before I even knew her. The further back, the worse. Even the idea . . . when I think of her as young . . . just young . . . in a short gingham dress, on a pavement, with a satchel, going to school, the idea of her life as an eight-year-old fills my heart with such terrible longing. Such a sense of loss. It makes no sense, it's ridiculous. My brain reels, I can hardly think. Images of someone I never even knew have a power to disturb me, to hurt me in a way which is more profound than anything I've known. (*He looks hopelessly to Valentina.*) What can I do? Just abandon her.

Sophia No.

Peter Just say, 'Well, that's it. You've had your glimpse. Now go home and do nothing but glue balsa wood on your own'? (*He shrugs.*) Plainly it's true, I'm not happy. I'm what the textbooks call 'seriously disturbed'. I wish I were stronger. I wish she didn't so upset me. (*A pause.*) But I think I have to go on.

There is silence. Sophia looks at him a moment.

Valentina I don't know. Why is that?

Peter Why?

Valentina Yes, why?

Sophia He just told you.

Valentina Yes. But what he feels will have an effect. On Grigor. On the children.

Peter I love the children.

Sophia They will live with us.

Valentina Will they? And when will you tell them about the separation?

Sophia does not answer.

Sophia?

Sophia I already have.

Valentina What?

Sophia Yes. I told them.

Valentina Why did you do that?

Sophia I felt it would be honest.

Valentina Please don't lie to me.

Peter Sophia . . .

344

Sophia Also . . .

Peter (*to Valentina*) I didn't know.

Valentina Tell me your true reason.

Sophia Many things.

Valentina Such as?

There is a pause.

Sophia There would be no going back.

Peter is looking across at her, alarmed. Valentina nods slightly.

Valentina Yes. And Grigor? Was Grigor there?

Sophia No. He wasn't with me. I did it this morning. He'll be home about now.

Valentina You told them without asking him.

Sophia Look, Mother, I've asked him often. He always says no. But they must know eventually.

Valentina You told them without his permission?

Sophia He will never give his permission. He claims I'm in the grip of a decadent fantasy. He says I am inflamed by the morals of the West. Mother, he's mad.

Valentina The children won't love you. They will never forgive you.

Sophia is shaking her head, now very agitated.

Sophia All right, I'll be there. I'll go home now. I'll tell him. I'll say 'Grigor, the children now know what you and I know.' I broke the news because if I didn't, nothing would have happened. Was that wrong? (*She suddenly cries out.*) Mother, don't look at me like that.

345

Valentina What did the twins say?

Sophia Well . . .

Valentina Tell me.

Sophia Look, what d'you think? Of course it isn't easy.

Valentina Well?

Sophia It's a long process. It's years.

Valentina Just today?

Sophia pauses a moment.

Sophia Nikolai was fine. At once he went back to playing. Alexandra said, would I please go away?

Valentina She's *eight*.

Sophia Mother, don't torture me.

Valentina turns to Peter.

Valentina Peter, are you shocked?

Peter No. (*He pauses, uncertain.*) Of course not. It had to be done. Eventually.

Valentina Is there anything worse? Is there anything worse than the weak when they try to be strong? They make such a job of it!

Peter That isn't fair.

Valentina Oh, I see. Is this how you would have done it?

Peter I'm not Sophia. I haven't suffered as she has.

Valentina How has she suffered? What does she suffer? Please. I would really like to know.

Peter Well . . .

Valentina In what way is she different from anyone in

Russia? What is her complaint? That she is not *free*?
That's what I've been told. Well, who is free? Tell me, am I
free?

Sophia No. No, Mother. But it's you who always say I am
docile . . . (*She turns to Peter.*) That's what she tells me.
That I'm passive; I'm second-rate, I agree to things too
easily . . .

Valentina I say this?

Sophia Today! Even today you said people take advantage
of me. Now when I make a stand, you insult me.

Valentina I do. Because it is doomed. Because it's not in
your character.

Sophia No?

Valentina It's just a little spurt. You don't have the
character to finish what you've started.

> *There is a pause. Sophia looks at her, as if finally
> understanding her objection. Then, with genuine
> interest:*

Sophia Is that what you fear?

Valentina Yes, it is. You'll fail. You'll lose heart.

Sophia Is that *all* you fear?

> *Valentina looks slightly shifty.*

Valentina Nor does he. I apologize for saying this. He's
ten years from dying.

Sophia Yes, thank you, Mother. Is there anything else?

> *She looks calmly to Peter who seems not remotely
> upset.*

Peter It's all right.

Sophia Perhaps you might explain. I suppose my mother did not tell you anything of her own life.

Peter Er, no.

Valentina We did not discuss it.

Sophia Valentina does not tell you why she's so hard on me.

There's a pause, the two women quite still.

My mother made a choice. Thirty-five years ago.

Valentina Yes.

Sophia I was a baby. She carried me in her arms into Russia, in 1921. She brought me here from Paris.

There is a pause.

Peter I see.

He waits for more, but the two women are still, both looking down. Eventually:

What . . . I don't see . . . I don't understand exactly . . . I mean . . .

Sophia Go on. Please. Yes. Ask.

Peter Well . . . I suppose I'm wondering . . . do you regret it?

Valentina How do you answer that question? At certain times everything is wrong.

Sophia smiles.

I was a wayward woman – that's the word. I lay around in beds, in studios, with men, smoking too much and thinking, shall I grow my hair? I had a child. Oh, I was like Gorki's mother, who stopped for fifteen minutes on a peasants' march to give birth in a ditch. Then she ran to catch up with the marchers. I was the same. I had my little Sophia in an atelier in the Marais, with two jugs of hot water and a homosexual friend who delivered her. And then I thought – well, is this it? This lounging about? This thinking only of yourself? This – what word should I use – *freedom*? Having a child changed everything. I suddenly decided that Paris was meaningless. Indulgence only. I had a Russian daughter. I had to come home. (*She sits back.*) An artist in Russia. Oh, when I came back, of course, everything was possible. (*She smiles.*) But now. I have not exhibited in seventeen years. (*She shrugs slightly.*) Foreign painters are exhibited in all sorts of style. But Russians may have one style only. It does not suit me. That's all there is to say.

There is another silence.

Sophia My mother is intolerant of those who complain.

Peter Yes. Do you ever think . . . you could have left here . . .

Valentina Exile, you mean?

Peter Yes.

Valentina It seemed to me cowardly. To give up seems cowardly. Finally that is always the choice. (*She gestures suddenly towards the canvas on the other side of the room.*) A painting, we are told, left by an aristocrat in his will. His last wish, to send it back to Russia. And he left in 1919! (*She laughs.*)

Peter I don't know, I mean, for myself I've never even thought of it, why should I? But for you . . . with your background . . .

Valentina No, of course not. My life is not happy. I say this to you. But it would also be unhappy if I'd been cowardly. (*She shakes her head.*) Your life is defined by an

349

absence, by what is not happening, by where you can't be. You think all the time about 'me'. Oh 'me'! Oh 'me'! The endless 'me' who takes over. 'Me' becomes everything. Oh 'I' decided. The self-dramatization. Turning your life into a crusade. A crusade in which you claim equal status with Russia. On the one hand, the whole of Russia, millions of square miles. On the other, 'I' think and 'I' feel. The battle is unequal. That kind of self-advertisement, it seemed to me wrong. And dangerous. And wilful. To drink wine or breed horses, and dream of elsewhere. (*Pause.*) I wasn't a communist. I know what has happened since. I'm still not a communist. How could I be? But I made a decision.

Peter And were you right?

Valentina I have no idea.

There is a silence.

Sophia Peter. Please. I want to be alone with her.

Peter What? Oh, of course.

Sophia Please, Peter, she and I need to talk.

Peter Of course. (*He is upset.*) Now?

Sophia Yes.

He stands a moment.

Peter When shall I see you?

Sophia What?

Peter See you? We haven't made an arrangement.

Sophia Oh no, that's right.

Peter Well, er . . .

Sophia Do we have to fix it now?

Peter Of course we do, yes.

Sophia Sorry, I can't think. You say.

Peter In three days, do you have . . .

Sophia Yes. Friday. The usual break after lunch.

Peter Three days.

Sophia Yes.

Peter I'll see you then. And we'll talk this over. Madame Nrovka, this has been a great honour. (*He goes across to Valentina.*)

Valentina I was pleased to meet you.

Peter To be honest I was scared. Not because of you. But because I care too much. I do crave her happiness.

Valentina Yes. That is clear.

   He stands a moment.

Peter Three days then.

Sophia Yes.

Peter I must go. (*Without looking at Sophia he turns and goes quickly out.*)

Valentina Now it's cold.

Sophia Yes.

Valentina It's cold suddenly.

Sophia They turn the heating off, I suppose.

Valentina All the money they must need to heat art. To keep art warm for the public. (*She looks across at Sophia.*) Tell me, is it money you want?

Sophia Yes, of course.

Valentina I guessed that. Peter's embarrassment was on

351

such a scale. I knew you must have told him to ask me for money.

Sophia I did.

Valentina He's too nice. He would have stood there for ever.

Sophia smiles.

How much do you need?

Sophia Two thousand.

Valentina When?

Sophia Well, after the counselling, and the advertisement, and the examination in the People's Court, finally you need the money for the Regional Court. But I felt . . . there's no point in my starting if at the end I can't pay.

Valentina You should have asked me this morning. Before speaking to the children. But it did not occur to you that I would say no.

She looks at Sophia who does not answer.

Why should I give you money when I do not approve?

There is a silence. Sophia just looks at her. Valentina turns away.

You're just unlucky. It's historical accident. In the twenties it was easy.

Sophia I've heard.

Valentina In the first days of the Soviet Union, you didn't need your partner's consent. You could sue for a divorce by sending a postcard and three roubles. There was to be a revolution of the sexes. I must say I had my doubts at the time.

Sophia smiles as well.

I had a lover for a while. Or rather I tried to. Another soldier. Like you, we had nowhere to go. After Paris, Russia seemed ridiculous. Because even then, people got upset if you showed your feelings. People disapproved. So we noticed that at stations people may embrace openly because they're always saying goodbye. So he and I used to go and pretend that one of us was catching a train. We embraced on the platform. We said a thousand goodbyes. Train after train went without us. Then an official came and said 'You've watched enough trains.' (*She pauses, lost in thought.*) And what will you have? A small room in the suburbs of Leningrad. No money. Children who dislike you for taking them away from their father. From prosperity. From someone who belongs. Who fits in. Who is happy here.

Sophia Yes.

Valentina Have you thought of the effect the divorce will have on him? A Party member?

Sophia Of course. But if I don't I will have no self-respect.

Valentina laughs.

Valentina Oh, please. You! No one cares. You have no status here. Be clear. You're a private citizen. Love in a small flat, it's nobody's business. But Grigor – he will lose position. Influence. Friends. He will be discredited. It's a sign of failure.

Sophia looks unapologetically at her.

Sophia Well, I can't live with the Party any more. (*She shakes her head.*) I've always known . . . after all, in my profession I work with young people. I spread ideas. I can't be considered for promotion unless I am also willing to join. The moment is looming when they will ask me.

(*She pauses a moment.*) This way the moment will never arrive.

Valentina Ah, well, I see . . .

Sophia I think the only hope now is to live your life in private.

Valentina So you choose Peter.

Sophia Yes.

Valentina Because he's ineffectual and hopeless and has no ambition. That's clear. You love his hopelessness.

Sophia It seems a great virtue. Is that wrong? After watching Grigor. The way Grigor is. It comforts me that Peter has no wish to get on.

Valentina Yes. That's attractive. But there's a limit.

Sophia You mean Peter is beyond it?

Valentina He is the Soul of No Hope. (*She smiles.*) Everyone here has a vision. How it might be other. We all have a dream of something else. For you it's Linitsky. Linitsky's your escape. How will it be when he becomes your reality? When he's not your escape? When he's your life?

Sophia I don't know.

Valentina Have you thought . . .

Sophia Of course.

Valentina It's possible you'll hate him? As you hate Grigor now.

Sophia No.

Valentina All the things that seem so attractive – that manner, the way he holds his hat in his hands, the gentleness – when they are your life, they will seem insufferable.

Sophia Perhaps. I don't know. How can anyone know?

Valentina smiles.

Valentina Everyone here lives in the future. Or in the past. No one wants the present. What shall we do with the present? Oh, Paris! Oh, Linitsky! Anything but here! Anything but now! (*She turns to Sophia.*) I had a friend. She loved a violinist. They could rarely meet. He was married. She worshipped him. Eventually he could not play unless he sensed she was in the audience. She went to all his concerts for over three years. She later said to me, rather bitterly, the violin repertoire is remarkably small. The man's wife died. He came to her and said, we're free. It lasted a week. She no longer desired him. (*A pause.*) It seems to me the worst story I know.

Sophia looks at her, holding her gaze.

What do you feel when he says that he'll die for you? That it's life and death.

Sophia Well . . .

Valentina Is it for you?

Sophia pauses a moment.

Sophia No. But we're different. I love him. I love what he is.

Valentina Do you wish he loved you less desperately?

Sophia That's how he loves me.

Valentina And is that a good thing?

Sophia Look, how can I say? He's kind to me. He'll never do me harm. I always feel I can rest with him. Yes, there is inequality. If you like, an inequality of need. Finally. But what's wrong with that? If we said, well, I can see this isn't quite perfect, we'd never do anything.

Valentina No.

There is a pause.

Even so.

Sophia What is the alternative? I know what you feel. But by your argument, must we put up with everything?

Valentina I have.

Sophia Yes. But now should I?

Valentina turns and looks at her, but does not answer.

Mother, will you give me the money?

Valentina Of course. (*She laughs.*) Mind you, I don't have it.

Sophia What?

Valentina Two thousand roubles, are you joking?

Sophia I assumed . . .

Valentina Oh yes, I act as if I'm rich. That seems to me simply good manners. Don't you see through it?

Sophia No.

Valentina Look at my life. How do you think I would have that kind of money?

Sophia begins to laugh.

Sophia I thought you were frugal.

Valentina Frugal? I'm poor.

Sophia Oh Lord, no, I don't believe it. I've been so nervous . . .

Valentina Well, so you should be. But not about money. You mustn't worry. I'll sell my flat.

Sophia Don't be ridiculous.

Valentina Yes. It means nothing. Goodness, if I couldn't throw money away I'd really be tragic.

Sophia No, there's no question . . .

Valentina Yes. I shall do it. To shame you.

Sophia Well, we shall see. (*A pause.*) You'll support me? You think I'm doing right?

Valentina There is no right. Until you see that, you will never have peace. (*She gets up. She walks right the way across the room, decisively.*) I will speak to Grigor. No, not for you. Not to help you. But on behalf of the children, I will persuade him not to oppose you, so that it's quicker in the Regional Court. He's frightened of women. Most bullies are.

   Sophia is about to speak but Valentina interrupts quickly.

Don't ask me any more. That's all I can do. Now please go. The man you want to live with is senile. Senile's the word.

Sophia Thank you, Mother.

Valentina You won't be happy. You'll die at forty.

Sophia Good. Well, I'm glad that you're pleased. (*She smiles, genuinely moved.*)

Valentina I'm not pleased.

Sophia Come here.

Valentina No.

Sophia Mother, please. Embrace me.

Valentina Don't be stupid.

Sophia is holding out her arms. Valentina doesn't move. So Sophia moves across and embraces her. Then she holds her head in her hands.

Sophia Hey, Mother, hey.

Valentina is about to cry. Sophia stops her.

Valentina You must go. Give my love to the children. Tell them to visit me.

Sophia Yes.

Valentina Whatever you do, this time you must live with it.

Sophia Yes. I've learnt that from you.

She looks at her a moment. Then she turns and goes out. There's a moment's silence. Then Valentina walks across to the chair and picks up the canvas from the leg against which it is propped. She holds it out at arms' length for five seconds. Then, without any visible reaction, she puts it down. Then she walks across the room and stands alone. Then her eyes begin to fill with tears. Silently the Assistant Curator returns, standing respectfully at the door.

Valentina You've come back.

Assistant Yes.

Valentina I didn't hear you.

Assistant Have you had time to look at it?

Valentina I've examined it.

There's a pause.

Yes. It's Matisse.

Neither of them moves.

Not, surely, the beginning of a sequence.

Assistant I'm sorry?

Valentina No, it's just . . . you said . . . there was nothing in the foreground, so you assumed this is where he started. Then later he put in the woman. Or the violin. But no. It was the opposite. He removed the woman. He sought to distil.

Assistant Oh, I see. Yes. That fits with the scientific dating.

Valentina Yes, it would. You could have saved yourself money.

The Assistant stands a moment, puzzled by her tone.

Assistant Do you need to take another look?

Valentina No. He said that finally he didn't need a model. Finally he didn't even need paint. *He* was there. He was a person. Present. And that was enough.

The Assistant moves, as if to pick the canvas up.

The giveaway is the light through the shutters. No one else could do that. The way the sun is diffused. He controlled the sun in his painting. He said, with shutters he could summon the sun as surely as Joshua with his trumpet.

Assistant Yes. I see what you mean.

She turns and looks at him.

Valentina And are you a Member?

Assistant What?

Valentina The Party. Do you belong?

Assistant Oh.

Valentina No. Don't tell me. I know. As surely as if you were a painting. (*She holds a hand up towards him, as if judging him. Then smiles.*) Yes. You belong.

Assistant In my job you have to. I mean, I want to, as well. If I want advancement. This painting is going to be a great help to me.

Valentina So Matisse did not paint in vain. (*She gathers up her coat.*) I must go. (*Before she is ready, she turns thoughtfully a moment.*) He was once in a Post Office in Picardy. He was waiting to pick up the phone. He picked up a telegraph form lying on the table, and without thinking, began to draw a woman's head. All the time he talked on the phone, he was drawing. And when at the end, he looked down, he had drawn his mother's face. His hand did the work, not the brain. And he said the result was truer and more beautiful than anything that came as an effort of will. (*She stands a moment, then turns to go.*)

Assistant I'll get you a car.

Valentina No. The tram is outside. It goes right by my door.

> *She goes. He stands a moment, looking at the painting. The background fades and the stage is filled with the image of the bay at Nice: a pair of open French windows, a balcony, the sea and the sky.*
> *The Assistant turns and looks to the open door.*

THE SECRET RAPTURE

For Blair

Characters

Isobel Glass
Marion French
Tom French
Katherine Glass
Irwin Posner
Rhonda Milne

The Secret Rapture was first performed at the Lyttelton Theatre, South Bank, London, on 4 October 1988. The cast was as follows:

Isobel Glass Jill Baker
Marion French Penelope Wilton
Tom French Paul Shelley
Katherine Glass Clare Higgins
Irwin Posner Mick Ford
Rhonda Milne Arkie Whiteley

Directed by Howard Davies
Settings by John Gunter
Costumes by Fotini Dimou
Music by Ilona Sekacz

Only half of us is sane: only part of us loves pleasure and the longer day of happiness, wants to live to our nineties and die in peace, in a house that we built, that shall shelter those who come after us. The other half of us is nearly mad. It prefers the disagreeable to the agreeable, loves pain and its darker night despair, and wants to die in a catastrophe that will set back life to its beginnings and leave nothing of our house save its blackened foundations.

REBECCA WEST

If you don't like my peaches,
Why do you shake my tree?
Get out of my orchard
And let a poor girl be.

POPULAR SONG

Act One

SCENE ONE

*Robert's bedroom. The curtain goes up on almost
complete darkness. Then a door opens at the back and a
dim and indirect light is thrown from the corridor.
Marion, in her late thirties, brisk, dark-haired, wearing a
business suit, stands a moment, nervous, awed, in the
doorway. She moves into the room which you can just
detect is dominated by a large double bed, in which a man
is lying, covered with a sheet reaching up over his face.
Marion stops a moment by the bed, looking down. She
then turns to go back towards the door.*

Isobel Marion?

*Marion lets out a scream, not having realized that Isobel
was sitting in a chair at the end of the bed.*

Marion My God!

Isobel I'm sorry.

Marion You startled me.

Isobel Don't turn the main light on.

Marion goes to the bed and turns on a small bedside lamp.

I needed some peace.

*Isobel is younger than Marion and blonder. She is in her
early thirties, and casually dressed in a shirt and blue
jeans. She is sitting at the end of the bed, facing us, not
moving. The room is seen now to be panelled, gloomy,
dark, old-fashioned. It is absolutely tidy, hairbrushes in
place, the body quite still beneath the shroud.*

367

I decided this would be the only place. For some quiet. There's so much screaming downstairs.

Marion moves gingerly towards the bed. She looks a moment.

Marion So were you with him?

Isobel There's actually a moment when you see the spirit depart from the body. I've always been told about it. And it's true. (*She is very quiet and still.*) Like a bird.

Marion looks across, nervous.

Marion Did he . . .

Isobel What?

Marion No, I wondered . . . who dressed him?

Isobel Dressed him?

Marion Yes. Is he in a suit?

Isobel I did it. And there was a nurse.

Marion stands a moment, not looking at the bed.

Marion Well, I don't know. Are you going to sit there?

Isobel Yes. For a while. Is that all right?

She smiles and holds out her hand. But Marion does not take it.

Marion Yes. Perfectly.

Isobel Did you want to be alone with him?

Marion No. I just wanted to see him for the last time.

Isobel does not move.

I'm sorry, you know, I feel wretched not getting here . . .

Isobel Oh, I'm sure Dad didn't mind. He was barely

conscious. He had no idea who I was. (*She smiles.*)

Marion I was wondering . . .

Isobel What?

Marion No, it's just . . . no, it's nothing. It's silly. I gave him a little thing. Six months ago. When I . . . when you first told me he was ill. I was shocked. I bought him a present.

Isobel Oh, was that the ring?

Marion I mean what I'm saying is . . . is he still wearing it?

Isobel No. We took it off.

Marion Where did you put it?

There's a silence. Isobel finally realizes what Marion wants.

Isobel It's in the drawer.

Marion nods slightly. Then she goes to the chest of drawers and opens the top drawer. She takes out a ring. Then closes it. She moves back across the room.

Marion Well, I must say, Isobel, you've been heroic. I wouldn't have managed it. I know myself too well. The times I came down to see him . . . I'll say this to you . . . it made me uncomfortable. I couldn't be wholly at ease. I find it hard . . . I mean if someone's, you know, as he was . . . I find it hard to strike the right attitude. Don't you find that?

Isobel I don't know.

There's a moment's silence.

Marion Look, about the ring.

Isobel It's all right.

Marion Isobel, please let me explain to you . . .

Isobel Honestly, Marion . . .

Marion I know when I took it just now, it must have looked bad. Did it look bad?

Isobel shakes her head.

You've always been kind to me. But there are reasons.

Isobel I'm sure. (*She looks down a moment.*)

Marion I know what you're thinking.

Isobel I'm not thinking anything.

Marion Oh, this is awful. It's absolutely ghastly. I knew when I took it, I should have waited. I should have come and taken it when I was alone. It's just the thought, if Katherine's got her hands on it, you know perfectly well she'll sell it tomorrow – he's left her everything – what, I'm meant to leave it in that drawer, so she can spend it on drink?

Isobel looks to the bed, disturbed by Marion's sudden loudness.

For God's sake, I mean, the ring is actually valuable. Actually no, that sounds horrid. I apologize. I'll tell you the truth. I thought when I bought it – I just walked into this very expensive shop and I thought, this is one of the few really decent things I've done in my life. And it's true. I spent, as it happens, a great deal of money, rather more . . . rather *more* than I had at the time. I went over the top. I wanted something to express my love for my father. Something adequate.

Marion has tears in her eyes. Isobel is very quiet.

Isobel Then by all means you must take it. I can't see why not.

Marion thinks about this a moment, looking judiciously at Isobel.

Marion I mean, God, I want to have something. It's a sort of keepsake. Every time I look at it, I'm going to feel sad. Because, you know, I think it's going to be a terrible reminder of . . . what do you call those things?

Isobel A *memento mori*.

Marion But I mean when it comes down to it, it's much better *that* than it's traded for eight crates of vodka for Katherine to pour down her throat.

Isobel looks at her a moment.

Isobel Shall we go down?

Marion Oh, for God's sake, I can't stand it.

Isobel What?

Marion Your disapproval.

Isobel gestures towards the bed.

Isobel Marion, please.

Isobel gestures again, uselessly, unable to express what she feels.

I don't disapprove. I'm just upset.

Tom appears at the door. He is in his late thirties, in a grey suit of artificial fibre, with a sober tie. He is tall, thin, and his face is boyish.

Tom Oh, you're in here.

Isobel Yes.

Tom Right.

Marion Tom, have you unpacked the car?

Tom I've done that, darling. (*He stands a moment, puzzled.*) Is anyone coming?

Marion Where?

Tom Downstairs.

Isobel In a moment.

Tom It's just a little odd all crowding in here. (*He frowns slightly.*)

Marion I'm just furious with Katherine.

Tom Katherine?

Marion I mean, have you seen her? She's drunk.

Tom I'm not sure that's true. I mean surely . . .

Marion One day, you would think, just *one day*. Was she drunk earlier?

Isobel When?

Marion You know, when . . . earlier, in his last moments . . . (*Marion gestures uneasily towards the bed.*)

Isobel I didn't notice.

Marion I think it's disgraceful.

Isobel Well, it hardly matters. Least of all to Dad.

Tom No, he's fine. He's in the hands of the Lord.

Isobel frowns slightly at this, then makes as if to leave.

Isobel Mmm. Well, perhaps . . .

Tom Is an ambulance coming?

Isobel No. An undertaker. We have a certificate. That's all been done. Time of death. Cause of death.

Marion Was Katherine much help?

Isobel What do you mean?

Marion Was she any help to you? When you were nursing Dad?

Isobel She was fine.

Marion I bet you had to do everything yourself.

Isobel No. Katherine helped.

Marion looks ironically at Tom.

Marion Isobel can't resist being kind about people.

Isobel I'm not being kind. (*She hesitates a moment.*) Also . . . Dad loved her. You must allow him that. He wouldn't have married unless he genuinely loved her.

Marion You know my views about that.

Isobel Yes, I do.

Marion An old man was taken for a ride.

Isobel I know you feel that. Honestly, I don't think it matters much. The great thing is to love. If you're loved back then it's a bonus.

Marion looks pityingly to Tom, as if this were too absurd for comment.

He saw himself as a failure . . .

Marion (*at once*) He wasn't.

Isobel Of course not. But that's how he felt. In the world's eyes. A small-town bookseller. The only thing that distinguished his life – as he felt – was this late passion for a

373

much younger woman. So now he's dead, Marion, you mustn't take that away. (*She turns, a little overcome by her own eloquence. She turns to Tom.*) What do you feel, Tom?

Tom Feel?

Isobel About what I've been saying?

Tom I couldn't find fault with it.

Marion Oh really?

Tom I'm sure both of you are right. (*He looks a little nervously at Marion.*) It's wonderful being a woman because you have that knack of knowing what's going on. Men just don't seem to have it. What is it? A sort of instinct? Still, *vive la différence*, eh?

Isobel is for the first time able to smile to herself.

Isobel Yes, well, certainly. Shall I make some supper?

Tom Oh, I'm defrosting some stuff. I got individual roast-beef dinner-trays from a freezer on the motorway. I didn't think anyone would need more than that.

Isobel gestures to the door.

Isobel So, shall we go?

Suddenly Marion speaks with unpredicted vehemence.

Marion I'm not going to forgive you.

Isobel What?

Marion You've tried to humiliate me.

Isobel Marion . . .

Marion You've made me feel awful. It's not my fault about the ring. Or the way I feel about Katherine. You make me feel as if I'm always in the wrong.

Isobel Not at all.

Marion Oh, yes. Well, we can't all be perfect. We do try. The rest of us are trying. So will you please stop this endless criticism? Because I honestly think it's driving me mad.

Marion turns and rushes out of the room. She is beginning to cry uncontrollably. Tom looks down. Isobel stands, pale.

Tom Well, goodness.

Isobel Oh, dear.

Tom I'm sorry.

Isobel No. It's not her fault. You lash out in any direction. Marion's in grief. It's her way of grieving. She chooses to lash out at me. (*She smiles, shaken.*)

Tom All the time, I must say, we were driving, she was sitting there seething. She kept saying, 'I hope we're not late.' Late? I didn't know what she meant. Then she said, 'I'll never forgive myself if I get there and that ring has gone.' I was rather shocked. But you're saying, what, it's because the death was such a blow?

Isobel I think so.

Tom And that's her reaction?

Isobel It's a way of coping.

Tom Gosh, well that's interesting. I do hope you're right. (*He frowns, thinking about it.*) You see, it happens quite often. She gets angry. Why? I mean, she's got everything she wants. Her party's in power. For ever. She's in office. She's an absolute cert for the Cabinet. I just don't see why she's angry all the time.

Isobel Don't you?

Tom Well, no.

Isobel Do you ever get angry?

Tom Angry? I don't think so. There's no need to, since I made Jesus my friend.

Isobel nods slightly.

Isobel I suppose that does make things easier.

Tom Oh, incomparably, yes. He transforms your life if you'll let him.

Isobel Really?

Tom Oh, yes. And he'll do it for anyone. That's what I like. He'll save anyone. I mean on the surface I was completely unsuitable . . .

Isobel You were never very sinful.

Tom Oh, God, yes, I was. Oh, yes. Perhaps you didn't notice but I was genuinely disgusting. Still am, of course.

He thinks a moment. Isobel is staring at him.

I'm the most horrible sinner. But he forgives me, and that's all that counts. (*He suddenly shakes his head.*) This morning Marion was already on her way to the Department. She's incredible, she's on her way at six, so I get the children's breakfast before I go off to work. Anyway, you called and told me what had happened, I thought, I don't want to break this to Marion on the phone. I'll drive in and tell her in person. I go to the car. Won't start. I open the bonnet. Spark-plug leads have perished. I can't believe it. I think, what on earth am I going to do? Then I think, hey, six days ago an old mate called in and left, in a shopping bag, a whole load of spare parts he'd had to buy for his car. (*He smiles in anticipation of the outcome.*) And, you know, as I go in and look for it, I tell

376

you this, I don't have a doubt. As I move towards the bag. I've never looked inside it and yet *I know*. It's got so I know. I know that inside that bag there is going to be a set of Ford Granada leads. And *then* you have to say, well, there you are, that's it, that's the Lord Jesus. He's there when you need him. I *am* looked after. He wanted Marion to hear the news from me. So that's when he'll decide, right, I'm going to help this person, I'm going to get hold of a few people and just . . . pick them up and move them around.

Isobel What, you mean you think that's why your friend dropped by in the first place?

Tom Certainly. No question.

Isobel Six days earlier.

Tom You're right.

Isobel Well, well.

Tom Of course my friend didn't know. He didn't drop round *knowing*. None of us know when we're part of God's plan.

Isobel Who perished the rubber?

Tom Oh, that's different. That's a natural thing. (*He smiles.*) People are so full of anger. Really it mystifies me.

Isobel is looking at him nervously.

Isobel Tom, I wonder . . . I wanted a favour. I've no right to ask this.

Tom Go on.

Isobel It's just, you know how much I love Marion. I wondered if you'd let me know if you sensed . . . (*She stops.*)

Tom Please.

377

Isobel If you felt she was seriously angry with me. If you felt it was serious.

Tom No problem.

Isobel I don't want you to feel you're betraying her.

Tom I'll make that promise. I'll let you know.

He smiles, full of reassurance. Isobel looks away.

Isobel Is the undertaker here?

Tom I should think so.

Isobel looks a moment to the bed.

Isobel Then we'd better go down.

At once we hear Katherine's voice. The set parts and we are on the lawn at the back of the house. There is a little garden furniture, seemingly at random. A table with a couple of chairs, then a couple more chairs set further away. Bright sunshine. A warm English day. Katherine is coming in, in a black suit, with a tight skirt. She is dark-haired, in her early thirties, thickset, pale, quick. Her voice is quite loud.

SCENE TWO

The lawn of Robert's house.

Katherine The priest was awful. It was clear he never knew him. (*She sits in one of the chairs.*) To be honest, I was relieved. When the coffin came in, I thought, oh dear, this is going to be unbearably moving. And then mercifully the vicar opened his mouth.

Marion appears at the back, now also in black. She walks on and remains standing, thoughtful.

378

It's quite extraordinary. The church must send them on some sort of training course. Called Trampling on People's Feelings.

Tom appears, dark-suited.

Tom Do we want a drink?

Katherine Yes, please.

Tom There's lemon squash. Orange squash. Coffee. Marion?

Marion Squash. (*She looks significantly at Tom.*) Squash would be nice.

Tom turns to go out, as Isobel appears from another direction, already changed back into blue jeans and a red shirt.

Isobel That was my fault.

Katherine It's all right.

Isobel I feel terrible. Dad never spoke to a priest in his life. So I tried to give that man some sort of briefing.

Katherine When he said . . . what was the word?

Isobel 'Mr Glass was respected as a local cricket umpire. A task he performed adequately.'

Katherine I mean, really!

Isobel 'Adequately'! It's pretty grudging.

Katherine You might expect better when you've just died.

Marion turns, disapproving.

Where'd he get that thing about 'known as Ginger'?

Isobel I have no idea.

Katherine He was never known as Ginger. Was he?

Isobel No.

Katherine Not since I've known him.

Marion He was doing his best. I thought he was very sincere.

Katherine looks at her a moment.

Isobel I stressed forty years of opposition to nuclear armaments. Typical Gloucestershire village. Of course the vicar never used any of that.

Marion I asked him not to.

Isobel Oh.

Marion I thought it would be inappropriate.

Katherine It's what he believed.

Marion Maybe. There's such a thing as a suitable time. Funerals shouldn't have politics dragged into them.

Isobel Is anyone hungry?

Katherine What d'you mean, 'dragged'?

Isobel is standing, trying to distract them. Katherine does not turn to look at Marion behind her.

He didn't want a funeral. The only thing *dragged* in was him. He wanted to be burnt and scattered. He said, 'Shoot me from a cannon into the English Channel.' I'd have done it. It was only at your insistence . . .

Tom appears, holding a tray.

Isobel Ah good, everyone, look, here's the squash.

Tom sets it down.

Tom I don't know what to do. There's a whole lot of people . . . (*He trails off, gesturing towards the house.*)

Isobel I'll go. (*At once she goes out to deal with them.*)

Marion I thought the family made it clear. We wanted some privacy.

Tom They've just drifted up.

Katherine Fuck them.

Marion Katherine, please.

Katherine Fuck them. Let them go somewhere else. Go to the Drum and Monkey. They can all claim him. It's safe. Now he's no longer there. (*She turns.*) Well, it's true. There's nothing people like more than claiming great friendship with people who aren't in a position to deny it. It's this immediate appropriation that I find so disgusting. (*She is suddenly quiet.*) Robert wasn't anyone's.

   At once Isobel returns.

Isobel They're going to the pub.

Katherine What did I tell you?

Isobel They asked us if we'd like to join them.

Marion Later. I think we should look after Katherine right now.

   Her tone is so threatening that Isobel shifts uneasily.

Isobel Look, Marion, why don't you leave me with Katherine?

Marion I mean, have you decided?

Katherine About what?

Marion Tom and I were wondering what you were going to do.

Katherine Oh, that.

Marion I'm not saying you need to make your mind up

immediately. Perhaps you should go on a holiday first.

Katherine I mean, sure, I'd be happy anywhere, I wouldn't mind where I went if I could just go somewhere and not have to put up with *me*.

Marion Oh, God . . .

Isobel Please, Marion . . .

Katherine Look . . .

Marion Let me . . .

There is sudden heat in all this, until Katherine rides in decisively.

Katherine All right, look, I know, you all think I'm hopeless. I'm not hopeless. I've had time to think. I do have a plan. I'm not going to stay in this house for the rest of my life. I decided. I'm going to work with Isobel.

Marion So.

There's a pause. Isobel doesn't move.

Isobel?

Isobel What?

Marion You didn't mention this.

Isobel Didn't I?

Katherine I want to sell up and, with the money I get, move to London. I think I've got a pretty good business head.

Marion What does Isobel feel?

Isobel does not turn.

Katherine It's just for one reason or another I never had a chance. I left school so suddenly.

Marion Mmm.

Katherine I wasn't ready. I had this ridiculous relationship with drugs. Which, thank God, I got over. But while that was going on, it was fucking hard to hold down a job. Then I put on four stones. I couldn't concentrate. I was fat and spotty and all over the place. So I never got going. Before I met Robert. And then down here with him, what was there? I helped out in the shop. But that's not really work. I know I'm ready now.

Marion If Isobel's happy.

Isobel Actually . . .

Marion What?

Isobel is about to say something, but changes her mind.

Isobel No.

Marion I thought your firm was very small?

Isobel Yes, it is.

Marion Just the three of you.

Isobel Yes.

Marion Can you afford another?

Isobel just looks at her, not answering.

When did you two decide about this?

Katherine For God's sake, Marion, we haven't decided. There's been a funeral.

Marion (*to Isobel*) Has she even asked you?

Isobel is silent, reluctant to speak.

Isobel Not in so many words.

Tom Marion, I think . . .

383

Marion Well, what do you feel about it?

Isobel Nothing. For the moment. I need time to think. We're all in shock. It's too hard. You think you're ready. Over and over you tell yourself it's coming. But when it happens, it cuts you off at the knees.

There's a pause.

Katherine Yes, that's right.

Isobel Why don't we talk later?

Katherine God, I need a drink.

Tom Squash?

Marion We all need a drink. It's only out of consideration for you that we're not all having one.

Tom It was Marion's idea. She felt if we all abstained from alcohol, it would be easier for you.

Katherine Well, thank you. (*She pauses a second, savage.*) Any chance of a Scotch? (*Before anyone can respond, she puts her hands up.*) All right, well fine, I didn't ask Isobel. No, I didn't. I assumed. That was wrong. I apologize. However, thank God Isobel is a generous person. I think she knows what I can contribute. She isn't going to say no.

At once there is a ringing noise from Marion's handbag.

What's that? Is that your handbag?

Marion is getting a phone out of her handbag.

Marion Sorry, everyone, I had to turn it back on.

Katherine Can't you leave it off the hook?

Marion There is no hook. (*She speaks into it.*) Hello, yes, it's all right. The funeral's over. Hold on, I'm going indoors. (*She walks off towards the house.*)

Katherine I see there's no chance of escaping this Government.

Isobel I heard it all night.

Tom I know.

Katherine How do you put up with it?

Tom Oh, I'm not interested in politics.

Katherine No. But you must hear the phone.

Tom No. Not really. It's just part of Marion. She's just someone who permanently gives off a ringing tone. (*He smiles and shrugs.*)

Katherine I just hate it. The idea of what she's doing. Someone at a party once said to me – they hadn't met Robert – they said, 'Oh, I hear you've got two step-daughters.' 'Yes. Marion and Isobel.' They said, 'Where are they at school?' I said, 'Marion's not at school actually, she's Junior Minister at the Department of the Environment.' They looked at me like I was nuts.

Isobel I can see.

Katherine I have to explain to everyone. She's just my step-daughter. It's absolutely nothing to do with me. What this Government is. Its loathsome materialism. The awful sanctification of greed. It's not my fault. That's what I say to people. I can't help it. Please don't blame me.

Isobel Nobody does.

Katherine Well, good.

Isobel looks uneasily at Tom, who is still standing.

It's why I love the idea of joining your business. I like what you do. Your designs. There's something decent about them. When I pick up a book with one of your covers – or a record – I always think, this is something which gives nourishment to people.

Isobel Some of them do.

Katherine I thought the best thing would be if I came with you this evening.

Isobel This evening?

Katherine Is that all right?

Isobel looks quickly at Tom.

Isobel What, you mean . . . I hadn't realized . . .

Katherine I don't want to sleep here. The idea . . . now Robert's gone. I'd like to start work in the morning. Put this whole thing behind me.

Isobel I'm not sure. Remember, it's all very recent. I think you should rest – at least for a week or two.

Katherine looks sharply at her.

Katherine What are you saying? You don't want me?

Isobel No, of course not. It's just . . . it's difficult. There's me and Gordon and Irwin, that's all. The three of us. We're very small beer. Each of us knows what each of us does. Inside out. We've been years together. We know each other's ways. And, to be honest, we're not making a great deal of money. If we wanted to expand, we'd have to be sure of the work to pay for it.

Katherine But exactly. That's what I'd do. (*She smiles enthusiastically.*) I can sell.

Isobel I'm sure.

Katherine That's what I'd be good at. Going to publishers. Getting you new contracts.

Isobel We know all the publishers. (*She smiles, trying to make light of it.*) It's a very small world.

Katherine Yes, all right. But I've got a knack.

She waits a second, Isobel lost for an answer.

You're saying no.

Isobel I'm not saying no.

Katherine Isobel, for fuck's sake, I need help.

Isobel I know. I know that. I will give you help. So will Tom.

Tom Absolutely.

Isobel Please come to London, certainly. For a while. You can sleep on my floor.

Tom That's a fair offer.

Isobel For the moment I just can't promise you a job.

There's a moment's delay, then Katherine gets up furious.

Katherine I'm going to the pub.

Isobel Now, look . . .

Katherine I don't give a fuck. I'm sick of being patronized. There's only one person who ever believed in me.

Isobel We all believe in you.

Katherine There's just one man who ever gave me a chance. The rest of you – well, yes, Isobel, in a way you're the worst. The others don't pretend. But you – it's all this kindness and tolerance and decency. Then just ask for something, some practical demonstration, just a small act of faith, then it's no. 'Fuck off.' It's so *fucking* English.

She goes out. Isobel puts her head in her hands.

Tom I'll go after her.

Isobel It's all right. They won't let her in. She's been banned for life from the Drum and Monkey.

Tom (*puzzled*) Isn't she English herself?

Isobel is suddenly exasperated.

Isobel Oh, God, it makes you feel so powerless. I saw all this coming. I saw it weeks ago. And I just delayed doing anything. I thought, just leave it, I've got more than enough. Nursing Robert. I was doing almost nothing. Most of the time I was just holding his hand. Often as he slept. Once in a while, Katherine would put her head in. She'd kiss him on the forehead. I remember thinking, as she bent over the bed: When Robert dies, the trouble will start.

Marion comes back in.

Marion What's going on?

Isobel ignores her, not noticing her.

Isobel And there's *nothing* you can do. You can see it coming, and you still can't do anything.

Marion Katherine's going mad.

Tom She won't get into the pub.

Marion She's in the kitchen. She seems to be taking up floorboards.

Isobel Oh, God, she must have a hiding place.

Marion anticipates Isobel's departure by shaking her head.

Marion It's too late. She's already got it.

Isobel I thought I'd looked everywhere.

Marion She says you won't give her a job.

Isobel Well, I can't.

Tom I'll go.

Tom goes out towards the kitchen. Marion is looking at Isobel with disdain.

Marion How can you have been so incredibly stupid?

Isobel What was I meant to do?

Marion I'd have thought it's fairly obvious. You have to pretend.

Isobel Pretend? Pretend what? That I have lots of money? That I don't have any partners? That we don't all have to work alongside each other, three to a rather small room?

Marion Why didn't you say, 'Well, I don't know yet. Come to London.'

Isobel That's exactly what I said.

Marion Keep her calm. String her along.

Isobel I tried.

Marion *Lie* to her.

There's a moment's pause.

Isobel No.

Marion Why not?

Isobel Because I can't. She pushed me. I could have said, 'Yes, fine, there's a job.' But there isn't. She'd have found out pretty quickly. What's the point of lying? (*She looks at Marion a second.*) Anyway it's wrong.

Marion Well, that's it.

Isobel What?

Marion There you are. *That*'s what it's about. That's why she's crying in the kitchen. With a bottle of whisky in her hand. Because *you* can't understand there are actually more important things in life than your wretched sense of honesty.

Isobel looks at her, not rising to the charge.

Isobel Well, in that case why won't *you* offer her a job?

Marion Don't be ridiculous. I'm in the Conservative Party. We can't just take on anyone at all.

Isobel What, and I can?

Marion It's different.

Isobel How?

Marion You know perfectly well. It's quite a different world. With extremely high standards of intellect and conduct. Civil servants have an extremely competitive and highly ordered career structure. In which you get very few marks for being an abusive alcoholic.

Isobel Oh, so you think she's just right for me.

Marion shakes her head, angry.

Marion No, it's you who always says there's nothing wrong with her. You always say, 'Oh, she's fine. Just restless.' But when the moment comes . . . that's the end of your so-called principles. You're so like Dad.

Isobel It's nothing to do with principles. (*She sits down, lost.*) I'd just like to be sure we do the right thing.

Katherine returns, silently. She appears quite quickly, then moves towards them, a new gentleness in her manner.

Katherine Well, this is much nicer. I apologize. I was being shitty. (*She leans over the top of Isobel's chair and kisses her.*) Isobel.

Isobel It's fine. (*Characteristically, she takes Katherine's hand for a few seconds.*)

Katherine I've spoken to Mrs Hurley. I was in the kitchen. Lunch will be ready in three-quarters of an hour. She's planning a rabbit and vegetable pie.

Suddenly Tom appears. He has obviously been running in pursuit of Katherine. Katherine smiles.

I outsmarted him. I've hidden the bottle again.

Tom I'm sorry, Marion. I tried.

Marion looks at him unforgivingly. Now Katherine is suddenly emotional, the alcohol flowing round in her and coming out as tears.

Katherine It gives me confidence, and I must say today I should be allowed a little confidence. Given what lies ahead. (*She smiles bravely, wiping her eyes with her sleeve. She sits down.*) Your dad never told you, he actually met me when he stopped one night in a motel. It was in the Vale of Evesham, he was coming back from the North. I don't know how I'd ended up there. I was working the bar. It was appalling. Trying to pick men up – not even for money, but because I was so unhappy with myself. I wanted something to happen. I don't know how I thought these men might help me, they were travellers, small goods, that sort of thing, all with slack bellies and smelling of late-night curries. I can still smell them. I don't know why, I'd been doing it for weeks. Then Robert came in. He said, 'I'll drive you to Gloucestershire. It will give you some peace.' He brought me here, to this house. He put fresh sheets in the spare room. Everything I did, before or

since, he forgave. (*She sits, tears in her eyes, quiet now.*)
People say I took advantage of his decency. But what are
good people for? They're here to help the trashy people
like me.

Marion looks disapprovingly from the back.

Marion Well, I suppose that's one way of looking at it.

Katherine It did make me laugh. The ring you gave
Robert is missing.

Marion I'm sorry?

Katherine Yes. Today I went into his room. I was planning
to give it to you. The funny thing is, I guess you'd already
taken it.

Katherine smiles. Marion looks cornered, shifty.

Marion Oh, yes. Actually I did pick it up. For its
sentimental value, that's all.

*There's a pause. Isobel and Katherine are smiling. Tom
is looking down.*

Isobel Katherine, I'll take you tonight.

Katherine No, really.

Isobel You say you want a job. You can start with me
tomorrow.

Katherine That's very nice of you, Isobel.

Isobel looks at her warily.

Isobel I'd like to feel it would mean you gave up the
whisky.

Katherine I can't promise. I can promise I'll try.

*Isobel stands. She smiles. Katherine gets up and
embraces her.*

Oh, Isobel.

Tom stands admiring the couple in each other's arms.

Tom Perfect.

Marion I must say I'm pleased.

Marion and Katherine embrace now.

Katherine.

Tom Praise the Lord.

Marion What?

Tom No. Nothing. I'll shut up.

The three women look at him. He stands a moment, cheerful, embarrassed.

I'm sorry. It just slipped out.

At once the sound of Irwin's voice, almost overlapping as the scene is replaced by Isobel's studio, which is a room half office, half studio, in which there are three dominating draughtsmen's desks, each with its own stool. Late evening. The lights are burning, Irwin is returning to his desk with a sheet of tracing paper. Irwin is an apparently modest man, in his late twenties, his curly hair smartly cut short. He wears blue jeans, more or less identical to Isobel's and a coloured sportshirt. He is calling offstage to someone we do not yet see.

SCENE THREE

Isobel's office.

Irwin I've got everything on file. I can't help it. I file everything. I even filed at school. (*He sits at his desk and resumes working.*) Every scrap of paper. Everything in

393

place. I don't know what it means. Someone once told me it meant I was prematurely middle-aged.

Now we see Isobel joining him, carrying two cups of coffee, one of which she sets down by his desk. She is still in her jeans, but with another sportshirt which is only subtly different from Irwin's.

Isobel Well, I don't like to say. I mean, about the filing.

Irwin I know.

Isobel And do you keep private things?

Irwin Certainly.

Isobel I'll bear that in mind. (*She smiles and goes to her own desk, where she also begins to work.*)

Irwin It's silly. I even have a file marked 'Smashed Dreams'.

Isobel Go on.

Irwin You know, when something goes wrong, something you've dreamt about, when you know it just isn't going to happen, I pile up all the bits and pieces, and then put them away.

Isobel smiles.

Isobel Give me an example.

Irwin There was a waitress . . .

Isobel I haven't heard this.

Irwin I was seventeen.

Isobel What was she like?

Irwin She was great. I painted her, actually.

Isobel I've never seen that.

Irwin Yeah. She has veal parmigiana in one hand and kidneys turbigo in the other. With peas. I was very keen on colour in those days. And she had one of those actual uniforms – like twinkies, you know? The black and white costume. With the colour of the food. The composition was excellent.

Isobel And what was the dream?

Irwin smiles.

Irwin The dream was – oh, you know – we'd have a cottage in Suffolk. We used to go to Liverpool Street, and buy all the local papers. Search through. Even now when I hear the words 'East Anglia', it's like a hand enclosing my heart.

Isobel has got down from her stool and is now standing behind him, looking at his work.

Isobel It's very good.

Irwin I like the gun. I'm pleased with it.

Isobel I like the wound.

Irwin Oh, really? (*He hands her a photo.*) I used Reagan's. I found it in a paper. I looked at Kennedy's. But it was too much.

Isobel is looking thoughtfully at the photo.

Isobel The only thing I remember is, Alexander Haig ran through the White House screaming 'I'm in charge! I'm in charge!'

Irwin It was funny.

Isobel I know. But I have to tell you – this is shocking – it's the only time I've ever found a politician sexy.

Irwin God!

Isobel I know.

Irwin That is really not good.

Isobel I know. It's appalling. It makes no sense to me. It annoys me. (*She smiles.*) There ought to be some justice.

Irwin (*quietly*) That's right.

Isobel There is no justice. A woman responds to the most deplorable things.

She stands a moment. They are both completely quiet, not looking at each other. Then she blushes bright red, looking down.

Irwin You're blushing.

Isobel No. I'm sorry. (*She looks away, half giggling, very embarrassed.*) I was thinking of something you do.

There is a contented silence. Neither of them moves or looks at the other.

Irwin (*quietly*) Do you think we'll have a child?

Isobel Mmm. There's a fair chance of it.

Irwin Will you marry me?

Isobel turns and looks at him.

Will you marry me now? If I ask?

Isobel I think we *will* get married.

Irwin Uh-huh. (*He sits, thinking.*)

Isobel It's something Dad said – for no reason – a few days before he died. Absolutely no reason. It was weeks since I'd mentioned you. He only met you once. He said, 'Will you marry Irwin?' I said, 'Yes, I rather think I will.' (*She suddenly looks up, sharply.*) What's that? I heard something drop. (*She goes to the door and opens it, picking up an envelope as she does.*) It's a note.

Irwin Is anyone there?

Isobel No. They've gone.

She closes the door, having looked down the corridor. She opens the envelope and reads. Irwin hunches down over his work.

How extraordinary. It's from Gordon.

Irwin Oh, yes?

Isobel He says if he sees me, I'll dissuade him. But he's decided it's time to move on. (*She looks up.*) What has got into him? (*She moves quickly across the room to the telephone.*) Shit, what's his number?

Irwin He won't be home yet. If he dropped off the note.

Isobel What a fathead! Why couldn't he face me? Really! Irwin?

Irwin Because he can't resist you. He thinks you'd get him back.

There's a silence. She looks at the note, then at Irwin.

Isobel What's going on? Did he talk to you?

Irwin Just a little.

Isobel Did he tell you he was going?

Irwin Not in so many words.

There's a silence.

Is it Katherine?

Irwin doesn't answer. But Isobel is surprisingly calm and gentle when she speaks.

Why didn't you tell me if that's what it is?

Irwin Because, really, it's none of my business. He was slightly put out, it is true.

Isobel I should have asked him first?

Irwin Not that. You know she's quite difficult.

Isobel She's impulsive.

Irwin Yes. Also she's proprietorial. We work very hard, the money isn't brilliant . . .

Isobel I'm trying to improve it.

Irwin I know. I'm not criticizing. But before Katherine came, Gordon had job satisfaction to compensate. And I think he probably felt that had gone.

Isobel thinks a moment.

Isobel (*decisively*) I'll call him up.

Irwin Also – let's be fair – it was always a bit odd, even before Katherine came. He was in love with you.

Isobel You think so?

Irwin I haven't any doubt.

Isobel looks at Irwin uneasily.

Isobel He never said.

Irwin Of course not. He was fifty. And looked like Sydney Greenstreet. He was also very sweet. My guess is he'd never loved a woman. So think about it. He's living at a certain level of pain. But there are privileges. Like, he sees you every day. You give him your attention. Things are pleasant. And stable. Till Katherine.

Isobel is suddenly quiet, looking at Irwin.

Isobel You seem to understand this. Do you feel the same way?

Irwin puts down his pen, serious.

Irwin It's different for me.

Isobel Why?

Irwin Because we're together. I have you.

Isobel So you mean you'll put up with Katherine?

Irwin Partly. (*He looks down.*) Anyway, now it's a practical question. Who'll do the books?

Isobel Well, she can. Can't she?

Irwin Accounts? Katherine?

Isobel Katherine can do maths. She's not incompetent.

Irwin It's just we used to be running a business. Now you want us to do social work.

Isobel stands, brought up short by what Irwin has said. She looks at the telephone.

Isobel I can't call him. Not if that's the situation. Oh fuck, why is everything so *hard*?

She stands, lost. Irwin watches her a moment.

Irwin What actually happened at the funeral?

Isobel Oh . . . (*She waves a hand uselessly.*)

Irwin I didn't like to ask before.

Isobel No. I didn't like to say.

Irwin You never said anything. You just came back with Katherine.

Isobel I haven't had time to decide what I feel.

Irwin How was Marion?

Isobel All right. (*She laughs in anticipation of her story.*)

Did I tell you, they're building a swimming pool in their back garden?

Irwin That sounds very nice.

Isobel That's what I said. Till I realized it's for Tom to do his conversions. I was looking at his suit trousers, I noticed they were wrinkled. He said they're always like this. It's because he wades in. If you look carefully round his chest, you can see a sort of watermark. I said, why can't you baptize people in swimming trunks? He said, the Lord expects a certain level of decency.

Irwin is smiling.

Irwin What did Marion think about Katherine?

Isobel Oh. She was desperate I give her a job.

Irwin looks at Isobel significantly.

Don't look at me like that

Irwin I'm sorry.

Isobel I hate it. What are you thinking?

Irwin I don't know, I wasn't there at the funeral, I can't gauge. But it seems to me everyone landed her on you.

Isobel No, it's not true.

Irwin Does Marion like her?

Isobel Of course not.

Irwin Well!

Isobel That's not the point. I just feel – she hasn't said this – I just know that if I tried to get rid of her now, it would be disastrous for her self-confidence. She's just lost her husband. She couldn't face the future. She was frightened.

She was lonely. If I hurt her now, it'll put her right back on the drink.

Irwin pauses, doubtful.

Irwin Yes, I'm sure, but . . .

Isobel What?

Irwin Isn't that a form of blackmail? I've had friends who've been through all this. The threat is 'put up with everything I do, or else I'll drink again'. Don't alcoholics just drain everyone around them?

Isobel Yes, but she's stopped. She's *ex*-alcoholic. She's been here three weeks and not touched a drop.

Irwin Not in front of us.

Isobel That's really unfair.

There's a pause. Irwin looks down.

We're doing something for her. We're helping her. She's happy here. I know all the problems. But we can't just pull out of it now.

Irwin smiles.

Irwin Do you want to go to bed?

Isobel No. I did. I wanted to, ten minutes ago.

They are both smiling.

What are you laughing at?

Irwin Now Katherine's climbing into our bed.

At once Katherine comes in. She is wearing a large coat, and underneath it a smart shiny blue dress. Her arms are full of flowers.

Katherine Flowers! Flowers! Flowers for everyone!

She dumps armfuls down on the table, then takes some across to Isobel.

Look, Pacific orchids. They're incredibly rare.

She sets these down beside Isobel, then starts to take off her coat.

Isobel What on earth's going on?

Katherine The man's outside. I've bought his whole stall.

Isobel What time is it?

Irwin Nine.

Katherine Do you have any money? The wretched man's followed me. I've said I'll go back tomorrow.

Isobel Irwin?

Irwin shrugs slightly and goes out to pay the man

Katherine I walk that way every day. Why can't people *trust* you? Stupid little man.

Isobel What are you celebrating?

Katherine I've sold the house.

Isobel Dad's house?

Isobel stands astonished as Katherine now searches for vases in the cupboard. Irwin returns, wallet in hand.

Irwin It was seventy pounds. It's cleaned me out. Do you want to write me a cheque?

Katherine Don't worry. I'll do it tomorrow.

Isobel When did you sell it?

Katherine Today. To a sucker in computers. Just think, I'll never have to go back.

Irwin frowns and goes back to his work.

I'm going to get a flat in London with the money. I saw a place just round the corner from here. Only nicer. I just passed it with Max.

Isobel Max?

Katherine You know, the publisher.

Isobel Of course I know Max.

Katherine The man I went to see. And – listen – he says he will consider giving us exclusivity. We can do all his covers for an eighteen-month trial period. An exclusive contract.

Irwin Really? (*He looks at her doubtfully.*)

Katherine Well, ring him. That's what he said. Mind you, it was fucking hard work. I had to take him to dinner. I was crossing and uncrossing my legs. I thought I'd have to make the ultimate sacrifice on behalf of the company. (*She has moved across with a jar of flowers to where Irwin is working.*) What's this? The *Encyclopaedia of Murder*?

Irwin Yes.

Katherine No, that isn't right. There should be an exit wound. And that's not the effect. (*She puts the flowers down.*) Look, give me a pencil. There's one here.

Irwin grabs his drawing from the board before she can write on it.

Irwin Leave that.

Katherine Why?

Irwin Just leave it.

Katherine I'll show you. Look, another piece of paper. A bullet goes through like *this*. Do you see?

Irwin goes to the other side of the room, very deliberately. Isobel is still standing in disbelief.

Isobel You sold the house?

Katherine Yes.

Irwin now holds up a book, his voice raised.

Irwin I actually bought a book. I went to the library this morning, I may say before you were awake, you were snoring on the floor . . .

Katherine Point taken.

Irwin It's called *Criminal Pathology*. (*He points to it.*)

Isobel Irwin, hold on.

Irwin It has a series of extremely lurid photographs. Which I have copied with photographic accuracy.

Katherine Yes, can I say something I've been longing to say? I think that may be the trouble with your work. Its very accuracy. I've got a different idea of art. I think the artist should *add* something. He should add an extra layer. That's what you're not quite doing in some of your stuff.

She shakes her head slightly. Irwin is watching her, saying nothing.

You're very bound, you're very *earthbound* by all this accuracy business.

Isobel attempts to intervene.

Isobel Please, both of you, can we hold off on this?

Irwin Now look, hold on, just a moment, you said this picture wasn't accurate?

Katherine That's right.

Irwin Then you said I was too restricted by accuracy.

404

Katherine That's right also. It's incredible. You're losing both ways. (*She smiles at the irony of it.*) The funny thing is, Max was saying at dinner . . .

Irwin Were you two talking about my work?

Katherine . . . he wanted to give us a contract because he was so convinced I could bring something out in you. Maybe something you didn't even know was there.

Irwin Well, I'm sure *that's* true.

Isobel speaks with sudden emphasis.

Isobel She's sold the house.

Irwin What?

Isobel Our father's house. She didn't ask us.

There is a pause. Katherine seems offended for a moment. Then goes to get more flowers.

Katherine (*casually*) What's wrong? I rang Marion. She said the whole deal was fine.

Irwin looks across at Isobel, his earlier point proved.

I wanted to check I was asking enough money. So I knew Marion was the right person to ask.

Irwin Did Marion call you?

Isobel shakes her head, her voice now very small.

Isobel Marion hates the house.

Katherine Certainly she said she was never going to use it. I said I could never face going back. (*She smiles sweetly at Isobel.*) That only left you. (*She stops now, serious.*) I have no money, Isobel. It's as simple as that. Robert and I spent everything he earned. He had no investments, he didn't approve of them. He thought they were wrong. So do I.

It's immoral, all that disgusting trading in shares. He just
bought books. I loved that in him. His other-worldliness.
The way he just didn't give a damn about money. But now
of course we've got to pay for that other-worldliness. The
bill's come in. We've got to pay duties. (*She looks sadly
down.*) And I knew you wouldn't want me to starve.

Isobel No.

> *Isobel looks at her. Katherine looks back, the two of
> them staring at one another. Then Katherine suddenly
> cheers up.*

Katherine I'll make some cocoa. Then I'll come back and
tell you everything that happened at dinner.

> *She goes out. Irwin waits, tactfully, for Isobel to speak.*

Irwin Isobel.

Isobel I know. Don't say anything. (*She shakes her head.*)
What are they doing? I wish someone would tell me what's
going on. (*She looks a moment to where Katherine has
gone.*) For a start it's only three weeks ago. Are we not
allowed to *mourn*? Just . . . a decent period of mourning?
Can't we have that? Can't we sit quietly? Why on earth is
everyone running around? (*She looks to Irwin.*) I watch
my family now, it's like they have to be *doing*, it doesn't
matter what. Run around, sell this, change that. The day
he died, I was sitting in his room, just trying for a moment
of stillness. In came Marion. (*She shakes her head.*) Can't
we have a moment of grief?

> *Irwin looks at her, as he has for the past moments, and
> now, tactfully, moves over to her.*

Irwin Isobel, they're cutting loose. Now you've got to.

Isobel What do you mean?

Irwin They're saying the whole thing is over. Your father's dead. There is no family. You're the only person who's still hung up on it. Don't you see? (*He kneels beside her, his tone gentle.*) You have to let go.

Isobel But what does that mean?

Irwin looks her in the eye.

Irwin Sack Katherine.

Isobel Irwin, I can't.

Irwin You must. It's a farce, what she's doing. What she just said about Max.

Isobel I know. Don't. (*She shudders in horror.*)

Irwin The idea that Max . . .

Isobel Oh, don't.

Irwin . . . this lovely old man would sit at dinner while Katherine made a play for him. It's appalling. Katherine leaning over the table in that awful dress. Her bosom hanging out. I mean it's actually funny. It'll make us a laughing-stock. And for what? (*He pauses a moment.*) Because you have some misplaced sense of duty to your father.

Isobel turns and looks down at him.

Isobel, you owe her nothing. Get rid of her now.

Isobel looks at him a moment, then shakes her head.

Isobel There was something there for Robert. I can't just abandon her. Think, there was this middle-aged man. Very idealistic. Living a life of ideas. 'Yes, I know,' he said, 'Katherine's impossible. But without her I'd have had a much less interesting life.' (*She smiles.*) 'I'm timid,' he said. 'My big fault is, I live in my shell. She gets me out of it. She's confrontational.' He loved that.

He said that living with Katherine was like being on manoeuvres with a great army. You had no idea where you'd wake up the next day. Once he woke up at four. She was in the kitchen with a drinking friend. She had a gun in her hand, and was yelling, 'Go on, do it! Do it! I want you to! If you love me, shoot me in the leg!' He loved that story. He didn't mind what people called her awfulness. Along came this girl who was prepared to say what she thought, especially to all those people he didn't dare be rude to himself. That's what he loved. She dared to say what he was only thinking. She wasn't dependent on anyone's opinion. (*She smiles.*) You know what it was? He thought she was free.

Irwin is bewildered, assertive.

Irwin But she *isn't*.

Isobel Of course not.

Irwin She's chronically dependent. Mostly on other people's good will. What you're describing is what more usually is called bad behaviour. And it's always at somebody else's expense.

Isobel looks at him a moment.

Isobel Mmm.

Irwin All you're saying is, she found a sucker.

Isobel It made him happy.

Irwin That's not the point. It won't make you happy. Will it?

Isobel pauses again.

Isobel No.

Irwin Then that's it. You have no choice.

She looks at him. Then reaches and puts her hand on his cheek.

Isobel I don't want to do it. Not tonight. I want to bury my head in the sand.

Irwin You can't do that.

Isobel Why not?

She smiles. He kisses the back of her hand. At once she kisses him. He puts his arms round her, the feeling warm between them.

I like it. I've got great plumage.

Irwin I've seen your plumage.

He smiles. Katherine calls from the other room.

Katherine (*off*) Isobel! Isobel!

Irwin But you must do something now.

Katherine returns with a huge vase of flowers beautifully arranged. She is already talking. Irwin gets up and tactfully takes them from her.

Katherine Did I tell you . . .

Irwin I'll take those from you.

Katherine Marion said she wants to make an investment in the firm?

Isobel In us?

Katherine Yes.

Isobel How extraordinary! She's never said that before.

Katherine No. Well, she feels now I'm here, the whole thing's a much better bet.

Isobel frowns.

Isobel But why? I can't see we need it.

Katherine If we're expanding, I mean like if Max comes through, you're going to need extra artists. We're going to have to pay them.

Isobel Where would we put them?

Katherine waves her hand, confidently.

Katherine Oh, we'd get a bigger place. In the centre of town. If we expand now, get some capital investment, we could be making money like hay. (*She laughs.*) Everyone else is.

Isobel I'm not sure.

Katherine I admit, it all depends on me. I've got to keep Max's cock hot in my pocket. But you shouldn't worry. Tonight I made a pretty good start.

Isobel looks quickly to Irwin, who is standing watching.

Isobel Look, I'm sorry, Katherine . . . (*She stops, unable to go on.*)

Katherine What?

Isobel Max is my friend. I'm also very close to his wife. Who's called Julia. Max gave us our very first job. It's just incredibly offensive when you talk of him as if he were a prostitute's trick. (*She pauses again.*) You make me sound priggish. But it's a difference of style.

Katherine looks at her. She nods a little, suddenly quietened, sincere.

Katherine This isn't going to work. I felt it. I really did my best.

Isobel I know.

Katherine I put such effort into this.

Isobel I know you did, Katherine. I'm not attacking you. I'm just saying we go about things different ways.

Katherine smiles at a memory.

Katherine Yes, it's something Robert said. He said, 'You must always remember Isobel is very *narrow*. She has no vision.' That's right.

Irwin stirs uneasily.

Irwin I'm sure he didn't say that.

Katherine It's all right. I won't tell you any more of what he really thought. I promise you, I'm going to leave quietly. My shouting days are over. It's up to you to say. I'm not totally insensitive. Do you want me to leave?

Isobel looks in agony to Irwin for help.

Isobel Look, it's just I have lost Gordon . . .

Katherine We're not talking about Gordon. I'm asking *you*.

Isobel stands unable to answer. Then suddenly Irwin intervenes.

Irwin The answer is yes.

Isobel No.

Irwin Isobel just doesn't want to say it.

Isobel Irwin, please.

He holds up a hand. Stops. Looks steadily at Katherine.

Irwin We've just been talking. She's just too nice to say. I'll say it for her. She's been taken advantage of. She's desperate you should go.

There's a pause.

Look . . .

Katherine That's fine. Well, that's very clear. Thank you, Irwin. If you let me sleep here, I'll go in the morning. I'll say goodbye then.

She turns and goes out, silently. Isobel does not move. Irwin waits.

Irwin Well, there we are. Can we go to bed now? Isobel?

Isobel turns and looks at him blankly.

Come on.

Isobel Don't be ridiculous. No.

Irwin turns and goes to the desk, silently. He picks up the drawing and screws it into a ball. He throws it down into the wastepaper basket.

What's that?

Irwin No, she's right about the drawing. I'll start again. My work is tenth-rate. (*There is a pause.*) Please. Let's go to bed.

Isobel turns and looks at him.

Isobel I can't do this. She's got to stay.

Isobel goes out after her. Irwin turns towards us, his face darkening.
  Then the sound of women's laughter as the scene is replaced by Marion coming on in a pearl-grey suit, followed by Rhonda, a dark girl in her early twenties, with a great shock of long black hair, extremely lively and attractive, but with rather an academic disdain. They come from the garden into the living room of Robert's house, which is in the process of being stripped out. There is a bare wooden floor, no curtains, an odd selection of abandoned chairs, which are mixed up with

the open packing cases which are scattered round the room. But the library is still complete: walls of books from floor to ceiling. At the back a high, long line of windows gives out on to the lawn. It's early afternoon. The women are in great spirits.

SCENE FOUR

Robert's living room.

Marion Well, I must say I really enjoyed that. I can't remember when I had such a good time. I am actually good at it. I do actually enjoy a good political session.

Rhonda Oh yes, absolutely. I thought you were absolutely superb.

Marion Did you think so?

Marion stands, reliving the encounter. Rhonda flops down in a chair.

I don't like Greens. They're so self-righteous.

Katherine comes into the room from the hall. She is wearing a sweater and black trousers. She is carrying a book.

Hello, Katherine.

Katherine How are you?

She sits down to read her book in this half-empty room. Marion goes on as if she has been asked a question.

Marion I had to see a delegation. Those awful Greens. Green people. About radiation levels from nuclear power stations. A subject, I may say, about which I know a great deal more than they do.

413

Rhonda That was clear.

Marion They're always going on as if their case is moral. That's what annoys me. Ours is moral too. People need power. Nuclear power is a cheap and effective way to provide it. It gives a lot of ordinary, decent people a considerably improved standard of living.

Isobel appears in the doorway.

I think that's pretty *moral* as well.

She turns and sees Isobel, frowning. She has in her hands piles of old books for the packing cases across the room.

Isobel.

Isobel Who were those people?

Marion Greens. I said I'd meet them. I wanted to impress on them I had a country background. So I had the idea of showing them this house.

She smiles. Rhonda smiles too.

Isobel Where do they come from?

Marion London.

Rhonda Yes. It was brilliant. We said, 'You *can* meet the Minister. Of course. The Minister's happy to meet you. But wouldn't it be more appropriate to meet in the countryside?'

Isobel I see.

Rhonda It meant they had to drive down.

Marion I was going to be here anyway.

She shrugs. The two of them are grinning.

Rhonda You know her parting shot?

Isobel I don't.

Marion It's just I hate exaggeration. That and self-righteousness. Those two things. I said, 'Come back and see me when you're glowing in the dark.'

Rhonda Brilliant.

Marion I'd invited a journalist. His pencil went crazy. It's so easy. It's like throwing fish to seals. I was giving him the headline for his story. 'Minister Says Come Back When You Glow.'

Rhonda laughs again.

Isobel Isn't that a little bit risky?

Marion Why?

Isobel I mean, I don't know, isn't it a little bit extreme?

Marion It's a *little* bit extreme. That's why it's brilliant. That's the whole art of publicity for a politician. You roll back the boundary just that little bit. A year ago you couldn't have said it. But now – let's face it – everyone hates Greens. (*She sits down contentedly.*) They're bored. It's a seventies problem.

Rhonda That's right.

Marion points at Rhonda from across the room.

Marion I despise their briefing. I'm so much better briefed. You know, they had absolutely no understanding of the method of accounting for plutonium rods. I cottoned on to that. Something that man with the blue shoes said very early on. It was a very small slip. But I got it. (*She smiles at Rhonda.*) From that moment on, they were dead.

Rhonda Very good.

Marion You know, they were expecting an idiot. That's

the first mistake. Because you're a Conservative. And a member of the Government. They expect you to be stupid.

Rhonda That gives you an advantage.

Marion Yes, that's right. (*She turns and cuts the air decisively with her hand.*) You blast them right out of the water. Hey, at this moment I could take them all on. The gloves are off. That's what's great. That's what's exciting. It's a new age. Fight to the death.

Irwin has come in. He is wearing gumboots which in a moment he will sit down to take off. The sound of distant gunfire.

Irwin God, the countryside. You do forget, don't you?

Isobel What?

Irwin Hello, my love. (*He kisses her cheek before going to sit down.*) Saturday afternoon. It's like the trenches out there. Bang! Bang! Bang! What is it about country people? They want to kill everything that moves.

Katherine looks up for the first time.

Katherine Irwin's back. Are we ready for the meeting?

Marion Let's get Tom.

She nods at Rhonda who at once leaves the room on her errand.

Irwin We don't do it in London. We don't say, 'Great, let's go out and shoot some cats. That would be *fun*. Murder some dogs for exercise.'

Rhonda sweeps back into the room.

Rhonda He's coming.

Irwin Outside the cities England seems to be one big rifle range.

At once another explosion of gunfire and Tom comes in, carrying a black briefcase, which he is opening on the way.

Tom Right, everyone, I have the proposal in here.

Isobel smiles, trying to make a joke of how brisk everyone has suddenly become.

Isobel Oh, Lord.

Tom Are we ready?

Rhonda Should I go?

Marion No, of course not.

Tom has already walked over to Isobel and handed her papers.

Tom This is the form. You would sign this.

Isobel Thank you.

Tom And this. Incorporation. Transfer of title.

Marion has walked across from the other side and is already offering a Mont Blanc.

Marion Pen?

Isobel Thank you.

Isobel looks round. The whole room is suddenly waiting for her: Katherine in her chair, book on knee, Rhonda leaning against the bare wall, Irwin looking at his gumboots, Tom and Marion standing on opposite sides of the room.

Tom Please go ahead. Ask anything you like.

Isobel smiles, embarrassed, trying to keep the atmosphere light. In the distance the guns fire again.

Isobel Well, I mean, you know I've already hinted, I don't mean to be difficult, it's just Irwin and I . . . (*She turns to him.*) Do you want to speak first?

Irwin shakes his head.

We both feel . . . I don't know how to say it . . . what you're suggesting is a very big step.

Tom It's a big step for us.

Isobel Of course.

Tom My company has the spare money. We want to use it. We want to help your firm expand. Because, well, our motives are wonderful. We happen to believe in you.

Isobel Yes, well, that's jolly good. It's just . . . the *form* of the arrangement.

Marion Isobel's worried about the idea of a board.

Tom frowns.

Tom Oh, I see.

Marion She's used to owning her own firm.

Tom Yes, but surely you'd expect us to protect our investment? (*He stands a moment, genuinely puzzled.*) I don't think there's anything sinister in that. It's pretty normal practice.

Isobel Your company would own us?

Tom Well, yes, indirectly. They wouldn't interfere. After all you'd have a board of your own.

Isobel Of which you'd be chairman?

Tom Technically.

Isobel And of which I would simply be one single member?

Tom frowns again.

Tom You'd also be managing director.

Marion (*firmly*) Isobel, Tom is President of Christians in Business. I think that makes it pretty clear he's a man you can trust.

Isobel turns at once, upset.

Isobel Oh, God, yes, please, honestly, this mustn't be personal . . .

Tom (*shyly*) It isn't.

Marion He's Chairman of his church's Ethical Committee.

Tom We meet six times a year. We try to do business the way Jesus would have done it.

Isobel You mean, had he come to earth in a polyester suit and with two propelling pencils in his top pocket?

Tom I'm sorry?

Marion looks angrily across the room.

Marion Isobel's making a joke.

Tom Oh, I see.

Marion Tom is out there in the community. He runs all these schemes. For youth. Don't you, dear?

Isobel Of course. Tom's honesty is not at issue. (*She stops a moment, having trouble now. She tries to speak quietly.*) It's just I fear I'd be losing control.

There's a short silence. The guns fire again. Katherine looks up, speaks quietly.

Katherine Isobel, you *are* the business. Everyone knows that. You are its asset. With all respect to Irwin. You are

419

what makes it work. No one is going to replace you. (*She shrugs.*) The whole board thing is just a technicality.

Isobel shakes her head, frustrated now, beginning to get angry.

Isobel Why don't you just *give* me the money?

Marion I find that question unforgivably naive. (*Suddenly Marion has flared up, a sister reminded of old arguments.*)

Isobel Now look . . .

Marion No, I . . .

Isobel (*exasperated*) Perhaps I don't *want* to get bigger.

Marion Don't be ridiculous. Are you crazy? There's money to be made. Everyone's making it.

Tom Remember, God gives us certain gifts.

Marion Tom is right.

Tom And he expects us to use them. That's our duty. If we fail to use them, he gets angry. Justifiably. God says to himself, 'Now look, why did I give that person those gifts in the first place? If they're not willing to get out there and make a bit of an effort?'

Isobel I *am* using them.

Tom Yes. But not to the full.

Isobel looks at him a moment, across a hopeless gulf.

Marion It's just the time. You must feel it. It's out there. It's the only thing I regret about belonging to the Government. Unfortunately I've got to help drive the gravy train. I'd rather be clambering on the back and joining in the fun.

Isobel What fun?

Marion Making money.

Katherine Darling, everybody is.

Marion Please wake up.

Katherine is suddenly animated.

Katherine You know I think this Government's appalling. But on the other hand, let's face it, given what's going on, it's just stupid not to go and grab some dough for yourself.

Marion It's more than stupid. It's irresponsible.

Katherine I mean, give it to the good guys. That's my philosophy. If we don't make the money someone else will. Well, in my book the arseholes have had it their own way long enough.

Isobel smiles.

Isobel But isn't there a chance that taking some will turn *us* into arseholes?

Rhonda laughs. Katherine smiles at her, compassionately.

Katherine Oh, Isobel . . .

Isobel Well?

Katherine I think I can live with that danger. Can't you?

Marion is moving quietly to the far side of the room

Marion If you don't take the money, then you insult us.

Isobel Now, Marion, come on . . .

Marion It's like saying you don't trust us.

Isobel You know that's unfair. You mustn't say that.

Marion I don't know how else to interpret a refusal. You're saying you don't think your brother-in-law will look after your best interests. (*Marion turns away, letting the accusation hang damagingly in the air.*) I don't know. Perhaps that's what you feel.

Isobel No.

Isobel looks to Irwin, desperate for help, but his eyes are still on his feet. The guns fire in the distance. Then Marion is very quiet.

Marion Also, you know, you must think of other people.

Isobel I'm sorry? (*She looks at her, not comprehending.*) What?

Marion I sometimes think, what sort of life is it if we only think about ourselves?

Isobel looks round the room.

Isobel I'm sorry, Marion, you've lost me.

Marion Katherine.

She is looking across the room to where Katherine now has modestly folded her hands in her lap. Isobel is quite still.

Isobel Ah, yes.

Marion That's who I mean. I don't know, it's difficult . . . Katherine, do you mind if I say?

Katherine Go ahead.

Marion One of the reasons Tom is so eager to put money in, is to help Katherine through this very difficult time.

Isobel I see.

Marion To me, let's face it, what's the best thing to happen to this family? In many, many years? The way Katherine's coped with bereavement so magnificently.

Isobel stands, her lips tight together.

I don't think you'd deny her a seat on the board.

There is a silence. Isobel goes slow, sensing a trap.

Isobel No. Well, of course not . . .

Marion Would you?

Isobel Don't be silly.

Katherine is quite still.

If the scheme goes ahead, of course, it's agreed, Katherine would be part of it.

Marion Good. (*She smiles to herself.*) Tom and I love the idea of Katherine having a long-term directorship. It's just the kind of security she's lacked in her life. (*She shrugs slightly.*) I mean, again, it's your decision. Katherine won't mind. Will you, Katherine?

Katherine shakes her head. Isobel turns now to Irwin.

Isobel That leaves only one person. Irwin?

Irwin Yes?

Isobel What you were saying last night.

Irwin looks up mildly from his boots.

Irwin thinks it's folly to mix family and business.

Irwin I do think that. Normally, yes.

Isobel What d'you mean, 'normally'?

Irwin I don't know, I can see, I've been listening, it's all very tricky . . . (*He finally puts his boots decisively to one side.*) Let's face it, Isobel, we are a bit stuck. We do need capital . . .

Isobel Irwin . . .

Irwin Tom is cash-rich. From making paper napkins. Or whatever he does.

Tom smiles tolerantly.

It seems you would be getting a great boost. As far as I can see, with very few strings. The best way – I was explaining this to Tom and Marion this morning – to get good work in our field is to leave people alone and allow them some breathing space. (*He smiles confidently.*) Tom agrees with this. So it's not in his own interest to interfere in any way.

Marion looks across the room, pleased.

Marion Also Irwin did mention, you don't mind my saying this . . .?

Irwin What?

Marion He did think perhaps you were hoping to get married.

Isobel *Married*?

Irwin No!

Isobel Did Irwin say that?

Marion Irwin, you've landed me in it. Was that a confidence?

Irwin Isobel . . .

Marion Now you're being coy.

Irwin I said no such thing. Honestly.

Isobel Irwin, what have you been doing?

Marion I can't really see what's so wrong with the idea.

Isobel Please, Marion . . .

Marion holds up a hand in surrender.

Marion All right, disregard marriage, forget I ever said it. Whatever. It doesn't matter. Marriage or not, we are proposing to double Irwin's salary.

Isobel Double it?

Marion Yes. We did tell Irwin that.

Isobel Irwin, is this true?

Irwin shrugs and smiles, boyishly.

Irwin They said it.

Tom We rate him very highly.

Isobel Yes. So do I. (*Her voice is very faint now. She seems dazed.*)

Marion It does seem absurd. I couldn't believe it. Irwin says he doesn't even own his room in Kentish Town.

Irwin No, I don't.

Marion At his age, really, Isobel, that is ridiculous. For an artist of his talent.

Isobel Oh, yes.

Now she is staring at Irwin, her mind miles away, as if trying to work something out. Marion takes a few paces, almost talking to herself.

Marion If someone comes along, says, 'Look, you'll do exactly the same job, in the same hours, in the same way, the only difference is, you'll be paid double . . .' (*She smiles to herself.*) You can't blame Irwin.

Rhonda Why do people think it's smart to be poor?

There's a silence, full of sadness. Marion frowns, surprised by Rhonda's sudden interruption. Then Tom breaks the mood, snapping his briefcase shut.

Tom I have to go. I've got a total immersion at six. Are you coming with me, darling?

Marion Yes. Rhonda's coming as well. Let's make some tea. Katherine?

Katherine Oh, yes.

She gets up from her seat. Tom and Rhonda go first as Marion stops a moment at the door.

Marion Think about it anyway.

She puts her arm round Katherine as they turn to go out. Isobel and Irwin are left alone in the empty room. Isobel is turned away from him, he behind her.

Irwin Isobel, please. Just look at me. Please.

She doesn't turn.

Things move on. You brought in Katherine. Be fair, it was you. It changed the nature of the firm. For better or worse. But it's changed. And you did it. Not me.

There is silence.

I wouldn't hurt you. You know that. I'd rather die than see you hurt. I love you. I want you. There's not a moment when I don't want you.

Isobel stands quite still, not turning. The sound of the guns.

Isobel The guns are getting nearer. God, will nobody leave us in peace?

The lights fade.

Act Two

Isobel's new offices in the West End. The draughtsmen's desks are noticeably newer and smarter than the old ones; there are more of them stretching away into the distance towards a back wall which is dominated by a large-scale, chic, designer motif. There are pools of light fashionably formed over each desk, but for the moment only one area is occupied. Irwin is sitting at his board, looking down at Rhonda who is on a rug on the floor. She is dressed only in a short blue silk dressing gown. There is a glass of champagne at her side, and Irwin has another. The place is deserted but for them. It's late.

Irwin What did he do then?

Rhonda Who?

Irwin This man of yours.

Rhonda Oh, well, of course. He was ready for the pounce.

Irwin What was the pounce like?

Rhonda As you'd expect. It was crude. (*She smiles.*)

Irwin No, tell me.

Rhonda He's a senior Tory politician. He's a Minister. Right? So he starts to talk all about his wife . . .

Irwin What, she doesn't understand him?

Rhonda Uh-huh, worse than that.

Irwin Worse? What?

Rhonda Guess. What's the worst thing of all?

427

Irwin shrugs.

Irwin You've lost me.

Rhonda You must have guessed.

Irwin No.

Rhonda She can't come.

Now Irwin smiles.

Irwin Good Lord, you astonish me. I'm trying to work out which one it must be. A Tory politician whose wife can't come.

Rhonda Have you got it yet?

Irwin Not really. To be honest, I'm spoilt for choice. Tell me more.

Rhonda Yeah, well, he's saying she's had some sort of accident. Ten years ago. A black man jumped out of an alley . . .

Irwin I see – what – and this has permanently damaged . . .

Rhonda Look, I don't believe it any more than you. A man is talking. Do you believe anything any man says? Especially on this subject? Do you have any idea what being a woman is like? By nightfall you're stuffed. You've spent the whole day sitting listening to men deceive themselves. If you're lucky. That's if they're not actually out deceiving you.

Irwin smiles, unworried.

Irwin Oh, really?

Rhonda Anyway, this man has spotted me in the Library at the House of Commons, researching for Marion . . .

Irwin And what's attracted him?

Rhonda laughs, suddenly embarrassed.

Rhonda No, I can't say.

Irwin No, come on, I'll tell you mine.

Rhonda Your what?

Irwin My most ridiculous sexual experience.

She looks at him a moment. Then tells.

Rhonda He saw me eating a prawn and mayonnaise sandwich. He says with my mouth half-open. So he could half see it. And this has simply driven him mad. (*She looks inquiringly at Irwin.*) Well? Have you got him yet?

Irwin Agriculture and Fisheries?

Rhonda No.

Irwin Is he in Defence? It's not . . .

Rhonda No, you're nowhere near.

They smile.

I said, well, if he bought me another identical sandwich, I'd be willing to go round and eat it in his flat.

Irwin And did he?

Rhonda smiles and gathers the folds of her robe, tucking them tightly round her legs.

Rhonda Why should I tell you? Isn't it more fun if you have to imagine?

Irwin And is that the point of this? Fun?

A pause. Rhonda looks down. Then she resumes decisively.

Rhonda Also, of course, he's fanatical about secrecy. The thing the electorate understands about Tory administrations is that the moment they get in, they take their dicks out of their trousers and all start waving them around.

Irwin I know. It's strange. It's never Labour.

Rhonda *Never* Labour, no. (*She pauses, puzzled a moment.*) So this makes him also, not only lascivious, not only a scuzzbag as you might say, but also very security-conscious. He's worried sick about where and when we're going to meet.

Irwin Do you meet?

Rhonda Yes. Eventually.

Irwin And?

She pauses a moment, thoughtful.

Rhonda It's the usual stuff. I don't know what he wants. Nor does he. He's like a man, that's all I can say. He's so out of touch with his feelings that he's like some great half-dead animal that lies there, just thrashing about.

Irwin Mmm. (*He thinks a moment, struck by her sadness.*) Not good.

Rhonda No. Seldom is, though. In my experience.

Irwin What does that mean?

Rhonda It means men are cunt-struck. But they rarely know why.

There is a silence. Irwin sips champagne.

Irwin Do you think that?

Rhonda Well, I do really.

Irwin Is it always true?

Rhonda Not always. Often. I find men cry out. I don't know why. 'Oh, no,' they say. Like they're shocked by what they feel.

Irwin Good Lord. You make it sound sad.

There is a moment's silence. Rhonda looks away.

Have you been back?

Rhonda Where?

Irwin No, I mean, with the politician?

Rhonda Oh, you're joking. He calls. He calls all the time.

Irwin Do you answer?

Rhonda One day I'm going to give him a shock. I'll get Marion to take it. And that'll be the end. (*She smiles.*) I already told her about him.

Irwin You told Marion?

Rhonda Certainly. We laughed ourselves silly.

Irwin Goodness. *Marion*?

Rhonda Yes. She loves gossip. Perhaps because her own life's so dull. I think that's why she employed me. She likes the idea . . . (*But she stops in mid-sentence.*)

Irwin What?

Rhonda No.

Irwin What are you saying?

Rhonda She likes the idea that I cause chaos.

There's a pause.

Irwin And do you?

Rhonda Not always. Sometimes I do. (*She looks at him.*) Tell me yours.

Irwin What?

Rhonda Don't you have a story?

Irwin Oh. Not really.

Rhonda You said you did.

Irwin Not at the moment. But somehow I feel I'm just about to.

Rhonda Oh, really? Why?

They look at each other now.

Irwin You used a dirty word. It excited me.

Rhonda What word?

Irwin Chaos.

There's a silence. Then Rhonda smiles.

Rhonda Yes, I've noticed. It has an effect.

The door opens at the back. Isobel stands in the doorway. She is harassed, tired, carrying a soft overnight bag and a big design portfolio. Seeing Rhonda and Irwin, she stands in the doorway, not moving.

Irwin Isobel. My goodness.

Rhonda Good evening.

Rhonda quickly gets up from the floor, guiltily. Isobel puts the bags down and closes the door.

Irwin What happened to Glasgow?

Isobel It was called off. (*She has moved into the room now and dumps the portfolio on his desk.*) Here, take this. It's yours. I won't be needing it. It's the industrial logo.

Irwin What happened?

Isobel I missed the last plane.

Irwin But you set off hours ago.

Both Rhonda and Irwin are standing, not moving, while Isobel keeps up a chain of action, collecting a pile of written messages from a pigeonhole, going to her own desk, sitting down to read them.

Isobel Have you dealt with these messages?

Irwin Rhonda came round. To see our new premises.

Isobel Ah.

Rhonda I think they're great. Irwin said you even had an en-suite executive bathroom. We were talking on the phone . . .

Irwin Yes . . .

Rhonda I mentioned my water was off. He said you had a new shower. I couldn't resist it.

Isobel Was it good?

Rhonda Oh. I haven't had it yet.

She walks across the room to the bathroom. Isobel now carries on working, opening her diary, ticking off items on lists.

I'm just about to.

Isobel (*to Irwin*) Did you do the layout for the publisher's ad?

Irwin It's here.

Rhonda I can't wait. I hear there's a bidet.

Isobel There's no bidet. There's everything else. But if that's what you need you can always do handstands in the shower.

Rhonda stands a moment in the doorway, taking in this remark.

Rhonda (*quietly*) I'll be back in a mo.

Rhonda goes out. Irwin is already holding the ad in his hand, and now very quietly he walks over to Isobel's desk and slips it in front of her, then stands waiting, like an expensive butler.

Isobel It's good.

Irwin Thank you. (*He waits a moment.*) I sometimes wonder . . . I don't know . . . whether you still care about my drawing.

Isobel I've said I like it.

Irwin It hurts me. You don't always seem as if it means what it did. I draw for you. That's why I draw. To please you. To earn your good opinion. Which to me means everything.

Isobel Well, you have it. So you're all right.

She is steady and quiet, still working. Irwin moves away.

Irwin I've just been talking to Rhonda.

Isobel Uh-huh.

Irwin I rather underestimated her. She's actually a quite interesting girl.

Isobel Yes, I'm sure.

Irwin She has a first-class degree in economics.

Isobel has no answer to this. Irwin shifts feet.

I mean I'm sure you probably think she's shallow . . .

Isobel No. Actually, I don't. I don't think anything. Why is everyone always so eager to tell me what I think?

Irwin Isobel . . .

Isobel I don't have an opinion. I have no opinion on the subject of Rhonda. I am absolutely neutral.

Irwin No, I just felt . . . from the way you greeted her . . .

Isobel turns suddenly, quite savage.

Isobel *What?*

Irwin shrugs.

Irwin Well, I think she seemed a bit put out.

Isobel You felt that? And you also felt that this was my fault?

She is looking at him now, her anger low and dangerous.

Irwin Isobel, you know I've been meaning to talk to you. You've not been looking too well.

Isobel No, that's true. I look like hell.

Irwin I'm worried for you.

Isobel Oh, really?

Irwin is quiet.

Irwin Why do you turn all my concern away?

Isobel carries on working, trying not to let any feeling she has show.

Look, you know I can tell when you're really angry . . .

Isobel Oh, I see. Now I'm being told that I'm angry.

Irwin Well, you are.

Isobel No, I'm not. I'm actually stopping myself. On the grounds that it would be counter-productive. I can see it's what you want. That I should get angry. But I am refusing to. And because today has been unspeakable, I am now going to go home. (*She has got up and gone to another desk where she collects a diary, and some cosmetics.*)

Irwin What are you getting? Those are Katherine's things. What's happened?

Isobel turns and looks at him.

Isobel Do you really want to know? Why not just . . .

Irwin Yes?

Isobel Continue whatever it is you were doing.

Irwin I was working.

Isobel Good. Then continue working.

Rhonda calls from the shower, loudly.

Rhonda (*off*) Is there any soap?

Isobel Do your work with the soap, Irwin. And I shall go home.

Irwin Isobel. Where's Katherine?

Isobel, who is once more about to leave, is suddenly stopped now.

Why don't you tell me? I don't get it. What's going on?

Isobel turns reluctantly and looks at him a moment.

Isobel She's in a clinic. That's where I've been. They called me at Heathrow and I came back into town. I had to get her admitted.

Irwin What happened?

Isobel A whole lot of stuff. Some joker gave her a drink. (*She nods.*) She'd taken out those clients . . .

Irwin Is that the video company?

Isobel Yes. It was stupid. I should have gone with her. They were unbelievably important. Over dinner they said they'd decided against our submission. So Katherine picked up a steak knife and plunged it straight for the managing director's heart.

Irwin My God!

Isobel It's fine. It's not a problem. He's an ad-man. His heart presents a very small target. He's got a few cut ribs. And Katherine was already too drunk to take aim.

Irwin looks down.

Irwin Oh shit, I'm sorry.

Isobel You don't have to be sorry. It's not your fault. How often did you tell me? It was my decision. I employed her.

Irwin So what will you do?

Isobel What can I do? We actually needed these people. They were good business. We're grossly over-extended. Look at this place! (*She gestures round the room.*) Instead . . . tonight we have a lawsuit. No, Katherine has a lawsuit. Mercifully she's under sedation. She'll wake up in the morning. And then I will face all her problems again. (*She smiles and turns to go, picking up her bag.*) Will you lock up after you?

Irwin Isobel!

Isobel What?

Irwin You can't just leave now.

Isobel Why not?

Irwin I want to help. I'd like to help you.

She smiles at him generously, then goes over and touches his arm.

Isobel I'm grateful for that. Honestly. But if you really want to help, best thing is to let me sleep.

He looks down, miserable.

Irwin I've got to talk.

Isobel Why?

Irwin I need it.

Isobel What, you all night and Katherine in the morning? (*The remark slips out. She at once looks down, contrite, apologetic, quiet.*) Please let me go, I've got problems enough.

Irwin That isn't fair.

Isobel No, it isn't. I only say it because I'm tired. That's why I want to go. Please? Is that unreasonable? I want to go because I've no fairness left.

But Irwin is still looking at her pleadingly.

Irwin Isobel, you've started avoiding me. You tolerate me, yes. But every time I look at you now, you look the other way.

Isobel I'm sorry. Yes.

Irwin Why do you do that?

Isobel I don't know. (*She smiles.*) I suppose a mistaken idea of kindness.

Irwin It isn't kind to avoid me.

Isobel No.

Irwin Perhaps it's more like cowardice.

Isobel Yes. (*She looks at him almost absently, smiling again.*) Shall we leave it at that?

Irwin No. I won't leave it at that.

Isobel Look, all right . . . (*She is suddenly vehement as if finally accepting that she cannot avoid this argument.*) I don't understand. What do you *want* from me? Like for instance tonight. I come in. What's in the air? A smell of cheap sex . . .

Irwin No!

Isobel And I think, oh yes, I see, I know what this is for. This is to make me into the one who's responsible. There is no purpose to this except to make me feel awful. Because I'm the girl who can't be giving this man all the love he needs.

Irwin I never said that.

Isobel You didn't need to. All I had to do was walk in the door and I was handed a role. My role is: the woman betrayed. Well, Irwin, I don't want to play it. I've no interest in playing it. Because it's humiliating. All I get to do is make catty remarks.

Irwin protests, outraged.

Irwin You're way off, we were just talking . . .

Isobel The next thing, you mention I'm looking terrible. Do you know how shabby that particular remark always is? You destroy a woman's confidence, then you say, I'm so worried about you, darling, you just don't seem to be yourself. Well, no. I'm not myself. I'm being turned into a person whose only function is to suffer. And believe me, it bores me just as much as it bores you.

Irwin is shaking his head.

Irwin I can't believe this. How long have you been thinking this?

Isobel Please don't be innocent. We've both been aware of it. You as much as me. We should have parted some months ago. We should have parted . . . (*She stops.*)

Irwin When?

Isobel You know when.

He suddenly points at her.

Irwin It still annoys you, doesn't it? That I talked to Marion and agreed to the restructuring.

Isobel No. It doesn't annoy me. It's just . . . (*She stops again.*)

Irwin What? Go on, please. You must say.

Isobel Oh God, I can't explain. Don't you understand? It's why I never talk to you. It's why I never look at you. I can't find a way of describing what's happened, without seeming to be disgustingly cruel. (*She looks at him, suddenly assertive.*) There we are, you see, now I look at you, you're flinching already . . .

Irwin Isobel . . .

Isobel And I'm standing here thinking, this is just stupid, I'm no longer in love with you. Why don't I just give you the push?

Irwin Is that what you want?

Isobel Why don't I just tell you to leave? As any sensible girl would. Why? Because, actually, there's a good part of me which is very fond of you. And wants to work with you. And hold on to what is best in you. (*She is suddenly*

gentle again, looking at him with affection.) So the fact is,
I find it very hard.

   Irwin looks down, moved.

Irwin I love you.

Isobel I know. I know you love me. God knows, you say it
often enough. (*She stops him before he can protest.*) I
don't say that to be cruel. But I never hear the words
without sensing something being asked of me. The words
drain me. From your lips they've become a kind of
blackmail. They mean, I love you and *so* . . . *So* I am
entitled to be endlessly comforted and supported and
cheered . . . (*She smiles.*) Oh, yes, and I've been happy to
do it. I comforted. I supported. I cheered. Because I got
something back. But it's gone. (*She shrugs slightly.*) We
both knew it. Yet you want some period in which we both
flounder together. Hang on tight while we get sad. But I
don't want to be sad. No one can remember now, but the
big joke is, by temperament I'm actually an extremely
cheerful girl. That's what's so silly. I'm strong. You sap my
strength. Because you make me feel guilty. I can never love
you as much as you need. Now I see that. So I've done a
great deal of suffering. But that's over. I'm ready to move
on.

   Irwin is looking at her disbelievingly.

Irwin I don't believe you.

Isobel You do. You do actually.

Irwin It's all because I failed some stupid sort of test . . .

Isobel No.

Irwin I wasn't *loyal*. I talked to your sister.

Isobel That's nothing to do with it.

Irwin Yes, it is. That was my crime.

Isobel tries to interrupt.

Isobel No, you're wrong. It's not that. It's just . . . I had an idea of you.

Irwin I know that idea. You saw me as poor and under your spell. As soon as I looked round and said, 'Hold on, this is ridiculous, please may I now have a living wage?' then . . . *then* of course you didn't like it. Because I was no longer in thrall. To the lady of the manor. I'm not under your patronage.

Isobel Good. (*She smiles.*) Then you have what you want.

Irwin No. (*He is quiet.*) I want you.

Isobel *Why*, for God's sake, if I'm what you say I am, if I'm – what? – patronizing . . .

Irwin No . . .

Isobel If I'm – what then? – possessive of you, if I'm this terrible influence, then plainly you're better off free of me.

Irwin No. That's not right. (*He looks her straight in the eye, suddenly calm and strong, as if knowing he has a strong hand to play.*) I'm still in love with you. I always will be. There's nothing I can do. It's just . . . (*He pauses.*) It's time you faced up to some truths.

Isobel is quiet, mistrustful, as if fearing what will be said.

Isobel What truths?

Irwin It's hurt me to watch you. Lately. You know very well. You must change.

Isobel How?

Irwin You must grow up. You have this crazy idea of integrity.

Isobel Crazy?

Irwin Yes. You have this idea because your father was a failure, because he sat in Gloucestershire, losing money hand over fist, but universally pleasant and kind, you think anyone who lives differently has to be some sort of traitor. You think I betrayed you. Well, don't you? (*He waits a moment.*) Not everyone can be your father, you know.

Isobel is already shaking her head.

Isobel That's really naive. You're nowhere near it.

Irwin Aren't I?

Isobel Of course not.

Irwin Then why, tell me why you will sacrifice your whole life for Katherine?

Isobel Don't be ridiculous. That's not what I'm doing.

Irwin Isn't it?

Isobel No! (*She moves away, uneasy.*) 'Sacrifice'! Irwin, really, what a word.

But he presses his point home, insistent.

Irwin Like tonight. The knife business. Did you notice? She reserves it for the big contracts. She doesn't flash a knife for the little guys, you know. She has priorities. She waits for the really major customer. With a great deal of money. Which we desperately need. Then . . . *then* she gives us a glimpse of her act.

Isobel turns to him, panicking slightly.

Isobel What are you saying?

Irwin I'm saying, look, like right now, her head is on a nice white pillow in a hospital – where?

Isobel North London.

Irwin All right. Now if at this moment we did a brainscan, tell me, what do you think we would see?

Isobel I don't know.

Irwin *What?*

Isobel shifts again, unhappy.

Isobel Vapours. Alcohol. Confusion. Loss. I don't know. (*Suddenly she shouts.*) *I don't know*.

Irwin Yes, you do.

There's a silence.

Isobel, she's dreaming of ways to destroy you.

Isobel No.

Irwin Yes.

Isobel Don't be absurd. You mustn't say that.

Irwin Why not? Just tell me. What state was your father in when he died? He'd had the life beaten out of him.

Isobel No.

Irwin I know, you think she's just unhappy. She's maladjusted. She hates herself. Well, she does. And she is. All these things are true. But also it's true, Isobel, my dear, you must learn something else. That everyone knows except you. It's time you were told. There's such a thing as evil. You're dealing with evil.

Isobel turns round, about to speak.

That's right. And if you don't admit it, then you can't fight it. And if you don't fight it, you're going to lose.

There's a moment's silence. Then Rhonda comes

*through from the bathroom. She is now fully clothed in
a smart skirt and pullover, her hair still wet from the
shower. She is cheerful.*

Rhonda That was great. This place is a major
achievement.

Irwin Ah, good.

Rhonda I don't know how anyone ever has baths.

Irwin No.

Rhonda Baths are disgusting. Sitting in your own dirty
water. Just lying there while the water gets muckier around
you. It must be unhealthy. I think everyone should shower,
don't you?

Irwin What?

*He is looking at Isobel, who is standing thinking, taking
no notice of Rhonda.*

Oh, yes.

Rhonda Well, anyway, I'm going to the flicks. Excuse me.

Isobel We'll come with you.

Rhonda I'm sorry?

Isobel I'd like to come.

Irwin looks across in amazement.

Rhonda It's very violent. I saw the trailer. It's one of those
Los Angeles crime things. Rooms full of blood. Then the
cop says, 'Right, I want everyone here to help look for his
ear . . .'

Isobel That's fine. My car's outside. (*She turns and looks
at Irwin.*) Let's have a big bag of popcorn. Then we can
have a good time.

445

Before they can leave, we hear the sound of Marion's
voice as she approaches from the back. The scenery
changes as the others leave, and we are in Tom's
office – an anonymously decorated room of glass and
wood panel, dominated by a big, bare leather-topped
desk. The glass runs unnaturally high, giving a feeling
of airy emptiness. Tom is already at his desk to greet
his wife, who approaches, putting down her coat as
she comes.

SCENE SIX

Tom's office.

Marion I can't see the problem. There really is no
problem. People so love to talk problems up. Family things
actually belong at the weekend. A drink on Sunday is
lovely. Or lunch. Or walking after lunch. That's the right
time for the family. It's crazy when it starts infecting your
weekend.

Tom gets up from behind the desk. He is nervous.
Marion sits down, impatient.

Tom I'm sorry. I can't help it. I'm worried.

Marion Why be worried?

Tom They may be angry.

Marion There's no point in being angry. They know you
already own the firm. It's simply an administrative
decision. Which makes total economic sense.

Tom To you. To me also. I'm just hoping they will see it
that way.

At once Irwin appears at the door. He is subtly changed.
He is glossier, better dressed, more outwardly confident

in a grey and white herringbone coat and cashmere scarf. He stands a moment, saying nothing.

Oh, Irwin, it's you.

Irwin Yes.

Marion Where's Isobel?

Irwin I don't know. Isn't she here?

Tom Why, no.

Marion We thought she was with you.

Irwin No. I haven't seen her.

There is an uneasy silence, no one moving.

You wanted a board meeting?

Tom Yes.

Irwin smiles and spreads his hands.

Irwin Here I am.

Tom Do you think we should start?

Marion I can't wait. Unless you've got time to help rehearse my replies. Here. (*She gestures with some postcards she is riffling through in her hand.*) Electricity costs in major industrialized countries. Test me.

Tom and Irwin smile, not sure if she's serious.

Tom Technically, you know, the meeting isn't necessary. The parent company has executive control. That said, it's obviously important you should all be happy.

Irwin Yes. (*He looks at Tom a moment, a little nervous.*) Look, actually, I think we might as well begin.

Tom Oh, really?

447

Irwin Yes. Isobel isn't around much.

Marion I see.

Irwin No.

Tom Who's been running the business?

Irwin I have.

Marion What, on your own?

Irwin More or less, yes.

There's a silence.

Marion We heard a rumour. We heard that you'd parted.

Irwin just looks at her.

What a stupid girl.

Tom I'm sorry . . .

Irwin No, it's fine.

Marion We did hear that.

Tom But surely it shouldn't affect the running of the firm?

Irwin looks embarrassed, but Marion interrupts.

Marion What happened?

Irwin Well . . .

Marion Rhonda did tell us something.

Irwin takes a quick look to Marion, taking this in.

Irwin Of course. She was there. We all went to the cinema. During the film, I looked round and Isobel had gone. I assumed to the ladies' room. Or to buy popcorn. What can I say? It was terribly embarrassing. I mean, explaining to Rhonda.

They stand a moment, frowning.

Isobel went and she never came back.

Marion With no explanation?

Tom When was this?

Irwin Three weeks ago. In fact it turned out she'd gone straight to Heathrow. Got the first plane at dawn and left the country.

Tom is puzzled.

Tom Goodness me.

Marion But she's back now?

Irwin Oh, yes. She came back quite quickly.

Tom She's looking after Katherine.

Irwin Yes. She's living there. She also bought back your dad's house.

Marion (*shakes her head*) It's just deplorable.

Irwin It was the first thing she did. She stopped the sale. Katherine was going to use the money to buy a flat. Well, Isobel's going to buy a flat for her. The one thing, however, she hasn't done . . . (*He stops, suddenly overcome, as if about to cry.*)

Tom Are you all right?

Irwin (*nods*) Well, anyway, we don't see her at work. (*He stares ahead a moment.*) So.

Tom I'm sorry, Irwin.

Marion It's so typical, isn't it? She's feckless. She was born irresponsible. Someone said, 'Do you know what politics is? Finally? Politics is being there every day.' And you

know it's true. You have to be there. I'm there every day.
Aren't I, darling?

Tom You are.

Marion And I'm there the next day. And the next day.
And the next day. For ever. Isn't that right?

Tom Well, yes . . . (*He stops, embarrassed.*)

Marion What?

Tom No, I mean, at least, I was going to say . . . at least
till you die.

Marion Of course. Why say that? That goes without
saying.

Tom Yes. No, you're right. I was just . . . pointing it out.

But Marion has already moved on.

Marion But, Isobel, oh no, if there's trouble, straightaway,
'I can't face it,' she says . . .

Tom Well . . .

Marion 'I've had a little tiff with my boyfriend.' Soon as
that happens it's upsticks and a wave and, 'Oh, off I go.'
She's totally unfocused. (*She leans forward in her chair.*)
Did you hear what happened before the funeral?

Irwin No.

Tom I'm not sure . . .

Marion After Dad died? Actually in the room Dad was
lying in? She asked Tom to spy on me.

Tom Darling . . .

Marion It's true. You told me. She actually took Tom
aside and said, 'Does Marion hate me?' It's *true*. 'If she
does will you promise to tell me?' She asked Tom! Really!

Is this the act of a normal, well-adjusted person? Please. Spare me. All my life I've had people say, 'Oh, she's the nice one.' (*Marion sits back.*) Nice? I think I call that paranoid, don't you?

Irwin looks down, embarrassed.

Irwin It's very difficult. You see, since she got back, Isobel won't speak to me.

Marion is immediately triumphant.

Marion Well, pardon me, I think that says it all. Let's face it, we've all been through it, we've all known people we've been fond of . . . (*She casts a reassuring glance.*) Before I was married, of course . . . I mean, however badly it ends, you don't just not speak to them. Do you? Is that normal? Please! We've all had our hearts broken. But really! (*She shakes her head.*) I'm sorry to say this. I wouldn't say it unless I were seriously concerned. But I think we should be considering professional help.

Tom Marion . . .

Marion I do. I've said it. I'm sorry. Get someone in who's experienced. These days there's no stigma attached. As far as I'm concerned, it's like fixing a car. If it breaks, just mend it. It's all avoidable. Nowadays they have brilliant people.

Irwin is looking down.

Irwin I'm not sure things are quite at that stage. It's more . . . (*He stops.*)

Tom What?

Irwin It's just wretched, I think, with Katherine. She sees no end to it.

Marion Yes. They make a fine pair.

Irwin The problem is, Isobel has made herself indispensable. And she sees no way to get out.

Tom is puzzled, worried.

Tom But what about work? Today, I mean, we have a crucial decision. We've had an excellent approach. We're being offered twice what we paid for the premises. It's a very good offer. We need to respond to it.

Irwin I'm afraid she seems to have no interest in the firm.

Tom It's extraordinary.

Irwin No, not really. It's all of a piece. While I work there, I don't think she's going to come near it. (*He smiles sourly.*) My guess is she's made some sort of vow.

The phone rings. Tom answers it on his desk. Marion is extremely provoked by what Irwin has said.

Tom Yes?

Marion I don't believe this. This is most peculiar. What is this? A *vow*? It's outrageous. People making *vows*. What are *vows*? Nobody made vows since the nineteenth century.

Tom holds his hand over the phone.

Tom It's Isobel.

Marion Well?

Tom She's downstairs. She says she won't come up until Irwin leaves.

There's a moment's pause only. Then Irwin gets up from his chair and picks up his scarf to put round his neck.

Marion No, Irwin, please. I forbid you to go. This is ridiculous.

Tom What do I tell her?

Irwin Tell her I'm leaving.

Tom speaks into the phone.

Tom He says he's going. It's all right. There are two exits. (*Tom smiles as he puts the phone down.*)

Marion This is absurd. I will not have this.

Irwin Will you put your proposal in writing?

Tom Of course.

Irwin nods at Marion.

Irwin Marion. Excuse me. I don't want a scene.

Tom Any messages?

Irwin No. No, thank you, Tom.

He walks across and shakes his hand. Tom puts his hand on his arm.

Tom You're shaking.

Irwin No. I'm just cold.

He turns and goes out. There is a moment's silence as Marion sits, genuinely angry. Tom looks away. Suddenly she speaks, the anger high in her now.

Marion We live in this world. We try to make a living. Most of us just try to get on with our lives. Why can't we?

Tom I don't know.

Marion Why does there have to be this endless complication?

Isobel has appeared in the other doorway. She is also changed. She wears a long dark blue overcoat and thin

453

glasses. Her hair is swept back on her head. She appears tense, thin, but also strangely cheerful.

Isobel.

At once Isobel comes warmly across the room, smiling and embracing Marion when she reaches her.

Isobel Marion. Hello. How are you? I've missed you terribly.

Tom Hello.

Isobel Tom. How are you? (*She goes over to kiss him.*) It's such a lovely day out there. It's incredible. I'd forgotten how high the sun is at this time of year. It's beautiful. I've spent half an hour in the park. Have you seen?

Tom No.

Marion No, actually. We've been too busy.

Isobel I'm sure.

Marion I'd love to spend my day just staring at the sun.

Isobel catches her tone, but tries to ignore it, keeping cheerful.

Isobel I've never been here. What a nice office!

Marion Isobel. Please.

Isobel Yes?

Marion Could you just tell us what's going on?

Isobel smiles at Marion, who is looking at her unforgivingly.

Isobel Of course. I'm sorry we can't have a proper board meeting. At the moment it's difficult between Irwin and me. It'll get better.

454

Marion Now listen . . .

Isobel Forgive me, I don't want to talk about it. Shall we talk about business? (*She smiles cheerfully at Tom trying to make interruption impossible.*)

Tom Of course.

Isobel is suddenly decisive.

Isobel You want to sell the firm because it's not profitable and sack all the staff, is that right?

Marion (*rising at once*) Now that isn't fair.

Isobel Please. I'm not judging. Marion, I'm just asking for the facts. (*Isobel sits opposite Tom at the desk.*) We redecorated the premises you bought us. They're now commercially very attractive. You can make a profit by selling them. You can double your money. But then of course there's nowhere for us to go.

Tom That isn't quite it. (*He smiles.*) There is also the point you are losing money. Sadly, the expansion hasn't really worked.

Isobel Well, no. I did warn you.

Tom I mean, any responsible businessman would tell you at this point he has a duty to his own survival. We have no real choice. We have to get out.

Isobel smiles.

Isobel With a little profit?

Tom Well, certainly.

Isobel Is it true we didn't cost anything in the first place?

Marion Isobel . . .

But Isobel, who is quite calm and gentle, puts up her

455

hand to stop Marion's indignant interruptions.

Isobel Look, I'm just asking. Someone said you wrote us off against tax. Is that right? (*She has to put her hand up again to quell the next interruption.*) Marion, please. I'm not criticizing. Is it true, because of tax, we cost you nothing?

Tom In a sense.

Marion Why apologize?

Isobel No, I don't expect it.

Tom It is legitimate business practice.

Isobel Of course. (*She smiles a moment at Marion, calming her down.*) And now I imagine your tax position has changed.

Tom Exactly.

Isobel Selling is now advantageous.

Tom Yes, that's right.

Isobel And the extra workers we took on?

Tom They would be compensated.

Isobel How much?

Tom Three weeks' wages.

There's a pause, while Isobel thinks this over.

Isobel Uh-huh.

There's a silence as Isobel nods slightly, not moving. Then she sweeps her hand across Tom's desk.

Marion Now, look, Isobel . . .

Isobel Well, I guess that's it.

Marion I wouldn't call them workers. Ex-students, more like. And ex- is being kind. They've had six months' fun at high wages. Now they're back on the market. I don't think they'll want to complain.

Isobel No. (*She shrugs slightly.*) Then it's done.

Tom What d'you mean? Let's be clear. Are you agreeing? (*He is disturbed at the ease of his own victory, puzzled now.*) Isobel?

Isobel Why even ask me? I'm only one vote.

She smiles as if that were the end of it. Marion is looking at her suspiciously.

Marion Now listen, Isobel, what are you up to?

Isobel Up to? Nothing.

Marion You think you're being clever.

Isobel Not at all.

Marion I get the drift of your questions.

Isobel They have no drift. I've simply been establishing the facts.

Marion Oh yes, I know what you think of us.

Isobel What I think? Oh, really? How?

Isobel is half smiling. Marion is angry.

Marion I just *know*.

Isobel I don't think so. Perhaps you know what you yourself feel. But that's different.

Marion What do you mean? (*She is panicking now.*) I've nothing on my conscience. I don't feel anything.

Isobel Good. Then in that case, everything's fine. (*She *looks at her a moment, then smiles.*) I must be off. (*She begins to get up.*)

Marion Oh, no, you don't get away that easily . . .

Isobel Tom. Goodbye.

Marion Just tell me. What did that mean? About what *I* feel?

Isobel has walked across and taken her hands. She looks her straight in the eye, with great warmth.

Isobel It meant nothing. Marion. Please let's be friends.

Marion We're always friends.

Isobel Good.

Marion I have no worries. I'm fine.

She is abashed by Isobel standing so close to her, so friendly. But as soon as Isobel turns, she speaks again.

It's not *me*, I'm just concerned for Irwin.

Isobel Irwin?

Marion Yes.

Isobel Why, what did he say?

Tom looks uneasily to Marion.

Tom Now, Marion, please . . .

Marion It's none of my business. I'm just telling you, as an impartial observer. You're being very selfish.

Isobel I see.

Marion It's a fact. If you won't go in to work, then, let's be sensible, there's no future for the firm. In sheer business terms. It happens to need both of you.

Isobel Marion, you heard Tom. The firm has no future anyway.

Tom Good gracious, no, excuse me, I didn't say that. Not at all. I'm hoping the two of you are going to continue.

Isobel turns, bewildered, for the first time slightly raising her voice.

Isobel But, Tom, you just said, we've got nowhere to go.

Tom Actually, there is a place. In this very building. It's a stroke of luck. I was getting round to saying. Did you happen to come through the car park?

Isobel I did.

Tom Well, probably you saw it. It's over there.

There's a pause.

Isobel Oh, yes.

Tom It's ideal. It's there. It's available. It's a base if you want one.

Isobel I see.

She is just staring at him. He is waiting a moment.

Tom We could let you have it rent-free. We'd pay your heat and lighting for a year, say. I mean for nothing. We'd throw it in. Absolutely free. As a pure favour. Gratis.

Isobel Well, thank you. (*She is looking across the desk at him. Now she speaks very quietly.*) But as I'm not with Irwin, it doesn't arise.

Tom (*smiles*) No.

Marion Now wait, look, Isobel . . .

Isobel (*to Tom*) All right?

Marion I'm a bit shocked by this. Tom is making a very decent offer. He's giving you a chance. He's saying he'll overlook the fact that you messed up the expansion.

Isobel But of course I never wanted the expansion.

Marion Well, exactly. Isn't that the whole point? I think you deliberately sabotaged it . . .

Isobel Oh, I see.

Marion Just to make your point. And now when Tom's saying, all right, put that in the past, I'll give you a second chance, you seem determined to throw it right back in his face.

Isobel smiles, unable to avoid answering, her patience going, but still with humour.

Isobel Well, no, I don't think so, I mean, look, I'm not complaining, whatever's happened is my own fault, I was out of my depth, no, I was weak, but putting that aside I have just been – what is the word for it? – I think I have just been *asset-stripped*. Isn't that the term for it? 'Objectively', as you would say, I have just been trashed and spat out in lumps. And now Tom has a corrugated hut at the back of his factory between, as I saw it, the car park and the waste-disposal unit on an industrial estate in Welwyn Garden City. (*She turns to Tom.*) Forgive me, but I think even Jesus might have doubts about setting up a business in there.

Surprisingly Tom chuckles at this, but Isobel's energy has unleashed all Marion's incoherent fury.

Marion Now this is it . . .

Isobel I'm sorry . . .

Marion This is exactly it. You spoil everything you touch. Everywhere you go, there are arguments. God, how I hate all this human stuff. Wherever you go, you cause misery. People crying, people not talking. It overwhelms me. Because you can't just live. Why can't you *live*, like other people? (*She stares at Isobel, distressed, in tears.*) Irwin came in here. He's in agony. He's a nice man.

Isobel He is a nice man. Except to me. That's the difference. He's in the grip of an obsession. Which he can't help. He's furious because I'm no longer in love with him. He can't accept that. And because I know him very well, I'm fearful. Because in a way I think he never will.

Marion Don't be ridiculous. He's just an ordinary person. We talked to him. He's an ordinary man.

Isobel turns, ignoring this.

Isobel And so I decided, perhaps it's irrational, all my life I've got on with everyone. But this one time, all my instincts say, 'Do something decisive. Cut him off. Wake him up. Shock him. Make it final.' (*She turns, thoughtful now.*) 'Do what needs to be done.'

Marion Really?

Isobel Yes.

Marion Was flying off necessary?

Isobel smiles at the memory.

Tom Where did you go?

Isobel I took the first plane that came. Lanzarote, as it happened.

Tom How was that?

Isobel Paradise. I took all my clothes off and walked along the beach. Lanzarote was paradise. But unfortunately no use to me. (*She laughs.*) You can't get away. You think you can. You think you'll fly out. Just leave. Damn the lot of you, and go. Then you think, here I am, stark naked, sky-blue sea, miles of sand – I've done it! I'm free! Then you think, yes, just remind me, what am I meant to do now? (*She stands, a mile away in a world of her own.*) In my case there's only one answer. (*She looks absently at them, as if they were not even present.*) I must do what Dad would have wished. (*She turns, as if this were self-evident.*) That's it.

Marion You are insufferable. You are truly insufferable. Hide behind your father for the rest of your life. Die there!

Marion is suddenly screaming. Isobel looks down, undisturbed.

Isobel Yes, well, no doubt I shall.

She turns and goes out. Tom stands appalled.

Tom You went too far.

Marion No, Tom, please . . .

Tom I should never have done this. I didn't see what would happen. I can't believe it, I saw nothing at all. I'm going down to pray. I fear for her.

Tom goes. Marion is left alone, astonished by Tom's departure.

Marion Tom. Tom. Please come back.

At once Katherine's voice from the back as she advances towards us, the new scene replacing the old. We are back in the hallway of Robert's house, which is bare and stripped-out. There is no electricity, only candles. Katherine is in trousers and pullover, calling towards an unseen Isobel.

SCENE SEVEN

Robert's house.

Katherine I'm not going, I tell you. I don't want to go. Why should I? What gives you the right? You're so superior. Do this. Do that. As if you always knew. You don't know. I'm not doing what you tell me. So leave it. Just leave it.

> *She sits down on a small wooden chair. Isobel comes in with a hot dish between oven gloves. She sets it down on the table. Isobel is even more distant, her hair wispy across her face, her manner detached.*

Isobel I only said it would be nice to go for a walk.

Katherine Well, it wouldn't be nice.

Isobel No, plainly.

Katherine What's this?

Isobel Shepherd's pie.

> *Katherine looks up at her.*

Katherine Are you out of your mind?

Isobel Eat.

Katherine Your cooking is unspeakable. It's all good intentions. Fuck shepherd's pie. It sums you up.

> *Isobel takes no notice, just helps herself to some. Katherine watches with distaste.*

Katherine All right, let's go out. Let's go to a French restaurant.

Isobel Don't be ridiculous.

Katherine Why not? Why not, for God's sake?

Isobel does not reply.

Sell the house.

Isobel No.

Katherine Then you'd have some money.

Isobel Not much.

Katherine Mortgage it.

Isobel It's already mortgaged.

Katherine It's just sitting here. Like us. (*She turns away impatiently.*) I'd rather be a drunk. Why don't you let me have a drink? At least when you drink you're alive. (*She gets up.*) What's life for? Jesus! Life means getting out there. Having some emotion. Is that right? When I went to all those terrible AA meetings, they kept saying people drink because they're angry. When you get angry, they tell you, count to five before you reply. Why should I count to five? It's what happens *before* you count to five which makes life interesting.

Isobel looks at her a moment. She has been eating automatically, in a trance.

Isobel Mmm.

Katherine What does that mean?

Isobel takes no notice.

This is the worst. This feeling we're just avoiding life. Look! Look!

She snaps her fingers in front of Isobel's face but Isobel does not react.

You won't even fight.

Isobel I don't want to. (*She pauses a moment, fork in hand.*) If you ask me, then I will go.

Katherine Go.

Isobel gathers up her supper, her plate, the dish, the fork, the knife, the salt, the pepper and goes out. Katherine stands a moment, not moving. Then Isobel returns, gets her big blue overcoat down from a hook, puts it on without saying anything.

Please don't leave me. Please, Isobel. Just stay for tonight.

Isobel stops a moment, then walks over to the mantelpiece where there is a packet of cigarettes. She lights one. She stands, still in the big overcoat. Katherine speaks quietly.

I don't know what to do. It's all such an effort. Like at school one term I worked really hard. I came fifteenth. I thought, this is stupid. Other people come second without trying. Why has God made me so fucking mediocre? The first boyfriend I had, it was the same. I adored him. I gave myself over. I couldn't get enough of him. Then one day he just stopped sleeping with me. Bang. Just like that. No warning. It happened again, the next three boyfriends I had. I thought, oh I see, there is something about me which is actually repulsive. After a while men don't want me. (*She thinks a moment.*) Well, that feeling is hard.

Isobel just listens, smoking her cigarette, not reacting.

Then I thought when your dad died – get out in the world. That night in the restaurant, I knew I couldn't do it. I just looked at them. I could see what they were thinking. She is not confident. I do not want to do business with her. They said, 'Oh, of course, you can't have a drink, can you?' It made me so angry. I thought, count to five. It's like they have to say it. Just to make you feel worse. So they all start

465

drinking vodka. In these really posh surroundings. They really get into it. And they laugh all the time, very loudly. They keep drinking more. And I think, oh God, you as well. Please give me a break. Just look at me as if you trust me. As if there were a little goodness in me. Then they say, 'Well, of course, you never really thought we'd give you the contract, did you? This can hardly come as a surprise.' (*She smiles.*) What do you do? I just want to hurt them. The managing director is eating a little bird. He keeps picking little bits out of his teeth. And drinking more vodka. And laughing. He says, 'No hard feelings.' I start counting to five. I don't even get to three. I suddenly yell out, 'Yes, there fucking well are. There *are* hard feelings. Because you have all the power. And you love to exercise it. And oil it with vodka. And smile your stupid shiny smiles. And you have just ditched me, you have just landed me, right back, right back into my terrible un-confidence . . .' (*She shakes her head.*) You know what happened. I reached for a drink. A few minutes later I picked up my knife. (*She shrugs slightly and turns to Isobel.*) It wasn't *so* wrong. Was it? At least I was alive. Not like now.

Isobel No.

Katherine Living here.

Isobel Mmm.

There is a short silence. Isobel's thoughts are unreadable. She moves.

I think perhaps we should both go to bed. (*She has gone to the main door.*) Look. The lock. Katherine. It's not enough. You must also put the bolt on. I told you.

Katherine I know.

Isobel Somehow Irwin's got a key.

Katherine Well, I didn't give it to him.

Isobel looks at her a moment, not believing this.

Isobel No. It's on. All right? Where do you want to sleep?

Katherine Oh, I'll take the bedroom.

Isobel is just about to leave the room when Katherine speaks suddenly.

Isobel.

Isobel What?

Katherine I never know what you think. I wish I knew what you thought of me.

There's a silence. Isobel smiles, before leaving.

Isobel I'll tell you one day.

Isobel goes out. Katherine does not move. Katherine goes to the door and undoes the bolt Isobel has just put on. She stands a moment, quite still. She is still by the door as Isobel returns, now in pyjamas with a book in her hand.

Help me with the bed.

They go to the sofa. They fold it down. Isobel throws a duvet on top. Katherine moves round to her side. Isobel looks at her a moment. Then embraces her, kissing her on the cheek.

Katherine Good night.

She turns and goes out. Isobel alone. She goes and picks up a book from beside the bed. She lies down and begins to read. Almost at once there is a sound from outside the door. She blows out her candle. There is absolute darkness. Then the door opens. Irwin stands in the lit doorway, a silhouette, as Marion was in the opening scene. Then he closes the door. Darkness. He clicks at the main light switch. Nothing. There is a pause.

Irwin I know you're there.

Isobel relights the candle. She stands quite still beside it.

Isobel You're wrong to do this.

Irwin Do what?

Neither of them moves.

Isobel Who let you in? I bolted the door. (*She calls through to the other room, not moving.*) Katherine! Katherine!

There is no noise.

She goes to bed with a Walkman.

Irwin She knows I phone you every day. She feels I've been badly treated. She wants you and me to make up.

Isobel Well, that's very good of her.

Irwin is very quiet.

Irwin May I just sleep with you?

Isobel No.

Irwin Why not? Please.

Isobel It's over. If you sleep with me, it'll be worse. It'll make you unhappy.

Irwin I can't be more unhappy.

Isobel It's still better you don't.

She is looking at him fearfully, still not moving. He walks into the room, she watching.

I'd make you some tea, but there's no milk.

*He has moved to the table. He takes out a small
handgun and lays it on the surface.*

What's that?

Irwin I bought it to kill myself.

Isobel You won't kill yourself. Is it loaded? Please. Give it
here.

*She takes a couple of steps towards him. But he is still
right next to the table and the gun.*

Irwin You're not frightened. Why aren't you frightened?

Isobel I don't know. I take what comes.

Irwin Make love to me.

*She is looking at him, very quiet. Very open, as if she
has already imagined his presence.*

Isobel Force me. You can force me if you like. Why not?
You can take me here. On the bed. On the floor. You can
fuck me till the morning. You can fuck me all tomorrow.
Then the whole week. At the end you can shoot me and
hold my heart in your hand. You still won't have what you
want. (*Her gaze does not wander.*) The bit that you want
I'm not giving you. You can make me say or do anything
you like. Sure, I'll do it. Sure, I'll say it. But you'll never
have the bit that you need. It isn't yours.

Irwin Don't say that.

Isobel It isn't.

There is a pause.

Irwin It's you. You've destroyed me. I don't sleep. I can't
make sense of life. Everywhere I go, there's nowhere to
hide. I can't rest. One day I tried to work, people said,
'Oh, where's that nice girl who used to be with you?' Now

I don't even work. I'm powerless. I only want one thing. To go back. To go back to where we were.

Isobel It isn't possible.

Irwin Why? (*He is suddenly passionate.*) All that time we were together, then once only, I do one thing, one thing which you think is wrong. That's it. I'm tipped out the window, like I'm rubbish. Because I've broken one rule. Katherine breaks a thousand rules. She breaks the rules all the time. All she does is betray you, day after day. Tonight, for God's sake, who do you think let me in? And why? So she can listen to me beat you round the head. And yet you go on taking care of her. Tell me, where is the justice in that?

Isobel smiles at the phrase.

Well?

Isobel I'm staying with Katherine. Someone has to take care of her. She has no resources. It isn't her fault. It's just a fact.

Irwin is suddenly quiet.

Irwin I have no worth. I can't feel my worth. When I was with you, it was there. Now it's as if you've withdrawn your approval. And I feel worthless.

Isobel I know.

Irwin Well? (*He waits.*)

Isobel What?

Irwin Why don't you help me? Come back to me.

Isobel No.

There's a pause.

Irwin Why not?

Isobel It wouldn't be honest.

Irwin Honest? Are you honest with her?

Isobel She's different.

Irwin Why? I was there when she landed on you. You didn't even want her.

Isobel No. She came my way. It was an accident, really. But I made a commitment. Why should I drop it just because the going gets hard?

Irwin is impatient.

Irwin You could say the same about me.

Isobel Yes, but you're an adult. And we were in love. And you have this idea that I can't accept.

Irwin What's that?

She looks hard at him a moment.

Isobel You want to be saved through another person.

There's a silence.

Irwin And?

Isobel It isn't possible.

Irwin Isn't it?

Isobel I don't know. I don't think so. (*She pauses a moment, then she begins to move.*) Now I'm going to bed.

Irwin Don't move.

Isobel I want you to leave.

Irwin I told you, don't move. (*He has begun to raise his voice, in panic.*)

Isobel Don't *move*? Good Lord, that will make life pretty difficult.

Irwin Please, I'm not making a joke.

Isobel Oh, really?

She moves towards the table where the gun is lying. He is still standing next to it. Now he screams.

Irwin I am telling you.

She stops.

Isobel Are you threatening me? What? (*She holds her hands above her head, in a little parody. She is very quiet.*) Will you hit me?

Irwin Isobel, please, don't make me . . . (*He stops, ashamed.*)

Isobel What? Make you what, Irwin?

He looks down, not able to answer.

No, please tell me. Go on.

Irwin No, nothing.

Isobel Please say.

He looks down, not able to answer.

If you kill me, will that be my fault as well?

At once Katherine comes in from the bedroom. She is fully dressed, now taking in the scene between them, but not yet seeing the gun on the table.

Irwin Katherine . . .

Katherine Oh, shit. I heard something.

Isobel Irwin, are you going to leave?

Irwin Not just now.

Isobel Then I'm sorry. Katherine, can you get the police?

Isobel is capable, clear. Katherine frowns.

Katherine Don't be silly.

Isobel I want Irwin to go. But he won't.

Irwin Please, Isobel . . .

Isobel I'm serious. He's threatening me.

Isobel is watching Irwin and the gun all the time now, not moving. Katherine makes a small move.

I want you just to walk out the door.

Katherine frowns.

Katherine Isobel, look, I don't get it.

Isobel It doesn't matter. Find someone in the street.

Katherine Are you sure? (*She smiles at Irwin for approval.*) Well, I mean . . .

Isobel Tell them we have an intruder up here.

Katherine He's hardly an intruder.

Isobel Katherine, just do it. I'm telling you. Just get on with it now.

Isobel has raised her voice. But Katherine, as she is about to accept this and move, sees Irwin reach out and pick up the gun. She stops dead still.

Katherine Lord.

At once Isobel moves towards the bed.

Isobel Then I'll go. Wait for me.

Irwin Isobel. No.

She has picked up the big blue coat from the bed and now puts it on. Irwin has called out to her in panic. Now she smiles down at her bare feet.

Isobel I haven't got shoes. Still you can't have everything.

She goes back to the main door. The gun is pointing at her back. She opens the door and just as she closes it behind her, Irwin fires five times at the door. It is deafeningly loud. The door splinters. There is noise from the other side.

Katherine No! No!

Irwin turns towards us, the gun now lowered. He looks beaten. There is a silence. Katherine moves towards the door and opens it. Isobel lies dead on the floor at the other side. Katherine looks a moment, then kneels down beside her. Irwin slumps on to a chair. Katherine puts her hand gently on Isobel's chest to feel for life.

Irwin It's over. Thank God.

There is a silence. Then the light begins to grow strongly from behind. The sound of high summer. Birds singing. Strong shafts of sunlight hitting the tall windows of Robert's living room and, in front of them, all his furniture as we left it at the end of the previous act, covered in white shrouds, and spaced about with packing cases. Katherine's flat moves away, and the next scene begins.

SCENE EIGHT

Robert's living room. Marion is moving slowly round the room, removing the shrouds from each piece of furniture, uncovering them, one by one. She is in a black dress. The

*ritual of removing the covers takes time. Tom comes in,
wearing a black suit. He is carrying a chair.*

Marion Over there.

*He goes and puts it down. Marion goes on taking off
covers.*

Tom There?

Marion Yes, that's right. Good. The carpet.

Tom Yes. I'll unroll it. (*He moves towards the rolled-up
carpet, pausing as he does to readjust the position of
another chair.*) This here?

Marion Yes, that's good.

Another chair moved.

Tom And this?

Marion Yes, that's perfect.

Another.

Tom This?

*Marion stands a moment, the sheets in her hand,
surveying the room.*

Marion It's as I remember it.

Rhonda comes in, in a short black skirt and jumper.

Rhonda There's a call from the Ministry.

Marion I don't want to speak to them.

Rhonda Fine.

*Marion goes across and hands her the sheets. Rhonda
goes out with them. Tom is on his knees now, unrolling
an old weathered carpet of many colours.*

475

Marion We played over there. Under the piano. Isobel had a kind of magic world.

Tom nods. Then Marion thinks, looking back towards the open door.

You must understand, Tom. I can't come to the church.

He looks up, stopping in his work, also to think. Katherine comes in, dressed as she was for her husband's funeral. She is carrying a large vase of flowers.

Katherine Flowers. Here we are.

Tom That's wonderful.

Marion Put them there.

She points to a table. Katherine sets them down. Marion is thoughtful.

Yes, they're fine.

Katherine Thank you.

Marion Good. (*She looks round a moment.*) When you were here, what else did you have?

Katherine Oh, ornaments. I think. (*She gestures vaguely.*) Lamps and things. Well, everywhere.

Marion goes to a packing case and takes out vases and ornaments which she sets on side tables.

Robert loved things. It made me jealous. He'd pick up a book. Or a photograph. His whole mood would change. Right away. Things consoled him. He was lucky.

Marion Yes.

Katherine It's a gift.

Rhonda reappears at the door.

Rhonda The people out there are waiting.

Marion is still surveying the room, adjusting objects, moving furniture. Tom has laid the carpet and is now standing.

They all want to walk in one group through the village. She does seem to have been amazingly popular.

There is a pause.

It's like everyone valued her.

Tom Yes.

Marion Except us.

At once Tom makes a move towards her, alarmed.

Tom Marion . . .

Marion It's all right. We'll be with them in a moment. Katherine, come here.

Katherine walks across to her. Marion kisses her on the cheek.

Just wait and we'll be along.

Rhonda and Katherine go in silence. Tom and Marion are left alone.

It's all obscure. It frightens me. What people want. Tom. It's frightened me, ever since I was a child. My memory of childhood is of watching and always pretending. I don't have the right equipment. I can't interpret what people feel.

Tom moves and stands behind her, wanting to console her.

I've stood at the side. Just watching. It's made me angry. I've been angry all my life. Because people's passions seem so out of control. (*She shakes her head slightly.*) You either say, 'Right, OK, I don't understand anything, I'll take some simple point of view, just in the hope of getting things done. Just achieve something, by pretending things are simpler than they are.' Or else you say, 'I will try to understand everything.' (*She smiles.*) Then I think you go mad.

Tom It's not that bad. The Lord Jesus . . . (*At once he stops.*)

Marion Yes, Tom? The Lord Jesus what?

Tom I don't know. I've slightly lost touch with the Lord Jesus.

He looks at her, then smiles. She smiles too. Then she gestures round the whole room. It is perfectly restored into an English sitting room – furniture, carpets, curtains, ornaments.

Yes. Well done. It's lovely.

There's a pause.

A perfect imitation of life.

Marion smiles and moves towards him. They embrace. He kisses her, with more and more passion. He undoes the buttons on the front of her dress and puts his hand inside, on her breasts. Then he runs his hand down the front of her body. She puts her head right back.

Oh God, you feel wonderful.

Marion Yes, so do you.

They kiss again. Then he takes a couple of steps back, smiling, slightly adjusting his tie.

Tom, I love you.

Tom I'll be back soon.

He pauses, and laughs a small laugh. Then turns and goes out. Marion is left alone. She sits on the sofa at the centre.

Marion Isobel. We're just beginning. Isobel, where are you? (*She waits a moment.*) Isobel, why don't you come home?